Women of the
American Revolution

Biographical Historical Fiction by Samantha Wilcoxson

But One Life: The Story of Nathan Hale

Luminous: The Story of a Radium Girl

Plantagenet Princess, Tudor Queen: The Story of Elizabeth of York

Faithful Traitor: The Story of Margaret Pole

Queen of Martyrs: The Story of Mary I

The Last Lancastrian: A Story of Margaret Beaufort (novella)

Once of Queen: A Story of Elizabeth Woodville (novella)

Prince of York: A Story of Reginald Pole (novella)

Women of the
American Revolution

Samantha Wilcoxson

PEN & SWORD
HISTORY

First published in Great Britain in 2022 by
Pen & Sword History
An imprint of
Pen & Sword Books Ltd
Yorkshire – Philadelphia

ISBN 978 1 39900 100 7

A CIP catalogue record for this book is
available from the British Library.

Typeset by Mac Style
Printed in the UK by CPI Group (UK) Ltd, Croydon, CR0 4YY.

Pen & Sword Books Limited incorporates the imprints of Atlas,
Archaeology, Aviation, Discovery, Family History, Fiction, History,
Maritime, Military, Military Classics, Politics, Select, Transport,
True Crime, Air World, Frontline Publishing, Leo Cooper, Remember
When, Seaforth Publishing, The Praetorian Press, Wharncliffe
Local History, Wharncliffe Transport, Wharncliffe True Crime
and White Owl.

For a complete list of Pen & Sword titles please contact

PEN & SWORD BOOKS LIMITED
47 Church Street, Barnsley, South Yorkshire, S70 2AS, England
E-mail: enquiries@pen-and-sword.co.uk
Website: www.pen-and-sword.co.uk

Or

PEN AND SWORD BOOKS
1950 Lawrence Rd, Havertown, PA 19083, USA
E-mail: Uspen-and-sword@casematepublishers.com
Website: www.penandswordbooks.com

'Remember the Ladies.'

– Abigail Adams, 1776

Contents

Contents

Chapter 1

The American War for Independence

W hen did the American Revolution begin? It cannot be simply defined as the war that broke out when shots were fired at Lexington on 19 April 1775. Tempting as it may be to give the easy answer of 4 July 1776, that ignores the years of unified resistance that led to the Declaration of Independence.

The American Revolution was more than the civil war that resulted in independence for a set of loosely united British colonies. The last decades of the eighteenth century saw a shift in a population of formerly loyal British colonists into passionately independent Americans. Those who had known only monarchy rejected the rule of a privileged few for the utopian promises of a republic. The war was a consequence of this shift in mindset – the final act in the revolution rather than the beginning.

The colonists who first resisted the Stamp Act in 1765 did not necessarily believe that they were taking a step toward the creation of a new country. They were standing up for their rights as British subjects. However, the unification that occurred when colonists claimed these rights did create the fissure with their mother country that eventually led to war and independence.

A failure to understand each other pushed the British subjects in the American colonies and the British parliament further apart as the eighteenth century progressed. Parliament saw taxes on the colonies as well within their authority and justified by the expenses of the Seven Years' War, known as the French and Indian War in the United States. It seemed unfair for that war debt to be charged to those living in England, who were already suffering under a stiff tax burden. On the other hand, colonists bridled at taxation without representation within the parliament and felt that they were being treated as second-class British citizens.

Actions to protest the Stamp Act began long before it was enacted, giving birth to the Sons of Liberty led by Samuel Adams in Boston, Massachusetts. These acts of resistance were successful. Parliament repealed the Stamp Act and passed the Declaratory Act in 1766. Removing the controversial tax, but restating parliament's authority over the colonies at the same time, left both sides with the illusion that they had been victorious.

In 1767, parliament, still coping with a mountain of debt related to defending land in the American colonies, passed the Townshend Acts, named for the new Prime Minister. In these acts, parliament felt it was dealing delicately with the unruly colonies, increasing duties and revamping customs administration to reduce smuggling without great expense to any individual colonist.

The American colonists held a very different view of the Townshend Acts. From their point of view, the issue remained the same – taxation without representation. The troops sent to Boston to ensure enforcement of the Townshend Acts were only fuel to the fire. Parliament saw the colonists' grumbling as treasonous, while colonists believed they were again being stripped of their rights as British citizens. As Mercy Otis Warren wrote, 'This inconsiderable duty on teas finally became an object of high importance and altercation; it was not the sum, but the principle that was contested; it manifestly appeared that this was only a financiering expedient to raise a revenue from the colonies by imperceptible taxes.'[1]

American colonists reacted to these acts with two forms of protest that helped unify them in a way they had not previously been and increased the chasm between British subjects in Great Britain and America. Nonimportation Associations were non-political groups of individuals or merchants unified in their efforts to boycott British goods. Committees of Correspondence also began to form, creating regular, organized communication between colonies. The phenomenon of us versus them was growing. Still, by the beginning of the 1770s, most American colonists were striving for equality as British citizens rather than independence. The colonies remained relatively ununited states. An incident in Boston on 5 March 1770 caused a shift in that perspective.

What became known as the Boston Massacre began as bored children taunting British soldiers on guard duty. With tensions high and both soldiers and Bostonians wondering about the motives of the other, it, unfortunately, escalated into shots fired and five dead colonists. The fact that this was more of a street brawl than a massacre is evinced by the fact that John Adams, future president of the United States, served as defending attorney for the soldiers, who were not found guilty of murder. That truth has been lost to history as propaganda images of defenseless colonists standing before a firing squad of British soldiers (a popular one engraved by Paul Revere) have replaced it in the minds of many Americans. 'Yet the accident that created a resentment which emboldened the timid, determined the wavering, and awakened an energy and decision that neither the artifices of the courtier, nor the terror of the sword could easily overcome, arose from a trivial circumstance; a circumstance which but from the consideration that these minute accidents frequently lead to the most important events, would be beneath the dignity of history to record.'[2]

Americans may have viewed this as a step toward war, but Great Britain was still focused on events closer to home. Unrest in the American colonies was not a high priority, and few seemed to fear escalation. Distance of thousands of miles and confidence in the British Empire created doubt that any serious issues would arise in America.

King George III had been twenty-two years old at his coronation in 1760. He had inherited the greatest empire of the age and was obsessed with retaining it. Intelligent and devout, he worked tirelessly, even acting as his own secretary.[3] He was also unforgiving toward those who disagreed with him and was irritated by disorder. Rebelling colonies were not a problem that King George III was well equipped for coping with through any method but force.

With what would later become known as the Boston Tea Party of 1773, the American colonies made another bold step toward independence. The trouble over tea demonstrates another failure of colonists and parliament to understand each other. While parliament felt that it was removing unfair duties and providing affordable tea to the American colonies, colonists saw monopolized trade in which they had no voice as they were forced to purchase tea through the East India Company. The fact that the tea was reasonably priced did not matter. In an effort to establish that the issue was solely with tea, those who carried out the Boston Tea Party, dumping forty-six tons of tea into Boston Harbor, did not destroy anything else on the ship. They had even given the captain the opportunity to leave with his cargo intact. They did not break locks (or fixed them when they did) or disrespect the ship's property, but they did dispose of every last leaf of tea on board.

Boston was not the only city that refused shipments of East India tea, and at least one British officer in New York understood the seriousness of events. 'All America is in a flame', he wrote to a friend in London.[4] It was not yet, but it soon would be. In the wake of the Boston Tea Party, parliament issued the Coercive Acts – Intolerable Acts to Americans – in May 1774. The Port of Boston was closed, threatening the livelihood of most Boston residents. By September, colonists were gathering for a Continental Congress. Although the goal remained reconciliation with parliament and restoration of colonists' rights as British subjects, the chance of reconciliation was shrinking.

Americans had some friends across the Atlantic. Thomas Howard, Earl of Effingham, demonstrated his support for the colonists by naming his Yorkshire hunting lodge Boston Castle. He also resigned his commission rather than fight against fellow British citizens.[5]

When war did break out, it was considered by many on both sides to be a civil war with each believing their actions were defensive. The colonists believed the presence of British troops and the Prohibitory Act made stockpiling defensive weapons a reasonable step. The British believed that seizing the colonial weapons at Concord and rebel leaders, Samuel Adams and John Hancock, in Lexington, Massachusetts would bring a swift end to their rebellion. In the meantime, the Conciliatory Resolution passed parliament in February 1775 to offer peace and tax relief to loyal colonies, but it did not arrive in America until after shots had been fired and sides had been taken. On 10 February 1776, George Washington wrote to Joseph Reed, 'We had born much – that we had long, & ardently sought for reconciliation upon honourable terms – that it had been denied us – that all our attempts after Peace had provd abortive and had been grossly misrepresented – that we had done every thing that could be expected from the best of Subjects – that the Spirit of Freedom beat too high in us, to Submit to Slavery; & that, if nothing else would satisfie a Tyrant & his diabolical Ministry, we were determined to shake of all Connexions with a State So unjust, & unnatural.'[6]

Mercy Otis Warren wrote, 'They were sensible the step they were about to take would either set their country on the pinnacle of human glory or plunge it in the abject state into which turbulent and conquered colonies have been generally reduced.'[7] By July 1776, the representatives included in the Continental Congress agreed that independence was the next step. They knew war would be the result – war with the greatest power in the world at that time. However, they also knew that the British would have to win a war and supply it from thousands of miles away. The newly declared United States only had to outlast them. Thomas Jefferson, writing the famous declaration intended 'to place before mankind the common sense of the subject, in terms so plain and firm as to command their assent, and to justify ourselves in the independant stand we [were] compelled to take. neither aiming at originality of principle or sentiment, nor yet copied from any particular and previous writing, it was intended to be an expression of the American mind.'[8]

What did this evolution in mindset and action mean for women living in the colonies and what roles did they fulfill?

Women's political opinions both before and during the Revolutionary War were diverse. Some held fast to their loyalty to their monarch and ancestral homeland and were forced to watch as friends and neighbors turned away from them. Others were passionate patriots or tirelessly supported husbands who were. Some did not have the luxury of forming a life based on loyalties and had to make do the best they could for themselves and their children as war raged around them. Women found themselves suddenly responsible for managing farms and businesses while their husbands were away. Many even made their way to the front lines.

Throughout the political upheaval and outbreak of war, women discovered, just as American men did, what they were capable of and how much they were willing to sacrifice for freedom and liberty. Their stories are as varied as the women themselves, from those who secretly assisted the armies with intelligence to those who became America's First Ladies. How they coped in a time of war and who they decided to support was just as significant as the actions of the troops in the field. They made incredible sacrifices for the public good.

It is a challenge to write about women of the American Revolution and keep their story the central one. These women lived in a patriarchal society that had clearly established gender roles. Because it is tempting to follow the chronology of the war and actions of their fathers, brothers, husbands, and sons, the women's story often winds up evolving into a story of the men in their life. Maybe that is, in part, fitting. Neither the men's nor the women's experiences through the Revolution would have been the same without each other, and their lives were indivisibly mingled. However, the objective of this book is to focus on women's experiences as much as possible.

War tends to be romanticized as time passes, making it easy to forget the horrors experienced, not only by the men who joined the army but also for those who remained at home and suffered shortages, loss, fear, and violence. Women were often left at home with children, forced to determine how to fill in for their husband as provider and protector. It is easy to envision patriotic women gathered at the fireside stitching clothing for men at war while their children sit at their feet. However, this image excludes many women who were turned from their homes, raped, and left to watch their children sicken and die for lack of food and care.

The integral role of women and their feelings about their circumstances is not often considered in any discussion of the American Revolution. That is about to change.

Chapter 2

Martha Dandridge Custis Washington

Her presence inspired fortitude.
— Pierre-Etienne Duponceau

Throughout her life, Martha Washington spent the first hour of her morning in prayer and Bible reading. This habit enabled her to maintain her faith and optimistic attitude through bearing and losing children, widowhood, war, public life, and widowhood again.

She grew up in the Tidewater region of Virginia, where the advent of tobacco had made fortunes that brought immigrants to the area in droves. The Dandridges had already been there for generations when Martha, called Patsy until her marriage to George, was born 2 June 1731 to John and Frances (Jones) Dandridge. As the first born of a genteel but not first-tier family of Virginia, Martha grew up learning to be a lady, run a household, and assist with her succession of siblings.

Besides the housekeeping chores that are familiar to us, Martha learned to raise and butcher chickens, sew and embroider, dye and weave cloth, and cook using a wood-heated brick oven. Eighteenth century women had a wearying number of household responsibilities, especially in America, where shipments from Europe could not provide for everything needed. Martha knew how to identify and use herbs – for food and medicine – and how to create most of what a family needed to survive. Martha became particularly fond of and skilled at making homemade jams and jellies. Even in a household with servants and slaves, as Martha's family had, the women of the house completed many tasks themselves and were responsible for supervising the others. Since she became a big sister before she was a year old, Martha would have helped lead her siblings in their studies. She modeled for them proper behavior at the dinner table and in worship service each week. One of Martha's most important jobs growing up was simply being a good example.

In addition to her household skills, Martha was taught to be a lady while confined in corsets that helped form her figure and correct her posture. Virginia ladies of Martha's time were trained to mimic British aristocracy in their manners and decorum. Simply walking and sitting could be a challenge in the full skirts that were the fashion. Martha apparently learned these skills well, because she flawlessly played the role of hostess as a married woman, even when thrust into the public world as America's original First Lady (although that title was not used during her husband's time in office). Her parents ensured that she could ride elegantly in a sidesaddle while maintaining perfect posture. Physical control and poise were also vital when learning to dance, a skill not to be underestimated in its importance in eighteenth century Virginia.

The objective would have been for her to eventually obtain a satisfactory husband, and in this Martha most certainly made her parents proud. Daniel Parke Custis belonged to the closest America had to an aristocracy. Rich and possessing thousands of acres of land, the Custis family was such a step up for Martha that Daniel's father initially forbade his son to marry her. This is where one gains the first insight into the woman Martha would become. Though only eighteen years old, Martha courageously stood up to her future father-in-law. He had threatened to disinherit Daniel and throw the family silver into the street rather than allow Martha to use it, but she managed to charm him into giving his reluctant blessing.[1] The couple was married when Martha was nineteen years old and her groom was twenty years her senior. This age difference was not uncommon or a barrier to their happiness. The skills Martha had learned at the Dandridge home made her a competent manager of the larger Custis plantation, prophetically named White House.

A large enslaved population made it possible for Daniel and Martha to profitably run the Custis estate. No evidence exists that Martha believed owning slaves was immoral or wrong in any way. While she did not support cruel treatment or sales that broke up families, Martha also could not understand when enslaved people ran away from what she felt was a comfortable home. It was a lifestyle she had been born into and never questioned, even as the colonies strived toward their freedom.

Within a year of marriage, Martha was pregnant. Given her love of children throughout her documented adult life, one can assume that Martha was thrilled to become a mother. Countering this excitement was the natural fear that all women faced during pregnancy and childbirth at this time. However, Martha's mother had safely delivered seven children by this time (another was born in 1756), so Martha might not have been greatly concerned. She likely kept up most of her activities until later in her pregnancy when Martha's status would have enabled her to rest if she preferred. Unlike poorer women or those who were enslaved, Martha would not be forced to work up until the time her labor began in earnest. When the time did come, Martha was surrounded by women – relatives, enslaved servants, and a midwife – to assist her through the birth. She may have consulted a doctor, but it is more likely that her younger sisters attended her. One of those sisters might have been left home to watch younger siblings, enabling Martha's mother to attend.

Daniel had his plantation duties to complete but surely also inquired as to his wife's progress and possibly visited her room. Husbands were not banned from the women's work but were not typically on hand throughout the delivery.

Little Daniel Parke Custis, named for his father, was born without known complications on 19 November 1751. Martha, like other women of her status, could enjoy a lying-in period after the birth of her babies. This was approximately a month of resting, recovering, and bonding with the baby. She probably nursed her baby, the practice known to be good for the mother's health and a form of birth control.

During their seven-year marriage, Daniel and Martha had four children, two boys and two girls. A daughter, Frances, was born in 1753, followed by John, called Jacky, in 1754, and Martha, called Patsy, in 1756. During this same time, however, began the experiences with grief that would be a consistent companion to Martha throughout her life.

Daniel and Martha's firstborn died of an illness in 1754, a heartbreaking but not uncommon occurrence for young children in an age before modern medicine. When Daniel Parke Custis and almost four-year-old Frances also died in 1757, Martha was left a twenty-six-year-old widow, grieving the loss of her husband and two children. Martha would experience grief more than most over the course of her lifetime. By the time of her death in 1802, she had outlived two husbands, her four children, all her siblings (despite being the oldest), and numerous extended family members and friends. She had no way of knowing this future was in store for her in 1757 when she was left alone to raise her remaining two small children and manage one of Virginia's largest estates.

According to historian Joseph E. Fields, this is where Martha's history begins to be available in her own words. The earliest existing correspondence of Martha Dandridge Custis is her letters to business contacts of her husband after his death. She informed them that she had become responsible for the administration of the estate in a style utilizing run-on sentences and eccentric spelling that she maintained throughout her life.[2] This style of writing is not particularly surprising for a woman of Martha's time and status. The household skills, decorum, and religious training that Martha had been given was considered more valuable for her future than learning to expertly read and write. However, she was literate, unlike more than half of American women at the time.[3] Martha had likely been taught math and grammar by her mother, and a love of reading improved her skill over time. Following the Revolutionary War, women began to receive greater education. The American mother was expected to teach her children intellect and morals, which she could only do if she had received such instruction herself.[4] During her years as First Lady, Martha arranged schooling for her teenage granddaughter and ward, Nelly Custis.[5]

In the 1750s, a young woman with small children and a large estate was not expected to remain unwed for long. Extensive mourning periods were romantic but impractical, although Martha was more fortunate than most with independent wealth that allowed her time to grieve and consider her future. She was soon receiving letters and visits from interested men. One offer of marriage came from a widower with a dozen children.[6] Even for a woman who loved children as much as Martha did, this prospect might have seemed a bit daunting!

Martha's heart was soon set upon a handsome, young man – eight months younger than herself in fact. In contrast to her first husband, who had been two decades her elder, Martha's new suitor was athletic and attractive. His wealth could not compete with the Custis estate, but Martha's position enabled her to be free of concerns regarding money. George Washington had begun making a name for himself, but neither he nor Martha could have imagined what was in store for them.

What George lacked in formal education and inheritance, he made up in charisma and ambition. He had begun purchasing land while still in his teens, motivated to improve his standing beyond what he had been born into.[7] Marrying Martha Dandridge Custis brought him a devoted spouse as well as her riches and social standing.

While there is no reason to believe that Martha did not love Daniel Parke Custis, one can imagine that being courted by and marrying a man her own age with the work ethic and magnetism of George Washington must have been an exciting, new experience for her. Martha was a petite brunette and George a tall, physically imposing man with auburn hair. They made an attractive pair, as well as a love match.

Little is certainly known of George and Martha's brief courtship, but he did order a ring from a Philadelphia jeweler on 5 May 1758. A month later, he was visiting White House, so it is possible that they became engaged during that visit.[8] That same summer, George was elected to the Virginia house of burgesses, continuing his upward movement in Colonial America.

George and Martha were married on 6 January 1759. She dressed lavishly in yellow brocade with silver lace and purple satin shoes. He forewent military attire in favor of a civilian suit.[9] The winter months that followed were spent alone at White House. Martha demonstrated that she would be fully devoted to her new husband from the beginning. Rather than remaining at White House once spring came, she moved her household to Mount Vernon, a work in progress that George rented from his sister-in-law. Although he had ordered fine goods and furniture from England to make Mount Vernon a fitting home for his new bride, George knew it did not compare to what Martha had grown accustomed to during her marriage to Daniel Custis.

If Martha ever complained or longed for finer quarters, she left no record of it. She would endure far rougher environments without complaining as long as George was there, as their future would prove. But those days were a long way off and would have been unimaginable to the young couple as they rode up the path to the construction zone that was George's dream. Mount Vernon as Martha first viewed it did not appear as it does to visitors today. The house built by George's father, Augustine Washington, was a four-room home with a wide passage down the center to allow breezes from the Potomac River to keep it cool in the summer. A half-story garret above was used for storage and bedrooms.[10] During the 1750s, a major renovation added a floor to the home, creating a second story beneath a third story garret. Small single-story additions were also built onto each end of the first floor. This is the work that was being completed when Martha was introduced to

Mount Vernon. More renovations would be undertaken later to create the familiar façade.[11]

Mount Vernon was farther from her childhood home than Martha had ever ventured at that time, but circumstances would make her adventurous and well-travelled by the end of her life. Although she never left the colonies that became the United States under her husband's leadership, Martha often found herself far from Virginia in the 1770s and 1780s. However, in April 1759, Martha's only thoughts were of making Mount Vernon the Washington family home. When Martha entered the central hall, she was welcomed by sunny yellow walls and fresh air blowing in from the Potomac. The grand piazza that Mount Vernon is recognized for today did not yet exist, but Martha was certainly still awed by the sweeping lawn that sloped down to the river's edge. One wonders what potential she saw in the estate as she unpacked furniture, linens, and luxury goods from White House.

As in many new marriages, Martha soon discovered that there would be a few challenges to being George's wife. She quickly demonstrated that nothing would come between them. These challenges came in the form of two women from George's bachelor days: his neighbor and his mother.

Sally Fairfax was married to George's friend, another George, and they lived near Mount Vernon at their own elegant estate, Belvoir. It would not have taken Martha long to learn that Sally was a tireless flirt and that George was susceptible to her attentions.[12] Martha may or may not have learned about letters that George and Sally had exchanged before Martha's arrival on the scene. Since Sally had been married throughout this period, she likely simply enjoyed leading on the young man and basking in his attention. If Martha felt threatened by the older, sophisticated woman, she left no indication of it. The Washingtons and Fairfaxes remained close until the Fairfaxes decided to return to England in the early days of the war.

George's mother was a different challenge. Mary Ball Washington was demanding and cold, characteristics that were not entirely missing in her eldest son. However, while George could be authoritative and closed-off from others, he could also be charming and affectionate with those he loved. History leaves us no evidence of this ability in his mother. Even as George became the foremost man in the young country, his mother seemed less than impressed. She had no relationship with his wife, and there is no record of her ever visiting the couple at Mount Vernon.[13]

If the lack of an affectionate mother-in-law bothered Martha, she made up for it with a vast array of extended family relationships. With six surviving siblings of her own at this time and four of George's, Martha had countless in-laws, cousins, nieces, and nephews to occupy her time and affections. She also expected that she would soon bear more children herself, and George would have also looked forward to having a son of his own, as much as he loved his stepchildren.

The fifteen years that passed between George and Martha's marriage and the outbreak of war were referred to as Golden Years by the Washingtons. Dedicating their time to Martha's children, each other, and improving Mount Vernon, the couple was content. Their most poignant disappointment during these years was their inability to have children. It is unknown why Martha experienced no further pregnancies after four in relatively quick succession with her first husband. George believed she had been injured in some way during her final labor, but it is at least as likely that he was infertile due to his case of smallpox.[14] Despite this disappointment, the Washingtons had a loving relationship and were famously happy together. Martha and her children had inherited vast Custis lands, but it was Washington's Mount Vernon that they called home. George inherited Mount Vernon, eliminating the need to keep up its lease, when his sister-in-law died in 1761.[15] He never desired to live anywhere else.

Before war could break the spell of life at Mount Vernon, a more personal tragedy struck the Washingtons. Martha's daughter, Patsy, suffered from epilepsy, an ailment that had no cure in the eighteenth century. George and Martha had spent a small fortune on doctors, potions, and even an iron ring in their efforts to cure their beloved daughter, but in June of 1773, Patsy died during an epileptic fit at age sixteen.

Martha, who had already experienced so much grief in her life and buried two other children, was crushed by losing her daughter. George Washington wrote that Patsy's death 'reduced my poor wife to the lowest ebb of misery'. Jacky Custis was Martha's only remaining child, and, though he was irresponsible and spendthrift, he did love and wish to comfort his mother. Upon hearing of his sister's death, he wrote to Martha. 'Her case is more to be envied than pitied, for if we mortals can distinguish between those who are deserving of grace and who are not, I am confident she enjoys that Bliss prepared only for the good and virtuous, let these considerations, My dear Mother have their due weight with you and comfort yourself with reflecting that she now enjoys in substance what we in this world enjoy in imagination and that there is no real Happiness on this side of the grave.'[16]

The death of her teenage daughter was more than the loss of another child to Martha Washington. Patsy had been a helpmate and confidant in a way that her son could never be. Martha spent the rest of her life taking in young extended family members in an effort to fill the gap left by Patsy. Eventually, she would even informally adopt two of her grandchildren. In the immediate aftermath of the death of Patsy Custis, Martha was comforted by the presence of her son's fiancé, Eleanor Calvert. This experience helped form a bond between the two women that caused Martha to support the youthful marriage between Eleanor and Jacky.[17] They were married at Mount Vernon on 3 February 1774. The friendship between Eleanor and her mother-in-law continued beyond the death of Martha's son and Eleanor's remarriage.

For much of their marriage, George and Martha Washington had been loyal British subjects who took a natural pride in their English heritage. They enjoyed Mount Vernon and each other, making careful use of Martha's inheritance from her first husband to bring George's dream for Mount Vernon to life. In the 1770s that life came to an abrupt halt. The couple who had eagerly ordered luxury goods from England began supporting boycotts and determined how to weave more cloth at home. It was not always possible to find colonially sourced substitutes for British goods, but more significant changes were still to come.

Although it occurred on 16 December 1773, news of the Boston Tea Party did not reach Mount Vernon until after the new year. The Washingtons must have wondered how the unrest in distant Massachusetts might impact their lives in Virginia. Perhaps underestimating the changes that were coming, George and Martha began another extensive renovation of Mount Vernon. George had added hundreds of acres to his estate in the years since his marriage, but the house had not been significantly improved since the addition of the second floor. In 1774, he began the work that transformed Mount Vernon into the mansion it is to this day. Several important features were added to the house as part of this renovation.

The New Room was a large, two-story addition that gave the Washingtons a place to entertain large groups of visitors in a style that would have felt familiar to sophisticated friends from Europe. The soaring walls were covered in bright green paper, the dye being an expensive demonstration of wealth. The opposite side of the house received a symmetrical addition that included a study and bedrooms.[18] The cupola was added at this time and served multiple purposes. Besides its aesthetic appeal, the cupola served as a lookout tower, offering a sweeping view of the Mount Vernon estate in every direction. With the windows opened, the cupola also served as clever ventilation for the large home. Heat could rise up and escape through the cupola as cool river breezes blew through the central hall of the first floor.[19] Finally, the two-story piazza that dramatically embraced the view of the Potomac was included in this series of renovations. This had the dual purpose of creating shade for the rooms on the east side of the house as well as creating an impressive outdoor space that maintained a comfortable temperature.[20]

While the Washingtons' renovations were started in earnest, reprisals for the Boston Tea Party from Britain were not slow in coming. In response to the Coercive Acts, or Intolerable Acts as they were referred to in the colonies, and the closing of the Port of Boston, a convention of the Virginia burgesses was scheduled for 1 August 1774. George Washington was in attendance. Delegates were selected to attend the Continental Congress that soon followed. 'God be with you gentlemen,' Martha said as she watched her husband leave Mount Vernon on 1 October 1774 for Philadelphia and an increasingly fuzzy future. The evening before had been spent in passionate discussion with those traveling with George: Edmund Pendleton, Patrick Henry, and George Mason.[21] Resistance to Britain had already begun with the Virginia boycott of British imports. The delegates planned to encourage other colonies, that had not already, to follow suit.

While George was in Philadelphia and tensions rose between England and her rebellious colonies, Martha managed Mount Vernon on her own, a responsibility that would continue to burden her for many more years to come. However, as 1774 came to a close and 1775 brought promise of war, Martha could have had no inkling of how much she and George would be expected to sacrifice to attend the birth of the United States of America.

At this stage, Martha actively participated in the boycott of British goods. Mount Vernon was almost a small village with multiple farms, a mill, distillery, and spinning house. They would forego European luxuries and make American homespun trendy, since the enslaved population at Mount Vernon could spin rope and rough textiles but nothing as fine as satin or silk.[22] Makeshift tea was made from herbs as colonists experimented to find palatable substitutes for the tea that now flavored Boston Harbor. Coffee saw a rise in popularity during the Revolutionary Era that would never disappear.

The autumn of 1775 saw Martha initiate a routine that would stay with her throughout the war for independence. She packed up wagons with supplies and trekked for almost a month through unfamiliar territory to join George and his troops in their winter camp. By the end of the war, Martha had spent almost half her time away from Mount Vernon due to her dedication to being at her husband's side.[23] That first winter at Cambridge, Massachusetts, Martha served as hostess and secretary, attempting to screen the many people who grasped at a few moments of the general's attention. George would have been hard-pressed to achieve anything that winter without Martha's contributions. She planned entertainment that gave everyone an opportunity to have a few words with her increasingly famous husband but protected his coveted privacy as well.

Away from the comforts of home and surrounded by strangers, Martha's natural cheer and optimism kept her going and was a balm to her stressed and under-supported husband. She was determined to make the best of circumstances, even when startled by artillery in the distance. 'Every person seems to be cheerfull and happy hear – some days we have a number of cannon and shells from Boston and Bunkers Hill, but it does not seem to surprise any one but me; I confess I shudder every time I hear the sound of a gun,' Martha wrote to her friend, Elizabeth Ramsay, on 30 December 1775. She goes on to describe her journey through 'beautyfull country' without mentioning the terror she must have felt during ferry crossings or the snow and cold to which the Virginian was unaccustomed.[24] Martha would not have her personal account be a reason for anyone's discouragement. She witnessed the dismal experience of the soldiers that inspired her to do all she could to assist them and support her husband, defending him and his decisions to any critic.

The Continental Army officially came into existence on 14 June 1775 and moved into New York City in April 1776.[25] Soon smallpox began infecting the troops, as it commonly did under the crowded, unsanitary conditions. George carried his smallpox scars as evidence of his immunity, but he was worried for Martha. He quickly took advantage of the need to consult congress to conduct Martha to the relative safety of Philadelphia.[26] Martha must have held hopes at this time that the war would not interrupt their lives for overly long. Rather than return to Mount Vernon, she stayed in Philadelphia and underwent smallpox inoculation. Given her lifelong fear of illness, this demonstrates what Martha was willing to endure that she might be more often in the company of her husband.

Once Martha had recovered from inoculation, the Washingtons sat for portraits painted by Charles Willson Peale.[27] One can only imagine the import of this task in Martha's mind, as she must have contemplated what losses the fighting would mean for American families, hers included. She had already lost one husband under much more mundane circumstances than war.

Peale had painted portraits of the Washingtons in 1772 as well, and there is a marked difference, especially in George's image. He appears more than four years older in the later portrait with greyed hair and worried lines upon his face. Instead of the navy and scarlet uniform of the Virginia Regiment, he wears the blue and buff for which he is remembered. Martha also received a miniature of this portrait to have with her while George was away and in case he never returned.

Martha's portrait reveals a woman still attractive at age forty-five with some rounding of the face that reveals her belief that a good host always partook of what was served to her guests. Her hair remains a dark chestnut and is accented with strings of pearls, a favorite style of Martha's. Her complexion is smooth and youthful. A miniature for George would have given him comfort during the couple's long separations.

Martha was in Philadelphia on 2 July when the Continental Congress voted for independence, learning of the Declaration before her husband, who was in New York with his troops and received the news on 9 July.[28] By the end of August, with no quick end to the war on the horizon as she had hoped, Martha returned to Virginia. She was anxious to meet her first grandchild, Elizabeth Parke Custis, born to Martha's son Jack and his wife Eleanor (Calvert) during Martha's absence.

Martha was cozy at home with her son and his family when George crossed an icy Delaware River on Christmas evening to bring his troops much-needed victories at Trenton and Princeton. While warm and comfortable compared to the Continental Army, Christmas at Mount Vernon was not as it had been in the past, missing George and the shipments of luxury goods that used to come from England. The Washingtons must have wondered what the new year held in store for them as the army settled into winter camp for the second time.

Morristown, New Jersey was selected for the chilly soldiers, already experiencing the shortage of supplies that would plague them throughout the war.[29] Travelling through wintery wilderness for about three weeks, Martha arrived in March to add her encouraging presence and helping hands to the bitter situation. Observers noted George and Martha's happiness together regardless of the circumstances.[30] Summer chores demanding her attention, Martha returned to Mount Vernon in June, no doubt hoping that George would be the one coming to her when next they met.

In the meantime, Martha kept busy with daily tasks as well as extra duties she felt compelled to accept. Having seen the value of her own smallpox inoculation, she took in two of her nephews to care for them as they underwent the procedure. When the boys' mother, Martha's sister, Anna, died on 17 December 1777, Martha was crushed by grief. 'She was the greatest favorite I had in the world,' Martha wrote to her grieving brother-in-law. 'She has I hope made a happy exchange – and only gon a little before us the time draws near when I hope we shall meet never more to part.' In the same letter, Martha requests that Anna's husband send his daughter, Fanny, to stay with her. 'My dear sister in her life time often mentioned my taking my dear Fanny if she should be taken away before she grew up – If you will lett her come to live with me, I will with the greatest pleasure take her and be a parent and mother to her as long as I live.' [31] This request was not fulfilled until 1784, when Fanny Bassett was sent to live with Martha at Mount Vernon and became a close companion.

Martha's grief over her sister's death was comforted by the birth of her second grandchild, Martha Parke Custis, on New Year's Eve 1777. With Jacky and his wife and children with Martha at Mount Vernon, she must have been as content as was possible while George remained in camp. He had entered winter quarters to brave winter of 1778 in a location chosen to provide for the troops better than Morristown had the year before. Valley Forge, however, would prove another harsh winter for the Continental Army.[32]

Snow and privation did not stop Martha from arriving in February, ready to provide whatever assistance of which she was capable. She became a substitute mother to young men who were wounded, ill, underfed, and freezing. Her compassionate heart must have broken when she was surrounded by so much need and so few sources of succor, but she never allowed discouragement to show. Martha offered supplies brought from Mount Vernon, spent time visiting those who were ill or wounded, and organized the ladies into sewing circles to mend clothing, knit socks, and make shirts for the underdressed men.[33]

The winter was not entirely free of entertainment. Evenings were frequently brightened with singing, and some of the officers put on a performance of *Cato* for George's birthday on 22 February 1778.[34] This play provided inspiration and strength during the long conflict, including quotes that would be paraphrased by revolutionaries, such as, 'It is not now a time to talk of aught but chains or conquest; liberty or death', and 'What a pity is it that we can die but once to serve our country'. When news arrived in May that France had recognized the independent United States of America, it was just the encouragement the men needed to shake off the pains of winter and prepare for the fighting season. The revived army retook Philadelphia as Martha returned to Mount Vernon.

Martha's routine of joining George at winter camp and seeing to Mount Vernon during the summer continued through each year of the war. The new year of 1779 was rung in at Philadelphia in circumstances quite different from Valley Forge of the year before. The riches of the city were a harsh contrast to the hardships endured by the soldiers, and George Washington worked to correct it. He could not have known that the following winter, back in Morristown, would be even worse. Martha, once again, left her comfortable home to make up for the lack of pay, supplies, and food in whatever small way she could. This depressing winter was followed by the fall of Charleston, South Carolina in May 1780, a devastating loss for the weary Continental Army. Amid concerns that the British might target Mount Vernon, Martha was provided with a protective guard when she made the trip home in June.[35]

The summer of 1780, Martha joined other women in building a Ladies Association that raised funds for the troops. Almost as frustrated as her husband with congress's lack of support and funds, the women decided to see to the work themselves.[36] When they raised $300,000, the women wanted something special for the soldiers or even to just divide up the cash evenly, but General Washington insisted that what they needed most was shirts. The Ladies Association acquiesced to his request and set themselves the task of sewing hundreds of shirts with cloth purchased with the money.[37] While some men were condescending toward the women's domestic efforts at supporting independence, the women were proud and took their work seriously. Martha was now almost fifty, and she must have thought of the young men who would wear the shirts that she sewed. Many of them were of an age with her son, but how many would survive the war? She likely prayed for their safety and health as she lovingly stitched together clothing for the anonymous men.

In September 1781, George Washington returned to Mount Vernon for the first time in six years and met his four grandchildren. One can only imagine Martha's joy at having him home while trying not to think about how soon he must leave. They slept side-by-side in their own bed, more grey and careworn than they had been the last time but finding no less comfort in one another. When George left, Jacky Custis went with him, determined to play a role in the war before it was over. They rode toward Yorktown. As Martha watched the two people she loved most in the world disappear, she surely prayed fervently for their safety and return.

Not accustomed to the rigors of camp life, Jacky soon fell ill. Knowing his mother's anxiety over his health, he wrote to her, 'I have the pleasure to inform you that I find myself much better since I left Mount Vernon, notwithstanding the change in my lodging.' [38] He provided her with a casual update on extended family he had been able to visit and his attempt to locate slaves who had run away from Mount Vernon, but he was not entirely honest. Jacky died on 5 November 1781, having witnessed the surrender of General Cornwallis but not really contributed to the patriotic effort. His mother had outlived all her children, and her beloved husband was at war. No correspondence of Martha's survives for the year after her son died, while she experienced deep, abiding grief. This she shared with her daughter-in-law, Eleanor, and their bond strengthened as they cared for the four young Custis children together.

The joy of the British surrender at Yorktown was firmly tempered for Martha due to the death of Jacky and the continued absence of George as he dealt with congress in Philadelphia. Victory did not taste as sweet as anticipated, but Martha packed up and left Mount Vernon again in December 1782 in order to be with her husband, who was frustrated with dragging treaty negotiations that kept him from home.[39]

On Christmas Eve 1783, George Washington rode up the tree-lined drive to his home, having won the war after sacrificing almost a decade of his life to the cause. Mount Vernon must have appeared oddly changed to him. The renovations begun in 1774 had been completed, but the entire estate had a somewhat dilapidated appearance. A caretaker could not take the place of a passionate owner, and George immediately got to work putting the estate in order.[40]

During George's extended absence, Jacky's widow, Eleanor, had remarried and come to an agreement with Martha. The two youngest children of Jacky and Eleanor were to be raised by George and Martha. This was not an unusual arrangement in the days of frequent remarriages and large families. Few things could have made Martha happier than having a second family to raise. The children put into the Washingtons' care were Eleanor Parke and George Washington Parke Custis, born in 1779 and 1781. Called Nelly and Washy, the children no doubt reminded Martha of Patsy and Jacky of earlier days. Martha wrote to friend Hannah Stockton Boudinot in January 1784, 'My little family are all with me; and have been very well till with in these few days, that they have been taken with the measles – the worst I hope is over, and that I shall soon have them prattling about me again.'[41] Martha's contentment in her domestic situation is evident.

One can only imagine her joy when her niece, Fanny Bassett, also came to live at Mount Vernon that spring, as Martha had requested after Fanny's mother's death years earlier.[42] Fanny was sixteen years old and therefore able to help the aging Martha with the small children and the constant stream of guests who made their pilgrimage to meet the great general. Martha came to depend on and confide in this beloved niece. At about the same time, George's nephew, George Augustine Washington also came to live at Mount Vernon. Romance bloomed between young George and Fanny, and Martha must have been thrilled with the match. She seems to have had no reservations about the marriage, although there were concerns for George Augustine's delicate health. He was sent to Barbados and Bermuda in hope that his health might be made more robust before marrying Fanny on 14 October 1785.[43]

The Washingtons briefly experienced a home life much as they had been desiring for many years. George was passionate about improving his estate, while Martha occupied her time with the children. She had anxiety over their health, which may be forgiven considering she had buried her own four children. In a letter to Fanny Bassett Washington her niece who was now married to George's nephew, she reveals her fears. 'My Dear little children have all been very well, till today my pretty little dear boy complains of a pain in his stomach. I hope it proceeds from cold as he is much better than he was some months agoe and a good nights sleep I trust will carry of his complaints altogether – I cannot say but it makes me miserable if ever he complains let the cause be ever to trifeling – I hope the almighty will spare him to me.'[44]

The Washingtons were forced to spend more of their time than they would have liked on coping with the constant guests that visited Mount Vernon, friend and stranger alike. All of them eager to lay eyes upon the famous general and claim a few moments of his time. It was a strain on their time and their finances. Martha would soon have reason to look fondly back upon these relatively minor inconveniences, for her life would be upended again after George's participation in the Constitutional Convention during the summer of 1787. He had not planned on such a long absence from Mount Vernon, but he also surely realized that the young country would not soon stop needing him. On 6 April 1789, he was officially elected the first President of the United States.

Martha was not pleased. She wrote to her nephew, John Dandridge within days of receiving the news. 'I am truly sorry to tell that the General is gone to New York ... when, or wheather he will ever come home again god only knows – I think it was much too late for him to go in to publick life again, but it was not to be avoided, our family will be deranged as I must soon follow him.'[45] She was disappointed in the continued disruption of their private life, especially as they aged with no retirement in sight, and Martha did not hurry this time to join her husband. However, when she did reach New York several weeks after George, Martha reverted to her habitual optimism. She wrote to Fanny Basset Washington in June that she had 'a very agreable journey' to Philadelphia, and that Fanny would 'think me a good deal in the fashion if you could but see me'.[46]

In other letters to Fanny, Martha revealed her homesickness. 'Give sweet little Maria a thousand kisses for me', she wrote in July.[47] Followed by a heart-wrenching confession in October. 'I never goe to the publick place – indeed I think I am more like a state prisoner than anything else'.[48] The tedium of public life was difficult for the Washingtons, but they were dedicated to serving their country. In a Christmas letter to Mercy Otis Warren, Martha expresses her feelings about the ups and downs of life in New York. 'I am still determined to be cheerful and to be happy in whatever situation I may be, for I have also learnt from experience that the greater part of our happiness or misary depends upon our dispositions, and not upon our circumstances.'[49]

Martha's determination was continuously tested during the years of her husband's presidency. Not only was she longing for home, but frequent bouts of ill health caused her to wonder if she and George would ever enjoy Mount Vernon together again. The first scare came on the heels of Martha's arrival in New York City. A tumor, fever, and pain led to a diagnosis of anthrax for the president, and an operation was deemed necessary.[50] The tumor had grown deep into George's left thigh, and the surgery, performed without anesthesia, would have been agonizing. His recovery was long and painful, leaving him bedridden for weeks. Looking for solace to comfort her fears that she might lose her husband, Martha became friends with Abigail Smith Adams, the wife of George's vice-president, John Adams. Upon meeting Martha, Abigail Adams observed, 'Mrs Washington is one of those unassuming characters which create Love and Esteem'.[51] Abigail was a quick study of character.

As soon as George was able, the Washingtons resumed their dinners and receptions. Their time was in constant demand, so it was necessary to establish specific, limited times for the public to see and speak to the president and his wife. The friendly, easy-going Martha was the ideal partner for her more introverted husband, just as she had been during the winter camps of the Revolutionary War. George was intimidating and aloof, but his wife was able to put people at their ease. George decided to travel in the hope of improving his health and getting some much-needed exercise. As he toured the northern states, Martha, alone in New York City, slipped into depression. Abigail Adams attempted to cheer her with social events, but nothing made Martha happy until George returned.[52]

Less than a year later, George's life was once again feared forfeit. In a probable case of influenza that progressed into potentially deadly pneumonia, doctors warned Martha to prepare for the worst in May 1790.[53] Away from home and family, Martha must have felt scared and alone as she wondered again if coming to New York had been the right decision. She would not be in dire financial straits if George died, but her love and devotion to him were evident in their letters and physical interactions. She must have longed to take him home. After a miraculous recovery, she wrote to Mercy Otis Warren, 'For my part, I continue to be as hapy hear as I could be at any place except Mount Vernon'.[54] All was right with Martha's world as long as George was in it.

Her happiness was complete when the Washington household spent three months of autumn 1790 at Mount Vernon before joining the rest of the federal government in its move to Philadelphia. The brief respite allowed them both to restore their health, visit with family, and ensure that the estate was being properly cared for. For Martha, the time was spent catching up with Fanny and showering grandchildren with affection. It must have been difficult for Martha to pack up and leave again when they left for the Morris mansion of Philadelphia and the cares of a nation were placed firmly on their shoulders once again.

The government's move to Philadelphia had an unanticipated consequence. Since Pennsylvania law stated that slaves were considered free after spending six months in the state, the Washingtons found themselves surreptitiously sending slaves on trips to Mount Vernon to continuously reset the clock on this law without it being publicly known. George struggled with the institution of slavery, having fought for freedom but being economically dependent on slave labor. He also had the additional complication of many of the Mount Vernon slaves being part of the Custis estate and not his to free. Martha, on the other hand, left no evidence that she was troubled by owning human chattel. When one of her personal attendants, Ona Judge, ran away while the Washingtons resided in Philadelphia, Martha was shocked that the young woman did not appreciate her good position. While trying not to raise too much public notice, the Washingtons tracked Judge and unsuccessfully attempted to have her returned to them. Judge married, had children, and lived the rest of her life as a free woman in New Hampshire.

When discussions began regarding George serving a second term as president, Martha was wholly opposed to the idea. Besides her desire to go home, she had already feared for his life twice during the four-year term. George was unenthusiastic but felt duty-bound. Only a unanimous election convinced him to agree to stay.[55]

Martha's fears were soon justified when yellow fever seared its way through Philadelphia in 1793. The busy city was transformed as those who could leave the city did, and tar was burned in the streets to repel disease-carrying mosquitos. George encouraged Martha to go to Mount Vernon, but she refused to leave his side, even when close friend Polly Lear succumbed to the fever. They left together for Virginia in September. Congress reconvened in Germantown to avoid any remaining pestilence in the city, and the Washingtons took up residence there in November 1793. When winter brought an end to the epidemic, almost 12% of Philadelphia's population had died.[56] Martha refused to leave Germantown, even when George was often absent during the summer of 1794 due to the Whiskey Rebellion. To Fanny she admitted, 'The President thinks that the public business will keep him in this place all summer – and it would not be agreable to me to stay at mount Vernon without him'.[57]

If Martha had anxiety over George's health through the winter, she might have relaxed as summer progressed and a resurgence of yellow fever did not occur. She could have scarcely expected that George, known far and wide as an expert horseman, would injure his back when his horse stumbled. She was even more worried because she was not with him to serve as nurse. He had taken a quick trip home, leaving Martha and the children in Pennsylvania. Martha wrote to her closest confidant, Fanny, who was at Mount Vernon. 'I have been so unhappy about the Presidt that I did not know what to do with myself – he tells me in his letter of Wednesday that he is better – I hope in god that he is so – if I could have come down with any conveniance – I should have set out the very hour I got the letter I hope and trust he is better and that he will soon be able to return hear again if he is not getting better my dear Fanny dont let me be deceaved let me know his case and not say he is getting better if he is not – it would make me exceeding unhappy to be told or made to believe he is getting better if he is not.'[58] Poor Martha's anxiety drips from the page.

George recovered once again. It was Fanny who died of tuberculosis on 25 March 1796. She had contracted the disease from her husband, George Augustine Washington, who had died three years earlier. Once again, Martha had lost a dear female relative who had filled a special place in her heart. Mount Vernon would have felt quite different without Fanny's presence. With Fanny's death, history also lost a source of correspondence that illuminated Martha's inner thoughts and feelings.

While no one could quite replace Fanny Bassett Washington in Martha's heart, Nelly Custis was coming of age, making her available as a helper and confidant. Her brother, Washy, had turned out much like his father before him, lazy and irresponsible, if loveable, but Nelly was mature and devoted to her grandmother who was more like a mother to her than her real mother. In fact, Nelly was crushed when she was sent to spend a season with her mother, Eleanor Custis Stuart.[59] Nelly was no less devoted to her grandfather, and chose his birthday, 22 February 1799, as the date for her wedding to George's nephew, Lawrence Washington.[60] They did not realize they were celebrating George Washington's final birthday.

Lawrence and Nelly were a blessing to the elder Washingtons. In their late sixties and weary of public life, George and Martha depended on their young nephew and granddaughter to act as hosts to the steady stream of Mount Vernon visitors as well as help manage the estate. It was an arrangement that suited all participants and became an even greater comfort to Martha when George died after a brief illness in December 1799.

Martha was crushed by his death by all accounts. At his bedside as he struggled to breathe his last, Martha sat quietly while doctors bled George and burdened him with useless treatments of eighteenth century medicine. When he was gone, she said, 'Tis well. All is now over. I shall soon follow him. I have no more trials to pass through.'[61] She never slept in their shared bedroom again, deciding instead to take refuge in a small attic room.[62]

After the death of George Washington, his wife, wishing to preserve her privacy, burned the forty-one years of letters they had written to each other. This action demonstrates several truths regarding Martha Washington. Her marriage had been a long and loving one. She knew that her husband had taken an immortal place in history, and she did not wish for their private life to be a part of that history. Martha undoubtedly felt that she had offered up enough to the public good and deserved to keep some part of her adored husband to herself.

She did not attend the funeral, although it was held at Mount Vernon.[63] Her days of forcing herself to do what the public expected of her were over, and she mourned alone and in her own way, closeted away with her Bible. The attic room would have been cold as the December wind blew in off the Potomac and Martha grieved. The remainder of Martha's life was spent waiting to join her husband in the heaven she so fervently believed in. She took comfort from the presence of Lawrence and Nelly and even rejoiced at the births of grandchildren and great-grandchildren, but she longed for George.

Martha was also not left to grieve in peace. Condolences, to which propriety required she make response, poured into Mount Vernon at such a pace that Martha was hopeless to keep up. George's secretary, Tobias Lear, took on much of the responsibility, and congress granted Martha the right of franking, free postage for mailing, that she might not be burdened by the cost of responding to so much correspondence.[64]

George had left Martha with a difficulty in his will. Over time, he had begun to struggle with the institution of slavery in a way that Martha never did, and he had granted his slaves their freedom upon Martha's death. He might have meant for this to free Martha from the responsibility of coping with their emancipation, but it created a difficult situation where some of the Mount Vernon slaves knew their freedom was based on the elderly lady's death. In addition to that awkward challenge, the enslaved populations of the Washington and Custis estates had become intermingled during George and Martha's long marriage. Those that were a part of the Custis inheritance would legally transfer to Martha's grandchildren upon her death, while those that had been George's would be free. That not only seemed arbitrary and unfair but also left black families with some members anticipating freedom and others not.

Martha attempted to ease this tense situation by freeing George's slaves on 1 January 1801. She was afraid that some of the slaves plotted her death in order to gain their freedom, so she gave it to them.[65] Some eagerly took up their newfound liberty and left Mount Vernon, others stayed because of family who remained property or for the stability Mount Vernon offered.[66] Her thoughts about this event are not recorded, but Martha had previously expressed shock and dismay when enslaved servants ran away. She did not understand why they would choose an uncertain freedom over the life offered at Mount Vernon. For a woman who had been part of a lengthy revolution based on liberty, it was an ironic blind spot.

No longer bridled by public etiquette, Martha was outspoken about her late husband's political opponents. She made no secret of her deep dislike of Thomas Jefferson, describing a visit from him as 'the most painful occurrence of her life' excepting only the loss of her husband.[67] Considering all that Martha had endured – the loss of two husbands and four children, eight years of war, and eight more of the presidency – it was a hard-hitting insult.

Martha did not wait long to join George and the many other friends and loved ones she had mourned during her almost seventy-one years. On 22 May 1802, she died in her little attic room, surrounded by those who loved her. As she had bravely followed George on so many other adventures, Martha joined him once again.

Chapter 3

Agent 355

I intend to visit 727 before long and think by the assistance of a 355 of my acquaintance, shall be able to outwit them all.
— Abraham Woodhull, aka Samuel Culper, Agent 722

Some women of the American Revolution are well-known, their names immediately bring to mind a portrait or quotation. Others remain elusive to this day. Though some of their contribution to history is known, their name is not. Agent 355 is contradictorily famous for serving as a female spy in George Washington's Culper Spy Ring, yet completely unknown, for no one has ever positively identified her. The only name for which she is known is the assigned number in Major Benjamin Tallmadge's codebook. Who was the woman behind the number 355? Several theories exist.

The Culper Spy Ring was developed in 1778 in response to the American army's need for intelligence on activities of the British during the occupation of New York City.[1] Some of the early American attempts at spying had been tragic and ineffective. One of the best-known examples is that of Nathan Hale. Young, erudite, and patriotic, Hale was enthusiastic but naïve. The young schoolteacher had been quickly arrested and hanged during his mission to Long Island.

Nathan Hale and Benjamin Tallmadge had been good friends and classmates at Yale.[2] Hale's death on 22 September 1776 would impact the caution and care that Tallmadge invested in creating Washington's spy ring. Tallmadge's older brother, William, had also starved to death while held on a British prison ship.[3] Needless to say, Tallmadge was ambitious to see the patriot cause succeed.

Washington had begun intelligence efforts within a fortnight of gaining command of the Continental Army, writing, 'There is nothing more necessary than good intelligence to frustrate a designing enemy, & nothing that requires greater pains to obtain'.[4] The Culper Ring was one of the most extensive spy networks of the American Revolution. It was composed of people that Tallmadge knew personally and trusted implicitly. Abraham Woodhull and Caleb Brewster had grown up in Setauket, New York with Tallmadge, and they formed the center of the ring. Initially, Woodhull went by the alias Samuel Culper. Later, Tallmadge assigned him the code number 722.[5] Agent 355 was likely a woman known by Tallmadge or Woodhull in order to have been included in the Culper Spy Ring.

Was she the wife of a friend? Servant? Slave? Maybe she was not connected to Tallmadge and Woodhull at all but was brought into the ring by another agent. Morton Pennypacker, an early Culper Ring historian, first suggested in 1948 that she was the secret wife of Robert Townsend, an agent (designated by 723) living in New York City during the British occupation. This is the theory historian Corey Ford finds most compelling in his 1965 *A Peculiar Service*, which takes an in-depth look at 1770s New York.[6] This romantic possibility has been taken up by historical novelists, and it appeals to readers who love a tragic romance. But is it true?

It is even possible that the 355 code was utilized simply to refer to a woman who was not an agent, since the number refers to 'lady' rather than a specific person, whereas the known agents' numbers referred specifically to them. In fact, all of the known agents are assigned numbers in the 700s in Benjamin Tallmadge's codebook, but the 300s are a list of general terms rather than proper nouns. The term 'lady' does offer some clue that Woodhull referred to a woman of a certain class, for a man of his time would not typically have referred to an enslaved servant, for example, as a lady. Is there a clue in Woodhull's choice of words in the single reference we have to Agent 355? He wrote, 'I intend to visit 727 before long and think by the assistance of a 355 of my acquaintance, shall be able to outwit them all'.[7] Does the fact that he says the lady is of 'my acquaintance' rather than 'our acquaintance' imply that she was unknown to Benjamin Tallmadge to whom Woodhull was writing? Or does that simply reflect that she was unknown to George Washington, the ultimate consumer of the information provided?

Had Abraham Woodhull had his way, there would be no record whatsoever of Agent 355, if she existed, or any of the Culper Ring activity. He would often include a request to 'destroy every letter instantly after reading for fear of some unforeseen accident that may befall you and the letters get into the enemies' hands and probably find me out and take me before I have any warning'.[8] However, George Washington knew he was making history and took exceptional care to preserve his writing and correspondence. Much of what remains of Woodhull's letters are Washington's decoded transcripts rather than the originals.

Ford supports the theory of Agent 355 being Robert Townsend's wife with the fact that a boy named Robert Townsend Jr was born around 1780. When grown, Robert Townsend Jr joined an association that built a memorial to those Americans who had died on British prison ships. Could this be because his mother had been arrested as a spy and died aboard one of the fetid ships? This would explain stretches of silence and sudden reluctance on the part of Townsend. He may not have feared danger for himself, but he would have wanted to protect his wife, if he had one, especially if she had been pregnant, as Ford suggests. Conversely, some believe that Robert Townsend Jr was born to a servant in Townsend's household. A theory that seems more plausible if less romantic. Historian Kenneth Daigler points out that Robert Townsend Jr's most likely birthdate is after the Revolutionary War was over, discrediting the theory that his mother was an imprisoned spy.[9]

Agent 355 may only be a figment of overactive imaginations, and many historians remain unconvinced of her existence beyond being just what Woodhull said, 'a lady of my acquaintance'. Female spies were uncommon but not nonexistent in the American Revolution. Some operated on their own, sending information to husbands or brothers in the army, and others were part of more organized networks. In many situations, women found themselves the holders of important information simply because men assumed they were not listening or could not understand the significance of what they were overhearing or observing.

Margaret Kemble Gage, wife of British General Thomas Gage, is believed by some historians to have passed information to the revolutionaries, warning Dr Joseph Warren of her husband's plan to seize weapons at Lexington.[10] While she has never been proven a spy with certainty, her loyalty to the colonial cause was well-known. General Gage had been stationed in the Americas for most of their marriage, and Margaret was from a prominent American family. The fact that her husband sent her to England just as the war was getting underway serves as circumstantial evidence of the suspicions against Margaret. However, it is also known that the Gages were a close couple who had eleven children together. When Margaret left for England, she went along with 170 wounded British soldiers and dozens of widows and orphans returning home.[11] Did Margaret love her husband but hope to thwart his plans against the colonists? We may never know. Margaret remained in England the rest of her life, despite the end of the war and the death of her husband.

Lydia Darragh was not suspected of carefully observing and listening as she went about her business in Philadelphia during the British occupation. If the fact that she was a woman was not enough to remove suspicion, she was also a Quaker. Many in the Quaker community attempted to remain entirely neutral during the American Revolution, an objective that could be difficult with competing armies vying for loyalty and supplies. When British officers met in a room of the Darragh home, they felt confident of their security. Even when the Americans clearly had been warned of a planned attack at White Marsh, the British questioned other members of the household, but not Lydia, stating, 'I know you were asleep for I knocked at your door three times before you heard me. I am entirely at a loss to imagine who gave General Washington information of our intended attack.'[12]

Sixteen-year-old Dicey Langston of South Carolina not only spied on her Tory neighbors to pass on vital information to the Americans, she shielded her father from harm when those neighbors became suspicious enough to threaten him with a gun. She also braved the marshy wilderness all alone in order to take information to her brother, James, who was fighting with the patriots.[13]

Female spies were not only recruited by the Americans. Elizabeth Thompson of Charlestown, Massachusetts, aided British prisoners, carried information to British troops, and even escorted a disguised British officer to where he could observe the Continental troops.[14] The first time Lorenda Holmes of New York was caught carrying messages to the British, she was 'stripped naked and exposed to the mob'. Humiliated, but not physically hurt, she was set free. The second time, her foot was held to hot coals.[15]

Was Agent 355 like one of these women, eager to serve or forced by circumstances? As historian Corey Ford states, 'Any history of espionage is bound to contain some blank pages, where the writer can find no documentation or record to guide him.'[16] Information flooded through the Culper Ring while British Major John André was in New York but slowed to a trickle when he went to Charleston, South Carolina. Is this an indication that Agent 355 was a friend or member of his household? It is an exciting, if improbable, suggestion. André's notes include evidence that he was aware of the Culper Ring with possible knowledge of individuals involved. Had he not been executed as a spy on 2 October 1780 for his part in Benedict Arnold's downfall, his map of Setauket and suspicions of the spy ring there might have had terrible consequences for those involved.[17]

Morton Pennypacker believed that Agent 355 could have been a woman related to Robert Townsend, even if she had not been his secret wife. Pennypacker points out that Townsend's sister, Sarah (also known as Sally), could have discovered Major John André's letters regarding the West Point plot. She may also have eavesdropped on conversations of Colonel John Graves Simcoe when the British officer was lodged in her parent's home.[18] Simcoe made no secret of his romantic feelings for Sarah, even giving her what is believed to be the first Valentine in America. Was he too casual with military information in her presence? Another possibility is that a servant overheard British plans that they passed on to Sarah, who told Robert so he could see that General Washington was informed. Perhaps Sarah did more than we know for the Culper Ring. Could she have been Agent 355?

At the same time, General Arnold was attempting to discover the names of the Culper spies in order to turn them over to the British along with the fort at West Point. He requested 'to be informed who they are, as I wish to employ them, for the same purpose. I will engage upon them to make no discovery of them to any person breathing'.[19] Fortunately, Arnold was unsuccessful in his attempt to gain entry into the Culper Ring before he was forced to flee when his treason was discovered.

The members of the Culper Ring, however, were not certain that their identities were unknown by Benedict Arnold. Major Tallmadge wrote to General Washington on 11 October 1780, 'The conduct of Arnold, since his arrival at N.Y. has been such, that though he knows not a single link in the chain of my correspondence, still those who have assisted us in this way, are too apprehensive of Danger to give their immediate usual intelligence.'[20]

Despite his assertion that Robert Townsend's sister provided him with information, Pennypacker did not initially name Sarah or her servant as Agent 355. In the 1939 edition of his *General Washington's Spies on Long Island and in New York*, Pennypacker stated that Anna Strong of Setauket was likely the lady Woodhull refers to as 355. It was not until the release of his 1948 supplementary research that he preferred the theory that Agent 355 had been Robert Townsend's secret wife.

Alexander Rose, who is widely accepted as a leading modern expert and has written one of the most thorough investigations into the Culper Ring, simply describes 355 as 'Anna Strong, Woodhull's neighbor and wife of Selah Strong, an active Whig and delegate to the provincial Congress before the war who was currently jailed aboard one of the British prison ships as a suspected insurrectionist'.[21] Rose does not suggest any alternate theories for 355's identity.

Anna Strong does fit the requirement that a participant in the Culper Ring be known and trusted by Tallmadge and Woodhull. Although she was older, and therefore was not a childhood friend of theirs, Anna was also from Setauket and was married to the local judge. Her sister was the second wife of Abraham Woodhull's father. While she may not have been Agent 355, Anna could have had a role in the Culper Ring. Some historians believe she was responsible for alerting Caleb Brewster that Woodhull had a communication to deliver. Some believe she did so by hanging laundry on her clothesline according to prearranged signals. However, not all historians accept that this role was filled by Anna and warn that the clothesline story should be treated more like local folklore than settled fact.[22]

Mary Underhill could also have been the lady to whom Abraham Woodhull referred. She was his sister, married to Amos Underhill and running a boarding house in New York City with him. Woodhull could plausibly visit his sister and brother-in-law with some regularity without raising suspicion, but there is no evidence that she assisted him in any other way with his spy work, although Woodhull did utilize their boarding house. Given Woodhull's reluctancy as a spy, it may have been unlikely that he would get his sister involved as well.

Although women enjoyed the advantage of lessened suspicions during spy work, they also endured physical dangers inherent in lone travel and interactions with the enemy. Women found working for the Americans took many of the same risks that men did, including imprisonment and execution, but they also could be sexually abused and often had dependent children who might suffer alongside their mother.

While there are many theories about who Agent 355 could have been, the most likely explanation is that there was no Agent 355 at all. Many modern historians believe that too much has been made of Abraham Woodhull's single reference to a lady of his acquaintance. Whoever he refers to, it is unlikely that the lady providing him some assistance was an agent. Whatever the true identity of Agent 355, or whether she existed at all, the name reminds us of all women who courageously risked their freedom and perhaps their lives in the pursuit of liberty.

Chapter 4

Sybil Ludington

There is no extravagance in comparing her ride with that of Paul Revere and its midnight message.

— Willis Fletcher Johnson

The passage of time and the exceptional activities of war transform some historical events into myth. It might sound implausible that Washington led troops across a frozen Delaware River on Christmas night, but we know it is true. Sybil Ludington is, and was, relatively unknown, but is her story authentic or the stuff of legend?

The first of her parents' twelve children, Sybil Ludington was born 5 April 1761. She was, therefore, sixteen years old on 26 April 1777 when her father, Colonel Henry Ludington, learned that the British were headed toward Danbury, Connecticut to seize or destroy colonial military provisions. Her father, lacking a more appropriate messenger, sent his daughter to ride through the county (New York's Putnam County now, Dutchess County in 1777) to alert the militia.[1]

A young woman could encounter many dangers in the middle of the night on the tree-lined country roads of a nation at war. That April night is reported to have been stormy with driving rain and terrible conditions for travel. Yet, Sybil is believed to have ridden approximately forty miles under these conditions in order to spread her father's message that the British target was Danbury. She reportedly approached each household with the warning that the British were burning Danbury. Encouraging men to join her father at Ludington's Mill and spread the word.

Besides the darkness, poor weather conditions, and rough roads, Sybil would have had to be on the watch for even greater dangers. The area was populated with men who were referred to as cowboys and skinners, violent men of both armies looking for easy prey. The no-mans-land that existed between army camps was vulnerable to crime and those who would take advantage of the situation. 'Cowboys' referred to British or

Tory gangs, while 'skinners' were Americans. It was marauders such as these that captured the British Major John André after his secret meeting with General Benedict Arnold, and they could have even more easily snagged a young woman alone in the night.[2]

Despite the alleged efforts of Sybil and Colonel Ludington, Danbury was burned, and the supplies destroyed. However, the gathered militia was able to drive the British back to Long Island before they could raze their next target. The lack of a successful mission has not made Sybil's story less intriguing. She is remembered as a brave young woman who was willing to risk her life for the American cause of liberty.

After the war, Sybil was married on 21 October 1784 to Edmund Ogden, who had also served in the Revolutionary War. When he died, Sybil applied for a pension based on his service, never mentioning her own activity. Even when it was necessary to appeal the decision to deny her a pension, Sybil did not mention her midnight ride. This is one of the facts that has led some historians to question whether or not it ever happened.

Did Sybil Ludington really ride over twice as far as Paul Revere and avoid capture by the British? Revere's ride has become cemented in American minds largely thanks to the poem by Henry Wadsworth Longfellow. In 'Paul Revere's Ride', written in 1860, Longfellow credits Revere with warning 'every Middlesex village and farm', though he truly was captured before reaching Concord as the first shots were fired in 1775. It is because of 'the midnight ride of Paul Revere' as told by Longfellow that most Americans remember lanterns signal one if by land and two if by sea (really, the Charles River). Revere traveled about twelve-thirteen miles, dodging British patrols. His main goal was not necessarily to reach every village the British might target, but rather to warn Samuel Adams and John Hancock and avoid their capture.

If Sybil did complete a ride that made Revere's look like a Sunday stroll, why did she not point out her service in 1838 when attempting to obtain a government pension? This is not the only question that crops up when considering Sybil's story.

In 1848–1850, Elizabeth Ellet compiled a two-volume record of colonial women's lives, including women's contributions to the Revolutionary War. This exhaustive history, titled *Domestic History of the American Revolution*, does not make mention of Sybil Ludington. Neither does Jesse Clement's

Noble Deeds of American Women, published in 1851. Did early historians of the women's part in the Revolutionary War simply overlook Sybil's story?

The first mention of Sybil's midnight ride is found in Martha J. Lamb's 1880 *History of the City of New York: Its Origin, Rise, and Progress*. It was then elaborated upon in a 1907 biography of Sybil's father. Based on oral family history, author Willis Fletcher Johnson had included Sybil's ride in his book, *Colonel Henry Ludington*. It was from this point that the daughter began to outshine the father. It was Johnson who gave Sybil star power by claiming, 'There is no extravagance in comparing her ride with that of Paul Revere'. [3]

According to historian Paula D. Hunt, Sybil's current fame can be traced back to a local effort to increase tourism in Putnam County, New York. In 1935, commemorative historic markers were placed along a plausible route for Sybil's ride. Since then, they have become historic evidence in and of themselves.[4] The markers have even inspired a poem, just as Paul Revere inspired Henry Wadsworth Longfellow. In 'Sybil Ludington's Ride', Berton Braley even calls her 'a lovely feminine Paul Revere'.

In her article, *Sybil Ludington, The Female Paul Revere: The Making of a Revolutionary War Heroine*, Paula D. Hunt demonstrates that other books, pamphlets, articles, local events, and even commemorative statues grew from the historic route markers until no one any longer questioned whether Sybil's ride actually happened. Americans long for an everyday heroine to whom young women can relate and admire. However, that desire should not override the demand for historical accuracy.

We might never know for certain if Sybil made her legendary ride. Barring previously undiscovered evidence, proving or disproving Sybil's legend is impossible. The lack of concern regarding the proof of Sybil's ride, or lack thereof, demands another question. Why do Americans so eagerly want to believe that it is true?

Paula D. Hunt states that Sybil 'represents Americans' persistent need to find and create heroes who embody prevalent attitudes and beliefs'.[5] It is an explanation that holds up to scrutiny when one examines the actions that created Sybil's fame.

From Martha J. Lamb's first mention of Sybil, the story of a young girl sent on a dangerous mission by her father has been repeated, elaborated upon, and used as inspiration through America's social issues. When Lamb was writing in 1880, it was to keep the memory of the American

Revolution alive at a time when those who had experienced it firsthand were disappearing. A similar phenomenon is taking place today as historians and writers fervently document and memorialize the Second World War. Veterans of the American Revolution were their Greatest Generation, and including the story of a young woman in that history gave a greater audience ownership of America's victory.

Even Putnam County's historical markers that guess at Sybil's possible route were inspired by more than a desire to boost the tourism industry. When they were installed during the Great Depression, they reminded Americans of what they had overcome in the past and what could be accomplished by a common citizen.[6] Could the project's participants have foreseen that the markers would be used as evidence of the historical event that they had only made educated guesses regarding, perhaps they would have changed course, but little can slow the spread of Sybil's story today.

It is not only the roadside signs that have been referenced as the source of historical fact. A children's book by Erick Berry, *Sybil Ludington's Ride*, gave Sybil's horse a name, Star, and this name has also become part of the historical retelling. Each detail strengthens America's bond to Sybil and her story and reduces the chance that anyone will question it.

As Paula D. Hunt demonstrates, Sybil's story has been used to inspire throughout the twentieth century. 'In the context of Cold War anxieties, Sybil's ride was not simply an act of youthful courage but an affirmation of American exceptionalism that needed to be revived in an imperiled era.'[7] Putnam County even had a Sybil Ludington Camp, where young girls could learn to be brave and self-sufficient just like Sybil.[8]

In a growing age of feminism and diversity, Sybil's story is included among those of the Founding Fathers to demonstrate that women were just as important as men during the birth of the nation. Sybil's story is simple and undefined, making her malleable to a host of historical social issues. Her name has been used to encourage local tourism, survival skills, patriotic pride, and countless other causes. Sybil was included in a set of commemorative stamps issued in 1975 alongside other lesser-known heroes, Salem Poor, Haym Salomon, and Peter Francisco.[9] Maybe the important thing is not whether or not Sybil really rode those forty miles on 26 April 1777 but the fact that she could have.

Deborah Champion made a patriotic ride of her own, carrying intelligence to George Washington in Boston from her home in Rhode

Island. She even had the composure to bypass a British sentry who stopped her along the way.[10] Many women were compelled to step up and perform courageous acts that they would not have done otherwise during the American Revolution. Like Sybil, they filled a need, took on a role that would have normally been filled by a man, and did what was necessary for the sake of their country. Some of their stories are better documented even if they do not enjoy the level of fame that Sybil enjoys today.

Women's lives were changed by the American Revolution. Considered a civil war at the time, families were torn apart by split loyalties, inflation left households in poverty, and violence was not restricted to battlefields as armies roamed the countryside for provisions and whatever else they might take from undefended households. Whether women were willing or not, many of them had to show the type of courage for which young Sybil Ludington has become famous.

They maintained farms and plantations, performing physical labor they had never before had to endure. They managed businesses, some learning along the way the skills with numbers and letters they had not been taught as children. They followed the army, not having the resources or ability to maintain a home on their own, they served as cooks, laundresses, and less savory roles for the fighting men. At home or in the field, they served as nurses to wounded men and sick children. Some women rose confidently to these challenges. Others struggled. Some failed.

Through the eight years of armed conflict, it is safe to assume that every woman in America was tested, had their life changed, and was forced to do something they might not have otherwise done. There can have been few whose daily lives were not touched by the hardships of war.

Some other women share Sybil's legendary status. Betsy Ross is widely remembered for designing and sewing the American flag that we all recognize today, but this story is no better documented than Sybil's. In fact, there are other women who made similar claims, and each may have some truth to them given the number of battle flags suddenly required beginning in 1776. Betsy Ross, who actually only briefly went by that name since her first husband died after only twenty-eight months of marriage, may have shared a story with her children about George Washington entering her shop, but she was far from the only Philadelphian of the era to do so. Washington was revered almost as a king after the end of the war, so everyone wanted to emphasize any connection they had with him.

Historian Marla R. Miller has performed exhaustive research on the history of Betsy Ross and admits that Betsy Ross might not have created the 'Betsy Ross Flag'. She might not have even lived in the Betsy Ross House in Philadelphia, but 'her life nevertheless helps us to contemplate the Revolution and its aftermath in new ways ... Her story is worth knowing for what it tells us, too, about the working women and men who built early American cities.'[11]

Molly Pitcher, who is most likely a compilation of women who stepped in to assist men at the front, is another legendary story of women in the American Revolution. So many other stories remain largely untold.

Before any bloodshed of war, women became involved in the patriotic cause by boycotting British goods. In their domestic role, it was much more within their control than their husbands' to make calls for nonimportation successful. Women took this responsibility seriously, as is demonstrated by the Edenton Ladies' Patriotic Guild who created their own agreement on 25 October 1774. The fifty-one signers pledged their public support for boycott.[12] Esther deBerdt Reed joined with Sarah Franklin Bache to form a Ladies' Association in Philadelphia. Sarah was the daughter of famous patriot, Benjamin Franklin, and Esther was the wife of Pennsylvania governor Joseph Reed. She wrote 'Sentiments of an American Woman' to encourage women to simplify and sacrifice for the Revolutionary cause.[13] By joining with other prominent ladies throughout the colonies, the Ladies' Association was able to collect an incredible amount, over $300,000, that they hoped would be divided equally between American soldiers. Esther wrote that the 'extraordinary bounty intended to render the condition of the Soldier more pleasant', but in the end, she used it to have shirts made as requested by General George Washington.[14] Still, Reed had demonstrated the ability of women to work together and achieve great things.

Women who remained loyal to King George III faced hardship just as their patriotic counterparts did. Esther Quincy Sewall calmed a mob that had formed outside her Cambridge, Massachusetts home by giving them free access to her husband's wine cellar.[15] Faring much worse, Grace Growden Galloway of Philadelphia saw her riches confiscated by the Americans. When she insisted that, 'Nothing but force shou'd get me out of My house', the men sent to possess her home were happy to oblige.[16] Both women had enjoyed life in the upper stratus of society before their husbands took the British side in the Revolution.

Emily Geiger has a story similar to that of Sybil Ludington. In June 1781, General Nathanael Greene needed to get a vital message to General Thomas Sumter regarding a plan of attack that required the consolidation of American troops. Emily insisted that she made the ideal messenger. She believed that a woman would be less conspicuous on roads swarming with British scouts. She may have been correct, but Emily was still stopped and searched. Little did the British know that she had memorized General Greene's message. Thanks to her brave action, General Sumter joined General Greene and America inched toward victory.[17]

Some women were not as brave or fortunate as others in making their mark on history. Young Jane McCrea is remembered for being scalped by Native Americans during an attack on Fort Edward. She was staying in a house near the fort when she was taken. Her imprisoners later claimed that she had only been scalped after dying of a bullet intended for her captors. Since the war party's second hostage, a Mrs McNeil, was delivered to the fort, their version of events is plausible. The young woman, who by all accounts had been the beautiful daughter of a clergyman, was an unfortunate victim, and nothing was gained by her death.[18]

Women on both sides of the conflict were affected by war. Wives of British soldiers faced the same decision whether to follow their husbands or stay home alone, though to follow was often an option only open to officer's wives unless the soldier had married once in America. Mercy Otis Warren, an otherwise fiery American patriot, commits several pages to the devotion and bravery of Lady Harriett Ackland, whose husband, Major Ackland, was wounded and taken prisoner by American forces at Saratoga. 'She followed his fortune and shared his fatigues,' Mercy wrote. 'Lady Ackland lost not her resolution or her cheerfulness by the dangers she had encountered; but accompanied her soldier to the action ... Here among the wounded and dying, Lady Ackland with her usual serenity stood prepared for new trials.'[19]

New trials Lady Ackland certainly endured. When she learned that her husband had been taken prisoner, she presented herself at enemy lines, requesting to see him. She was given safe passage by General Horatio Gates and nursed her husband who had been shot in both legs until he was allowed to return to England the following year.

African American women in America experienced unique challenges during the American Revolution as well. Hearing the call for freedom but knowing it did not apply to them, many felt helpless to improve their conditions. Black men might decide to accept the British offer of freedom in exchange for joining their side, but that only left their wives, sisters, and daughters more vulnerable. Holding a family together was challenging enough for those who were enslaved and increasingly difficult as war engulfed the nation. Some took advantage of the chaos to run away and establish themselves in lands to the west or in Canada. According to historian Carol Berkin, most remained where they were, 'the desire to be in familiar surroundings and among friends and family in a time of chaos and violence kept them at home'.[20]

Free blacks in America had to decide whether the British or American side offered them better opportunities for the future. Black women sometimes resorted to becoming camp followers just as white women did. A living could be made as laundress, cook, or nurse, and, of course, some resorted to prostitution. Although they were dependent upon the soldiers, women who decided to follow the army did feel they were exerting some independence in making the decision to leave their home to do so.

Phyllis Wheatley is the most famous black woman of the Revolutionary era. Brought to the United States and sold into slavery in 1761, Phyllis was purchased by the Wheatley family of Boston, who saw that she was educated and treated much like a member of the family until they eventually freed her. Phyllis wrote and published poetry, no small feat for any eighteenth-century woman, earning her widespread praise and even a letter from President George Washington. Most African Americans, however, did not see their situations improved by the Revolution, and while northern states began prohibiting slavery in the post-war years, those in the south would not taste emancipation until 1863.

Women in America led varied lives before the American Revolution and took on just as varied of roles during the war. Some are remembered as heroines. Some paid the ultimate price. Many are not remembered at all. It is for those that the legend of Sybil Ludington lives on, inspiring generations of women to do more than they thought themselves capable.

Chapter 5

Mercy Otis Warren

I know of none, ancient or modern, which has reached the tender, the pathetic, the keen and severe, and at the same time, the soft, the sweet, the amiable and the pure in great perfection.

– John Adams

Mercy Otis Warren was a witness to the rise of the American Revolution. She soaked up the populist ideas that her brothers brought home from their studies and eventually convinced her father to allow her to join them with their tutor. At a time when women's writing was typically limited to household records and personal letters, Mercy wrote satirical political plays, poetry, and eventually a massive three-volume historical narrative. In an era of firm division between gender roles, Mercy made a name for herself on the political scene and lobbied for better education for women. Born in 1728, Mercy watched the Revolution from start to finish while raising five sons born between 1757 and 1766.

On 14 November 1754, Mercy Otis married James Warren, who had been a classmate at Harvard of her favorite brother, also named James. This brother was one of the first to speak out against growing tyranny in America when he argued against writs of assistance in 1761 and uttered the famous phrase, 'taxation without representation'.[1]

James Otis, nicknamed 'the patriot' by his adoring younger sister,[2] went on to speak loudly and publicly in support for colonial rights, criticizing Massachusetts Royal Governor Thomas Hutchinson and plural office holding. Mercy caught the spark of patriotic fervor and wrote poems and letters of her own, demonstrating her own fine political mind. In 1805, she completed her own *History of the Rise, Progress, and Termination of the American Revolution*, making a name for herself in America's history in a way that even her outspoken, intellectual brother never had. In it, she described her brother as 'the first champion of American freedom'.[3]

Before Patrick Henry's 'treason' speech in 1765, often considered the first formal call for independence, 'there were few, if any, who indulged an idea of a final separation from Britain ... Independence was a plant of later growth'.[4] Unfortunately, by this time, Mercy's beloved brother was also becoming infamous for his mental instability. James Otis had a reputation as an intellectual, but also as one who would switch topics mid-speech or suddenly grow angry without provocation. Mercy took up her pen where her brother had left off. According to historian Lester H. Cohen, 'Warren's major literary and political aims – to form minds, fix principles, and cultivate virtue – characterized her writings from the beginning.'[5]

The riot that destroyed Governor Hutchinson's house on 15 May 1765 was the topic of Mercy's first political satire. However, within a year, Mercy was writing about more private pain after the death of her younger sister, Abigail, who 'breath'd forth her soul on a soft tender sigh' in the poem into which Mercy poured her grief.[6] When news of the Stamp Act repeal arrived, Mercy was caring for five sons aged ten and under, including newborn George. Only later would she reflect how few realized the danger of the Declaratory Act of 1766 which proclaimed Britain's right to tax and govern the colonies as Parliament saw fit.

Mercy may have had her time largely monopolized by child-rearing and housekeeping in the 1760s, but that did not keep her from staying informed about the fast-moving political news of the day. Her letters from the pre-war years demonstrate Mercy's knowledge of and passionate opinions regarding current events. She harshly criticized women who did not participate in boycotts of British goods and insisted that women needed to do their part in America's fight for liberty just as the men did. Later, when writing her *History*, Mercy not only looked at the differences in the roles of men and women but the different points of view of colonists from different regions. She, of course, felt that inhabitants of Massachusetts were valiant in leading the cause for liberty. Of Virginians, she wrote, 'Perhaps it may be true, that wherever slavery is encouraged, there are among the free inhabitants very high ideas of liberty; though not so much from a sense of the common rights of man, as from their own feelings of superiority.'[7] She admired the virtues of individual men, such as Patrick Henry, of whom she wrote, 'He was a man, possessed of strong powers, much professional knowledge, and of such abilities as qualified him for the exigencies of the day', even as she remained suspicious of southerners in general who proclaimed themselves friends of liberty.[8]

While some Americans resisted the radical call for liberty, Mercy wrote regarding the inevitability of war from 1 October 1768 when British soldiers arrived in Boston. 'The American War may be dated from the hostile parade of this day'.[9] With their arrival, Mercy also would have been concerned about the safety of her brother, who had been speaking out against British tyranny for years. It was not unreasonable to anticipate his treatment as a traitor might have been severe.

Mercy's fears for her brother turned out to be well-founded. On 5 September 1769, James Otis was beaten by British soldiers and left with severe head wounds that diminished his mental capacity and exacerbated his mood instability. When Mercy heard of the attack, she wrote, 'Is it possible that we have men among us under the guise of the officers of the Crown, who have become open assassins?'[10] She was devastated by her brother's condition, and the attack fed her patriotic fervor. She wrote at length of the attack in her *History*, calling James 'the first martyr to American freedom'.[11] By November 1771, the Otis family was forced to accept that James's brilliant mind was permanently damaged. He was legally declared *non compos mentis* – insane.[12]

Much of Mercy's writing from this time was published anonymously. Women were not expected to follow or comment on politics, although the revolutionary movement was highly dependent upon them as household managers to boycott goods and replace them with homemade items. Mercy was concerned about revealing her identity as the author of satirical poems and harsh reflections upon British governance. Her brother's disability at the hands of angry British soldiers could not have reduced her reluctance to speak publicly.

At the same time, another woman was openly writing about politics. Catherine Sawbridge Macaulay was a British author who published *The History of England from the Accession of James I to that of the Brunswick Line* in 1763. She was also an admirer of James Otis before his decline, writing that his 'patriotic conduct and great abilities in defense of the rights of your fellow citizens claim the respect and admiration of every lover of their country and mankind'.[13] When her brother could no longer respond himself, Mercy took up correspondence with Macaulay. Therefore began a relationship that would enrich and embolden Mercy's political thought and writing. Correspondence with Macaulay encouraged Mercy to speak out regarding politics and reassured her that Americans had some support on the other side of the ocean. Decades later, when Mercy was compiling her *History*, she would frequently review her letters to and from Catherine which discussed the historical events as they occurred.

Macaulay was in correspondence with many leading patriots besides Mercy, including Benjamin Rush, Samuel Adams, and Benjamin Franklin. She often shared these letters with others to build up British support for the Americans. By the mid-1770s, however, she was frustrated in her attempts. She wrote to John Adams, 'I believe no evil short of the entire destruction of their property will produce an effectual opposition to the career of power'.[14] The British public simply could not be convinced to support Americans unless they thought they might benefit from said support.

She made a radical attempt to gain public notice of the wrongs being done in the colonies with her 1775 *Address to the People*. In it, Macaulay holds back little in her criticism of the rule of George III and the 'slavery which they have imposed on the conquered'.[15] She boldly stated that the Americans were justified in their opposition since Parliament had deprived them 'of every part of their rights which remained unviolated'. with the passing of the Intolerable and Quebec Acts.[16]

It was not long before Macaulay took refuge in France, where she kept up her American correspondence. Uncertainty regarding her treatment should she be named a traitor caused her to make this choice. A rumor reached Catherine that a wax effigy of herself had been used in American espionage efforts, and she was glad that she was out of the reach of British authorities.[17] She regained her political bravery in 1778 when she published her *History of England from the Revolution to the Present Time in a Series of Letters*, which attacked parliament and its treatment of the Americans.

As for Mercy, Thomas Hutchinson, who often debated with Samuel Adams regarding the colonies rightful place in the world, became the first victim of Mercy's satirical wit. First, in *The Adulateur*, Mercy's Rapatio was so well known to be Hutchinson that the Sons of Liberty referred to him by that name.[18] This was followed by *The Defeat* in which Rapatio was revived as a more devious enemy who comes to a violent end. The plays were published in the *Boston Gazette*, but few knew the truth of their authorship.

After the evening that has become known as the Boston Tea Party on 16 December 1773, Mercy wrote, at John Adams's urging, a satirical poem titled 'The Squabble of the Sea Nymphs' to memorialize the event. In it, tea is sacrificed to aquatic gods by rebel nymphs. Upon reading it, Adams wrote to Mercy's husband, James Warren, that it was 'one of the incontestable evidences of real genius'.[19]

However, Mercy could not entirely devote herself to patriotic politics the way men like John Adams did. She was a wife with a household to maintain. More importantly, she was the mother of five sons. Much as she supported independence from an early point in the Revolution, Mercy was afraid of what might become of her boys if called upon to fight. She wrote to Abigail Adams, 'not to mention my fears for him with whom I am most tenderly Connected: Methinks I see no Less than five sons who must Buckle on the Harness And perhaps fall a sacrifice to the Manes of Liberty Ere she again revives and spreads her Chearful Banner over this part of the Globe.'[20]

Her fears were not assuaged when General Thomas Gage replaced Hutchinson as the governor of Massachusetts, placing the colony under martial law. His authority under the Coercive Acts, which had been passed in response to the destruction of the tea, left colonists feeling vulnerable and without a voice. Boston Harbor lay empty, relieving many of their livelihood, and tensions rose as many, including Mercy, wondered what would come next.

She wrote to Hannah Lincoln, 'As every domestic enjoyment depends on the decision of the mighty contest, who can be an unconcerned and silent spectator? Not surely the fond mother or the affectionate wife who trembles lest her dearest connections should fall the victims of lawless power or at least pour out the warm blood as a libation at the shrine of liberty.'[21] The cause of the Revolution could not be ignored. It was time to take sides, and Mercy was already compiling the letters, pamphlets and newspapers that would be used to write her *History*.

Britain believed that crushing the rebellious fervor in Boston would cause the colonies to fall into line. What they did not anticipate is that the reaction would prove to be quite the opposite. People outside of Massachusetts began to wonder if their port town could be closed down next or if their governor could be replaced with the military against their will. Instead of meekly accepting British rule, Americans began to stand up in support of the radicals in Boston. They sent supplies, food, and assistance to those who experienced hardship due to the port closure, and the colonies began to feel more like a cohesive unit than they had before. Mercy called it a 'kind of predatory struggle' that 'almost universally took place'.[22]

Still, she wondered if her sons would 'fall a sacrifice to the Manes of Liberty Ere she again revives and spreads her Chearful Banner over this part of the Globe'.[23] However, Mercy's more immediate concern was her husband. As a member of the Massachusetts Provincial Congress, James helped make decisions that were sent on to the Continental Congress in Philadelphia, where their friend, John Adams, served. Torn between anxiety and pride in her husband's service, Mercy wrote to him of a desire to 'retire to some remote and quiet corner of the earth, where we could sit down in peace and leave the busy world with all its bustle, confusion, animosity and tumult'.[24]

On 20 October 1774, the Continental Congress received word via Paul Revere that the Massachusetts Assembly had been dissolved on Gage's orders. This was the incentive they needed to approve and publish a Declaration of Rights and Grievances. They also called for another boycott to begin on 1 December 1774. Mercy was encouraged by the news, even as she wondered about the fate of her own little family.

James was frequently away at this time due to his position with the Massachusetts congress. Mercy could tend toward anxiety when he was away. She, like many other wives in her position, often wrote urging James to come home. Both James and Mercy were disappointed when their plan for her to join him in Concord in April 1775 had to be cancelled due to the presence of British troops. James wrote to settle her fears but was also forced to instruct her to prepare for moving the household to safer ground. 'We may perhaps be forced to move ... Don't let the fluttering of your heart interrupt your health or disturb your repose.'[25]

James was prescient in his warning. Within a fortnight, shots were fired at Lexington and Concord that shifted the colonies ever closer to outright warfare. James rushed home, and the Warrens set out for Rhode Island. Mercy later wrote in her *History* that 'A scene like this had never before been exhibited on her peaceful plains; and the manner in which it was executed, will leave an indelible stain on a nation, long famed for their courage, humanity and honor.'[26]

James and Mercy encountered many other travelers, some witnesses of the fighting at Lexington and Concord. One told them of a story so harrowing that Mercy included a retelling of it in a letter to a friend. 'I saw yesterday a gentleman who conversed with the brother of a woman cut in pieces in her bed with her new born infant by her side.'[27] Accounts such as this must have caused internal struggle in the patriotic but fearful Mercy.

It was not long before James was duty-bound to leave again, and Mercy took comfort in the correspondence of friends in similar circumstances. She and Abigail Adams exchanged frequent letters and found solace in their shared hardship and fears. Their letters are not overly demonstrative in their emotion, though they do refer to each other as esteemed and affectionate friends. Rather, they seem to take comfort in the sharing of news and their status as politically interested women. Mercy struggled to balance her strong patriotism with her anxiety for her husband and sons. She tended to suffer debilitating headaches when stress overcame her. It caused her to beg James to come home and decline political duties, even as she wrote about the importance of American independence. Writing became one of Mercy's key tools for balancing these opposing forces. It enabled her to keep a historical record of events, correspond with friends to give and receive emotional support, and ease her anxiety through the routine of putting pen to paper.

James understood his wife's temperament and frequently took the time to write to her during events that must have made this task difficult to make time for. The day after the Battle of Bunker Hill, with both sides reeling from the unexpected extent of bloodshed, James wrote to ease Mercy's worries and assure her that 'I long to see you, perhaps never more in my life'.[28] However, James could not go home. He had been named president of the Provincial Congress to replace Dr Joseph Warren, who had been killed at Bunker Hill while attending to the wounded.

Mercy, like Abigail Adams, was torn between her desire to be with her husband and her domestic duties. With five sons aged nine to sixteen in 1775, she had reason to be thankful that they were safe at home while at the same time begrudging the fact that they kept her from James. By July, Mercy decided that she would go to her husband. She found him much in need of her for support, and, unexpectedly, for her pen. The ongoing need for men and supplies meant that James Warren desperately required a private secretary. These duties also placed Mercy close to information that would be invaluable when she later penned her *History*. That same month, James was elected paymaster general for the Continental Army, placing the Warrens at the center of revolutionary activity.

Before the Declaration of Independence was written, Mercy Warren recognized that she was living through historic times and was determined to keep a thorough record. Besides always urging her husband to send news in his letters, Mercy asked Abigail Adams to send her accounts of current events – newspapers, handbills, and even private journals if possible. She also kept consistent correspondence with John Adams and requested that he send her as much information as possible. Like George Washington, who took meticulous care of his wartime papers, Mercy understood the importance of the time in which she lived.

She was also among the first to encourage said declaration and suggest a republican form of government. Mercy was less enthusiastic about her husband fulfilling a role in the new government. James declined various positions, including nomination to Superior Court. John Adams bristled under the Warrens' lack of dedication, writing to Abigail in 1776, 'he loves to be upon his Farm, and they both love to be together. But you must tell them of a Couple of their Friends who are as fond of living together, who are obliged to sacrifice their rural Amusements and domestic Happiness to the Requisitions of the public.'[29]

Besides their desire to be together, James and Mercy may have decided that it was best for him to remain in work that allowed him to be home because of troubles with their eldest son, James Jr. He had left Harvard in the midst of his senior year for problems that may have been related to drinking or, a more troubling possibility, mental illness similar to that which Mercy's brother, James Otis, had suffered.[30] The matter was kept understandably quiet, which makes it difficult to know the details of James Jr's condition. One can imagine Mercy's fear if she thought it possible that her son might repeat the decline of the brother she so loved.

News of the Declaration of Independence came but was somewhat tempered by the onset of a smallpox epidemic. James and Mercy went to Boston for inoculation, as did Abigail Adams and her children. James wrote to John Adams when a copy of the Declaration arrived in Boston on 15 July 1776, 'The Decleration came on Saturday, and diffused A general Joy. Every one of us feels more Important than ever. We now Congratulate each other as freemen. It has really raised our Spirits to A

Tone Beneficial to mitigate the Malignancy of the small Pox, and what is of more Consequence seems to Animate, and Inspire every one to support, and defend the Independency he feels.'[31]

By December, Mercy was frantic with worries again as James was offered military command, her elderly father suffered failing health, and her sons underwent smallpox inoculation and required constant nursing. Torn between her family duties, concerns for James, and her desire to write, Mercy often found herself overwhelmed and anxious. It was a state she was forced to endure when James was made a director of the Navy Board in May 1777. The fact that James accepted the post when he had rejected several others for the sake of his wife is an indication of his own passion for the navy position.

In the midst of war and separation from her husband, Mercy also had to cope with the timeless mother's pain of the emptying nest. When James went to Boston for the navy, Mercy had only the youngest two of her sons still at home. Winslow, the second oldest and her not-so-secret favorite, was working his father's farm and business. James Jr had recuperated enough to return to Harvard, where he was joined by his younger brother, Charles.[32] Because of the difficulty of importation throughout the war, some of Mercy's time freed up by the absence of her sons was spent processing wool into thread to be used for her own household and those in need. As more goods became difficult to procure, housewives like Mercy worked to replace them with homemade substitutes.

Another balm to Mercy during the absence of beloved family members was the arrival of Nabby Adams. The daughter of John and Abigail, Nabby was thirteen years old in 1778 when she was sent to stay with Mercy for tutoring. It was an ideal situation for Mercy who was missing her own sons, had no 'Little Good Girl' of her own,[33] and loved discussing intellectual pursuits. Mercy wrote to Abigail with updates on 'your Daughter who I Really Love, and Love her the more the Longer she Resides with me. In future I shall Call her my Naby and Back my Claim with the promiss of her papah to whom I shall appeal if you Monopolize too much.'[34]

When Nabby returned home, Mercy refocused on her writing, but not her *History*. Instead, she looked at the war profiteering occurring and penned the poem 'The Genius of America weeping the absurd Follies of the Day'. Some believe she also wrote the satirical play *The Motley*

Assembly. Mercy was disappointed that some people took advantage of circumstances to hoard riches rather than focusing on the common goal of liberty. She did not want America defined by ostentation and lack of virtue.

Given Mercy's preference for simple virtues, one can imagine her disappointment when rumors reached her that her second son, Winslow, was earning a reputation as a gambler. When he accepted a position as commission agent to the Netherlands, Mercy was terrified for his physical safety during Atlantic travel and sure he would fall into immorality in Europe. Her favorite, but troubled, son sailed for his post on 3 June 1780. Mercy was concerned that he would be led astray, but her fears increased when she learned that the ship, *Pallas*, upon which Winslow had sailed had been seized by the British. Before he could be influenced by the opulence of Europe, Winslow found himself a prisoner of war. However, Mercy did not fret long before she was relieved by the arrival of her eldest son, James Jr. He was posted on the Navy frigate, *Alliance*, which arrived in Boston on 19 August 1780 with news that the passengers of the *Pallas* were being well treated.[35] Not long after, Winslow was released into England, and his mother could resume worrying about his character rather than his physical safety.

In January 1781, the Warrens purchased the Milton home of former Governor Hutchinson. That they had the funds for this purchase near the end of the war is evidence of their affluence compared to most Americans. This would have felt like a victory to Mercy after satirizing the inept leader in her plays. In her *History*, Mercy describes Hutchinson as 'dark, intriguing, insinuating, haughty and ambitious, while the extreme of avarice marked each feature of his character', leaving no doubt regarding her feelings toward him.[36] However, just as the colonies had victory in sight, Mercy had personal concerns that would overshadow news of the surrender at Yorktown.

Mercy's son, Henry, fell ill with a cough that raised fears of consumption, and he took time away from Harvard to take in the sea air. Tuberculosis, the name later given to what was known as consumption in the eighteenth century, was a common cause of death at that time and would have been a scary diagnosis, even in the midst of war. The highly contagious nature of tuberculosis was unknown in the 1780s. Therefore, Henry and Charles, brothers and students at Harvard, spent much time together without fear that one was spreading disease to the other. Charles remained at school, pressing on with his coursework in spite of his health, which also began to suffer. However, Mercy soon had even larger problems.

On 9 June 1781, the *Alliance* again docked in Boston with James Warren Jr on board.[37] He had been badly injured in a naval battle. James Jr was forced to have his leg amputated, and Mercy doubted that it would save his life. He survived but lived the remainder of his life a cripple. Mercy rejoiced that James Jr regained his health, unaware of the dangers to her younger sons' lives at Harvard. Stress related to her sons' health exacerbated Mercy's problems with fatigue and anxiety. Her eyesight also suffered, a lingering side-effect of her smallpox inoculation. She wrote few letters through the last half of 1781.

For Mercy, the victory at Yorktown on 19 October 1781, meant that James was home, and her worries could abate. She could enjoy the Milton house and recover her own health. James declined a position in congress in preference of his farm and aversion to power-hungry politics. The war won, factions and power struggles immediately seeped into American politics, much to the dismay of the Warrens.

Early in 1783, Winslow returned from Europe, and his mother was ecstatic. She had not seen him in three years, and Winslow had not been a dependable correspondent. When he arrived in Philadelphia, his father quickly set to work obtaining a government office for him to replace the unprofitable business ventures the young man pursued on his own.

Just when Mercy was at peace with her sons' situations, a tragic blow came from another direction. James Otis had allegedly once said, 'My dear sister, I hope, when God Almighty in his righteous providence shall take me out of time into eternity that it will be by a flash of lightening'.[38] On 23 May 1783, that is just what happened. Mercy's outspoken, patriotic brother was standing in the entryway of his home watching a storm when 'his great soul was instantly set free by a flash of lighting'.[39] He had 'lived to see the independence of America, though in a state of mind incapable of enjoying fully the glorious event which his own exertions had precipitated'.[40] Mercy and others who loved him hoped that James Otis would be better remembered for his bold loyalty to his country than his later madness, and so he has been.

Just a few months later, the Treaty of Paris was signed on 3 September 1783, officially recognizing the United States of America as an independent nation, just as James Otis believed it should be. Mercy was both proud of the accomplishment and concerned for the future of the new nation. She continued work on her *History* as it unfolded around her. During this time of relative peace in the Warren home, Mercy began to work, at Winslow's prompting, on *Ladies of Castille*, which would be published in 1790. The play was a tragedy about the fight for liberty in sixteenth-century Spain and the role of women caught up in the struggle. It was a point-of-view Mercy was all too familiar with.

Shortly after the completion of *Ladies of Castille*, Mercy's youngest son, George, left home for school, leaving her feeling despondent. She still had James Jr to care for, and the house did not remain empty for long. Charles and Henry both fell ill once again. By the summer of 1784, Mercy's concerns for Charles's health had become severe. He was sent to Hispaniola (modern Haiti and Dominican Republic) in the hope that the tropical climate would relieve him. He was still there in early 1785 when he wrote to his mother that a new illness kept him from travelling.

Mercy began working on her play, *The Sack of Rome*, to distract her from her worries. Another story of patriotic values and tragic events, Mercy poured her concerns about the new United States into the Rome of her creation. She worried that the virtues that had led to the creation of the country – piety, honesty, integrity, and hard work – would be lost, as would the nation.

In 1784, Mercy was finally able to discuss in person politics, war, and its aftermath with the fellow female historian with whom she had been corresponding for two decades. Catherine Macaulay visited the newly created United States and meeting Mercy was on her agenda. The two upon meeting each other were as pleased in person as they had been with their epistolary relationship. This despite Macaulay's marriage to a scandalously young man, a situation of which Mercy would typically disapprove. While they had managed civil discourse over many more significant topics, the women had a minor falling out over Boston fashion.

The *Sans Souci* club of Boston was an elite place to meet for conversation, cards, and music. Mercy found it lacking in the virtues that had led to the Revolution. She wrote to Winslow that 'local vices are growing rampant among us'. [41] She saw John Hancock as a corrupt leader enamored with excess and the *Sans Souci* a reflection of his leadership. Catherine, used to British luxuries and more liberal in her femininity, found the club and the company far less offensive than her conservative friend. Macaulay's endorsement of the club made her a heroine among the very people that Mercy was afraid would ruin America. She wrote, 'The name of Macaulay as a subscriber to this frivolous society casts a shade on her character'.[42] Both women suffered some ridicule for their positions and the resulting feud, and Mercy was accused of writing a satirical play of these events. That both women felt the controversy was made too much of by the media and politicians of the day helped them to reconcile before Macaulay's return to England in 1785.

When Charles finally returned from his trip to the Caribbean, Mercy was disappointed to find his health deteriorated rather than improved. He was eager to join Winslow in Lisbon, Portugal, but Mercy was afraid she would never see him again, that he might not survive the journey. Her fears were well-founded. Charles did sail for Europe, and he died on 30 November 1785 in St Lucar, Spain. He was twenty-three years old. Mercy's sons and husband had survived the war, but grief finally fell upon her home. Mercy was crushed by the news, especially since Winslow had sailed home not realizing that his brother was coming, so Charles had died with no family present to comfort him.[43] Mercy found solace in her faith and the promise of heaven. She shared this with her sons in letters intended to ease their grief and help them look forward to a day when they would be reunited with Charles.

Winslow arrived in the US, not only unexpectedly, but in debt. The elder Warrens themselves struggled to manage their estates in the post-war inflationary period, they were forced to put the Milton country house on the market to cover their financial needs and assist their son.[44] James Jr, on the other hand, had improved more than once thought possible. Accustomed to his missing leg, he had recovered his health enough to take on a teaching position. It was a very different life than that he had lived at sea but fulfilling for a young man from an erudite family. Mercy was both happy for him and sad to see him leave her home once again.

Soon, matters of state occupied Mercy's mind once again. The Constitution, which had been drafted to solve the inadequacies of the Articles of Confederation, needed ratification of the states to become the law of the land. Mercy lobbied for its rejection, alienating her from her close friends, John and Abigail Adams. Mercy believed that the Constitution put too much power in the hands of the federal government and did not ensure the rights of individuals or states, issues for which the war of independence had been fought and won. She was not the only prominent citizen concerned about the Constitution's lack of a Bill of Rights. She enumerated her concerns in *Observations on the New Constitution* in February 1788.

The objections of Mercy and other anti-federalists were countered by the *Federalist Papers*. Written by Alexander Hamilton, James Madison, and John Jay, the *Federalist Papers* remain a definitive resource for Constitutional study, although, at the time of their publication, they were intended as defense of the Constitution rather than a study of it. The *Federalist Papers* were persuasive to those voting on ratification.

While the federalists believed a strong centralized government was vital to the ongoing success and survival of the new nation, Mercy believed that it crushed liberties only recently won by the blood of so many good patriots. She must have felt disappointed and betrayed when her state of Massachusetts, where many of those sacrifices had been made, ratified the Constitution while calling for the addition of a Bill of Rights.

The Constitution was ratified in June 1788, 'the system adopted with expectations of amendment'.[45] The battle over ratification past and the Milton house sold, James and Mercy moved back to Plymouth, Massachusetts and a simpler home more filled with happy memories. Mercy embraced the slower pace of life and was determined to give up politics and possibly the writing of her *History*. It was disheartening for Mercy to see former allies and friends drifting away as a political divide grew.

Mercy was increasingly a woman of contradictions. She had patriotic fervor but disapproved of what form the new nation was taking. She was insulted if James were not offered important positions, but she often insisted that he decline them in order to remain at home. Mercy encouraged her sons to not allow politics to impact their relationships, while her own decades-long friendship with the Adams family faded. She wrote of female independence while hating the idea of being alone. Virtue was highly valued, while she made continuous excuses and allowances for her son, Winslow. She enjoyed sharing her opinion but was easily offended. Mercy was highly critical of federalism but dedicated a book of her collected poems and plays to President George Washington in September 1790.

Early in 1791, the troublesome Winslow appealed to General Henry Knox for a military position to evade a lawsuit that was being revived against him.[46] The standing army that many anti-federalists held distrust for was skirmishing with Native Americans, and western posts in Ohio and Indiana needed defenders. Winslow's mother strongly disapproved of this course of action, regardless of her public humiliation over Winslow's misdeeds. Her son had survived the war, and she did not embrace the idea of sending him off to fight another. Besides this personal concern, Mercy believed the Native Americans were being mistreated by imperialistic federalists. They were the 'original proprietors of the soil', and deserved better.[47]

Winslow was sentenced to jail for his debts in May 1791, but he was safe from fighting.[48] James and Mercy felt betrayed by the country they had been a part of creating. Their son imprisoned and they themselves considered outsiders by the federalists in charge, the Warrens must have wondered where everything had gone wrong. Winslow was not incarcerated for long before he was released to take his place in the army.

On 1 November 1791, the Warrens celebrated the marriage of their son, Henry, to distant relative Mary Winslow. Enjoying the occasion and looking forward to grandchildren, Mercy could not have known that just days later, on 4 November 1791, Fort Jefferson would be attacked by a joint force of Miami and Shawnee warriors. Winslow Warren was one of the 646 Americans killed in the attack.

Mercy was beside herself with grief for her favorite son. She had not been prepared for his death as she had been with Charles, and she regretted that she had not spoken more fervently against his leaving. 'Oh, how I do regret that we did not all unite to prevent, if possible, our dear Winslow engaging in the late fatal expedition'.[49]

In December 1791, the Bill of Rights resolved many of the problems that Mercy had included in her *Observations*. With these amendments, even Mercy Otis Warren would eventually grow to appreciate and approve of the Constitution. However, coming as it did on the heels of Winslow's death, Mercy's passion for the ratification was understandably muted. Catherine Macaulay also died in 1791, ending the more than twenty-year friendship that had mostly occurred through letters.

Not until the birth of Henry and Mary's daughter, Marcia, did Mercy rise somewhat from the pit of her grief. Marcia, named for her grandmother, Mercy, also helped James heal from the loss of his two sons. Both James and Mercy resumed their writing and activities following their granddaughter's birth. They took comfort in each other, and, in 1795, the addition of a grandson.

In August 1796, Mercy received a conciliatory visit from Abigail Adams, the first they had shared in eight years.[50] Mercy may have aged, but this had not softened her political ideals. She still wrote fervently against federalism and for education for women, although she had yet to complete her *History*. Abigail agreed wholeheartedly with Mercy on women's rights and had learned how to be more diplomatic regarding areas of disagreement.

When John was elected president months later, Mercy wrote her congratulations but could not resist a snarky reference to obtaining a 'crown' in reference to what Mercy perceived as John's monarchical vision for America.[51] Nonetheless, the women remained friends, if not close confidants, and continued to correspond even as Abigail became a busy First Lady. Mercy attempted to balance friendship with the Adamses with her lack of support for John's presidency. With the passage of the Alien and Sedition Act, which criminalized writing against the government as treason, Mercy determined not to see her *History* published until after her death. She feared that one she had thought of as a close friend and mentor had become a tyrant. Having determined to delay publication of her own work, Mercy must have been dismayed when Hannah Adams, a cousin of John, published her own *A Summary History of New England* in 1798.

Mercy continuously worried over James's health, as he did hers. However, it was their youngest son George who fell ill in 1799. Mercy realized the illness was serious when George stopped writing, but she was unable to endure winter travel to Augusta, Maine, where he was residing, and George died on 5 February 1800.[52] Of Mercy's five sons, only two remained. It had long been her worst nightmare to consider losing her children, and she struggled with the burden of her loss, turning to her faith as comfort.

She also had James Jr to lift her spirits when he returned to Plymouth and opened a school near his parents. He had finally been awarded a pension as a wounded veteran, two decades after his amputation.[53] James Jr also began helping his mother prepare her *History* for publication following the election of 1800 that unseated the federalists. Mercy welcomed the author of the Declaration of Independence, Thomas Jefferson, to the presidency, seeing him as a more suitable leader than John Adams. With the reversal of the Alien and Sedition Acts, Mercy was ready to publish her *History*, but her eyesight had deteriorated over her seventy-three years, making the work nearly impossible for her to complete on her own. James Jr effectively became her secretary, and the project slowly began to take its final form. Finally, on 21 December 1804, Mercy signed a publishing contract.[54]

Mercy's concerns regarding the future of America and the loss of what she considered patriotic virtues are clear from the beginning of her *History*. 'The progress of the American Revolution has been so rapid, and such alteration of manners, the blending of characters, and the new train of ideas that almost universally prevail, that the principles which animated to the noblest exertions have been nearly annihilated,' the first volume published in 1805 warned.[55] She felt it was her duty as a historian to encourage readers to 'look back with due gratitude and respect on the fortitude and virtue of their ancestors, who, through difficulties almost insurmountable, planted them in a happy soil'.[56]

Mercy had maintained a tremulous friendship with John and Abigail Adams, but her portrayal of him in her published *History* brought it to an end. She feeling that she had written an unbiased, well-informed record of events and he believing that she had maliciously slandered his character and understated his achievements, the two exchanged sixteen letters full of anger and suggested corrections before rending the relationship completely.[57]

After the loss of the Adamses as friends, Mercy also lost her husband of fifty-four years. James Warren died on 28 November 1808. His devoted wife grieved him as the 'perfect man'.[58] The loss of so many of those closest to her may have caused Mercy to reconsider old friendships. After all that had been said between them, Mercy desired reconciliation with John Adams. His wife always holding great sway over him, Abigail presented Mercy with a ring containing a twist of hair combining her own, Mercy's, and John's 'at his request'.[59] John, almost as old and just as set in his ways as Mercy, continued to criticize her *History* to mutual friends if not directly to the author. Only when his friend, Dr Benjamin Rush, died on 19 April 1813 did John begin to feel the urgency of putting things right with Mercy. Then Nabby, John and Abigail's only daughter, died 1 September 1813, and John waited no longer.[60] With his conciliatory letter, John included a remembrance of Mercy's long-dead brother, James Otis, who she had nicknamed 'the patriot', and they began corresponding again with a focus on their shared past and those they had lost. After losing three sons, her husband, and many friends, the aged Mercy was touched by this gesture and found comfort in the renewed correspondence.

They must have both been devastated when the British burned Washington on 24 August 1814. Was America's independent history to be so brief? Mercy would never know the outcome of the War of 1812, sometimes referred to as the Second War of Independence. She passed away on 19 October 1814 at eighty-six years old.

Chapter 6

Margaret Shippen Arnold

All the sweetness of beauty, all the loveliness of innocence, all the tenderness of a wife and all the fondness of a mother showed themselves in her appearance and conduct. We have every reason to believe she was intirely unacquainted with the plan...

– Alexander Hamilton

Known as Peggy, Margaret Shippen was a Philadelphia socialite and consummate belle of the ball before she married General Benedict Arnold. The couple made history, but the extent of Peggy's role in Arnold's betrayal remains unknown. We can be sure that she was not as innocent as George Washington's men foolishly gave her credit for, but did she ensnare her husband in a plot he would not have taken up for himself? Before we decide, let's go back to the beginning.

Born in June 1760, Peggy was a vibrant sixteen year old when the Declaration of Independence was signed not far from her Philadelphia home. The youngest of the surviving Shippen children, she was a favorite, known for her charisma, intellect, and feminine beauty. Philadelphia was the largest, most sophisticated city in the colonies, and Peggy was comfortably secure in the affluent upper class of the city.

Peggy's father, Edward Shippen, was a lawyer connected with many great names of the day. Young Peggy may not have been interested in politics, but she would have met George Washington, Benjamin Franklin, and others deeply involved with the revolution. Peggy and her three older sisters, Elizabeth, Sarah, and Mary, received tutoring in the skills required by upper-class ladies, such as sewing, dancing, and music, but did not attend a traditional school. Given Peggy's intellect, she likely learned much in her father's extensive library.

According to one account, Peggy was 'particularly devoted to her father, making his comfort her leading thought, often preferring to remain with him when evening parties and amusement would attract her sisters from home'.[1] Contrary to some fictional accounts of Peggy, she was devoted to her family, a serious girl who disliked gossip.

When war broke out, it quickly impacted the Shippens. Elizabeth's cousin and beau, Neddy Burd, volunteered in 1775, leaving her father's law office where he had been employed. Peggy was close to her oldest sister and must have tried to comfort her when Burd left. Tench Tilghman, another cousin, later became an aide to General Washington. Complicating matters further, Peggy's brother, Edward, joined the British army late in 1776. Peggy's father attempted to maintain neutrality, an endeavor that became increasingly difficult as the war progressed.

It was with this goal in mind that Edward Shippen moved his family out of Philadelphia into rural New Jersey. Peggy loved her father, but she disliked country life and longed for the city. They did not remain for long. Not wishing to be labeled traitors for their lack of patriotic zeal, the Shippens left New Jersey for a farm outside Philadelphia after determining that the city remained unsafe with rumors of military action on the horizon.[2]

The war did soon impact the Shippens in two ways. Edward was taken prisoner during Washington's Christmas attack at Trenton. Washington graciously released the young man to his family. Then, as the British occupied Philadelphia, the Shippen family returned to their home, choosing the dangers of the British troops over the uncertainty of rural life trapped between two armies. The British were welcomed by the aristocracy of Philadelphia, either for self-preservation or passionate loyalty to the king. Either way, those in the city enjoyed dances, parties, and plays while the rest of America struggled to survive as prices soared and goods became scarce. It was during this winter of 1777–8 that Peggy Shippen befriended British Captain John André.

It was not the first time John André had been in Philadelphia, not that anyone, besides a few admiring ladies, had noticed him on his initial visit. On 5 September 1774, he had been an anonymous member of the crowd outside the Carpenters' Company Hall, watching as members of the Continental Congress arrived to discuss the growing tension between British America and the parliament on the other side of the Atlantic.[3] Then, he had been Lieutenant André of the Royal Fusiliers, a young man with lofty ambitions. André had not only begun collecting information as soon as he arrived in the Americas, he also began creating connections that he felt might become useful later. In his position as quartermaster, while stationed in Canada and during his long trek as a prisoner of war, André sought out correspondents who could provide him with a wealth of information regarding the state of the war.

André was described by one of his American contacts as 'rather under the average stature, of a light agile frame, active in his movements and sprightly in his conversation'.[4] Several portraits of him show a young man with serious, wide-set eyes and smooth, pale skin. He was attractive and charismatic, important characteristics in a man tasked with gaining trust and harvesting information.

On 30 September 1777, he re-entered Philadelphia with the occupying British army rather than as a prisoner of war. For eight months, the British were quartered in Philadelphia, but it was not the victory they thought it would be because they were still missing a vital, definitive defeat of General Washington. The time in Philadelphia may have seemed a waste to some, but John André made the most of his opportunities, wherever he was. His military journal goes frustratingly silent during his time in Philadelphia. This may be due to the leisurely quality of the stay, but it could also indicate secretive operations that André had been preparing for since his arrival in America. The dances and entertainment that marked the British occupation of Philadelphia were an ideal setting for a handsome, young officer to encourage the revealing of information and loyalty to the king.

André was quartered at the home of Benjamin Franklin, who was in France pleading the American cause.[5] For entertainment, he and some fellow officers laid claim to the Southwark theater and planned shows, calling themselves Howe's Thespians. André is known to have flirted with many Philadelphia ladies but not to have formed any serious attachments. The party atmosphere of Philadelphia reached a climax with the Meschianza of 18 May 1778, which served as a going away party for General Sir William Howe, who was returning to England after resigning his commission.[6] Peggy and other belles of Philadelphia dressed in exotic togas and turbans that scandalized some of the guests. Swathed in silk and jewels, did Peggy hope to gain the attention, and possibly a marriage proposal, from a British officer? Did she have particular hopes for André? Or was she just a seventeen-year-old having fun?

She was not paired with André for the Meschianza pageant, rather Peggy dressed to match Lieutenant Winyard. André accompanied another young woman with whom his name was sometimes connected, Peggy Chew.[7] Other reports claim that Edward Shippen decided at the last minute not to allow his daughters to attend, so it is not known with certainty that Peggy Shippen actually participated in the grand event. The opulent party was criticized from all sides, even many loyalists finding the wanton display tasteless as soldiers starved and froze at nearby Valley Forge.

The extent of Peggy Shippen's connection with John André is unknown, but Peggy did keep a lock of André's hair when he left Philadelphia.[8] A sketch André drew of Peggy still exists, showing her as a fashionable, beautiful young woman. Historian D.A.B. Ronald writes that Peggy was 'beautiful, bold, intelligent, determined, resourceful, ruthless, nerveless. Above all, she was willing and able to wear the "double faces" needed to fight his secret war'.[9] Did their plans go so far as discussing the ensnarement of an American general, or was it just a happy coincidence that General Benedict Arnold soon arrived in Philadelphia?

The women who had so willingly consorted with the British were briefly shunned once Philadelphia was back in American hands. However, the charm, beauty, and wealth that had made them the most eligible women in the city soon overcame any tarnish as traitors that some attempted to label them with. The ladies of the Meschianza were soon as welcomed by American soldiers as they had been by their British counterparts, enduring only a few jealous remarks about their 'high roll' hair and disloyalty before retaking their place at the top circles of society.

Some loyalists did choose to leave with the British rather than take their chances with the Americans, whom many Tories believed were fighting a losing battle anyway. This seems to indicate that if a love affair had been going on between Peggy and André, she could have married him and gone with him as some other young women chose to do with their British beaus. Peggy, however, chose to wed a rebel general twice her age.

Benedict Arnold's name has become the byword for traitor. Some who might accuse a betrayer of 'being a Benedict Arnold' might not even have a clear idea of why they are saying it. His treason is one of the most famous incidents of the Revolutionary War, and his wife played a significant role in it. However, even before his marriage, Arnold experienced problems with the Continental Army that made him ripe for betrayal.

He had never received the rewards he felt he deserved for his bravery and accomplishments, from the taking of Fort Ticonderoga with General Ethan Allan and especially after the Battle of Saratoga. General Arnold had been badly wounded in the leg but refused amputation. After a long, painful recovery, he was able to walk with a cane. He had been popularly credited as an American hero, but not rewarded or recognized as such by congress. General Arnold was bitter when he saw others receive positions and promotions that he felt were owed to him. General Washington, who had great confidence in Arnold's leadership and understood his frustrations, though clearly not to the full extent, offered him the military governorship of Philadelphia in 1778 after the city had been abandoned by the British.

In this position, Arnold began to demonstrate his willingness to put his own desires above his duty and honor, and he found the wealthy city more to his liking than the hardships of the field. In order to fill his own coffers with the rewards he felt he was owed, Arnold made deals with the merchants of Philadelphia and took for himself anything he saw that he wanted.

When he saw Peggy Shippen, he knew he wanted her. Arnold likely did not realize that Peggy had recently been entertaining John André. On the other hand, she might not have realized that he had recently been courting a teenaged girl in Boston. It may have been for loyalist purposes that Peggy now befriended the older general. Peggy's correspondence from this era was destroyed by her family, so we can only hypothesize as to her true feelings.[10] Did she see Benedict Arnold as a brave American hero who showered her with gifts and affection or as a cripple past his prime who could be easily manipulated? The truth may be somewhere in between.

Arnold's lavish lifestyle in Philadelphia captured the attention of congress, and he once again found himself the subject of an investigation that he found embarrassing and insulting. The fact that he was acquitted of illegal action did not assuage his ego. These troubles do not seem to have scared away the Shippen family. Arnold asked Peggy's father for permission to marry her, and he appears to have hesitated concerning Arnold's health more than his prospects. Arnold did not ask for a dowry, which must have pleased Shippen as the war stretched even the wealthiest families' finances. No evidence indicates that Peggy did not wish to marry Arnold, but her motivations and feelings are unknown. To secure the match, the already overextended Arnold purchased Mount Pleasant. The riverside mansion reassured Edward Shippen that his daughter would not be taken too far away and reminded Peggy that she would live in luxury. They could not have imagined at that time that the couple would never reside in the beautiful home. Those who were already investigating Arnold's use of government goods and funds might have raised an eyebrow at the general's extravagant purchase, but one might assume that his teenage fiancée was impressed. A quiet wedding ceremony took place at the Fourth Street Shippen home on 8 April 1779.[11]

Within approximately a month of their marriage, Arnold arranged for a Philadelphia merchant, Joseph Stansbury, to open negotiations with Sir Henry Clinton regarding Arnold's services.[12] Major John André was the ultimate recipient of Arnold's message, and he must have been elated at the possibility of turning such a prominent American leader to British espionage. Had he discussed such a possibility with Peggy before leaving Philadelphia? Was Benedict Arnold taking his place in a carefully laid plan? The fact that Arnold's contacts in the treasonous plot were Peggy's rather than his own indicates her early involvement, if not her encouragement or instigation.

At this point, André gave Arnold some tasks to test his abilities and dependability. He also gave him a code name, Monk, which was a reference to George Monk, who had turned on parliament in the previous century for the benefit of Oliver Cromwell.[13] André retained Stansbury as a messenger and added a second. Messages would also reach him through a friend of Peggy's. André received letters from Peggy by the same couriers, as is evidenced by a 'List of Articles' she requested from him on 18 July 1779. The items included 'Pale Pink Ribbon' and 'Clouting Diaper' – a not-so-subtle message that Peggy was pregnant.[14]

Arnold was ready to switch sides, but he also wanted assurance that he would be better appreciated by the British than he felt he had been by his home country. In June 1779, a letter to André pressed the compensation issue, demanding £10,000 but making no guarantees of his own contribution. He had offered some information during the weeks of correspondence, but nothing that made André willing to make a commitment of that amount.[15] Because of the ongoing investigations into Arnold's financial activities, it was reasonable for André to weigh how valuable of an asset Arnold would be. What sort of command were the Americans likely to give a dishonored, crippled general? Would Arnold be able to offer anything that could turn the tide of a war that was beginning to lose support from the other side of the Atlantic as well?

Arnold had obvious reasons for reluctance, especially if he felt that the British army was giving him no better treatment than what he had suffered at the hands of the American congress. This may have been his fear when he received condescending messages from André such as this: 'Join the army, accept a command, be surprised, be cut off – these things may happen in the course of maneuver'.[16] Tarnished though his reputation was, many still believed Arnold was the great hero of Saratoga. Dealing with the British would only be good for his future if they eventually won the war. For his part, Arnold may have believed the American cause was lost. He had believed in it and fought for it, but his betrayal may have been partially due to the belief that it was doomed. He said as much to André, 'The present struggles are like the pangs of a dying man, violent but of short duration'.[17]

Perhaps, Peggy and her husband felt that this switching of sides would be a benefit to them once America lost the war. 'Peggy would prove herself to be an adviser, a strategist, and a true partner', write historians Mark Jacob and Stephen H. Case.[18] Arnold would be a high ranking officer of the winning side, and Peggy would reign Philadelphia as its leading lady. They would have the riches they both craved, and their decision to serve the British would seem brilliant in retrospect. Maybe Peggy had alternative plans of her own. She wrote to André in the autumn of 1779 that her 'friendship and esteem for him is not impaired by time or accident'.[19] Some have interpreted this to refer to a relationship that the two hoped to rekindle once Arnold was firmly in hand.

Whether Peggy's plan included a happy future with Arnold or André, neither was to be. It is just as unclear if André had feelings for her beyond a shared desire to see England victorious. In a poem written after Peggy's marriage, André wrote, 'And shall then another embrace thee my Fair!' [20] Was he writing of Peggy, someone else, or simply writing what he believed to be a fine line? The only fact that seems clear is that once the plot was conceived, it was fully supported by Arnold and his wife.

However, as Jacob and Case point out, 'Arnold had taken a loyalty oath … Her only promise was to support her husband, and indeed she did so with fidelity'.[21]

Tensions rose in Philadelphia, which had become a different city than the one that had hosted opulent balls and the Meschianza. With Continental currency suffering from inflation that made it nearly worthless, merchants and farmers shipped goods to ports where they were more likely to find buyers with gold, silver, and foreign currency. Riots and feuds between revolutionaries and loyalists made the streets increasingly dangerous as the Arnolds determined their best way forward and Peggy's pregnancy progressed.

Peggy gave birth to a son on 19 March 1780. She, like other women of her time, may have been concerned about her own safety while giving birth, but little Edward, named for her father, was born without documented problems. Given her wealth and social standing, Peggy would have enjoyed the best medical care available, possibly that meant the attendance of her mother and sisters.

In the meantime, John André, promoted to major, followed General Clinton to Charleston, South Carolina, 'admitting that he could not win in the north'.[22] While Clinton and André were gone, the Arnolds worked on gaining a prize to entice their fellow conspirators into commitment. In May 1780, Arnold convinced General Philip Schuyler to speak on his behalf to George Washington. His request? Command of West Point. This was the prize he would offer the British. West Point protected possession of the Hudson River, and Arnold felt it should be worth the £10,000 he had previously requested (he later increased his request to £20,000), as well as a command as brigadier general in the British army.

Peggy lobbied so energetically for her husband to be posted at West Point that her sister-in-law, Hannah, suspected Peggy might be having an affair with one of the men she frequently petitioned for support. Robert Livingston did assist the Arnolds in their quest for West Point, but there is no evidence besides Hannah's accusatory letter to her brother of an affair. Since the bombastic Arnold was rarely quiet when offended, it seems safe to assume that he was satisfied that Peggy had done no more than encourage Livingston to take his part.[24]

Certain that the post would be offered, Arnold wrote to André of his expectations and the price he placed upon turning it over. George

Washington, therefore, was surprised when he asked Arnold to take an honorable field commission and the scheming general, 'appeared to be quite fallen; and instead of thanking me or expressing any pleasure at the appointment, never opened his mouth'. Peggy also heard the astonishing news while at a dinner party and went into one of her 'hysteric fits,' according to one witness.[24] The couple must have wondered what would happen to their plans. In addition, Peggy may have been skeptical of her crippled husband's ability to survive another field command.

They must both have been relieved when a change of plans caused Washington to assign Arnold to West Point after all. West Point was made up of a series of forts (including Fort Arnold named for the hero of Saratoga) strategically placed where the Hudson River makes tight turns leaving ships vulnerable to attack. Control of the Hudson River was vital for the movement of supplies and troops. With Arnold off to his post, correspondence with the British was then left to Peggy, and it was she who informed her husband that they agreed to his offer of West Point and his price of £20,000. He began a campaign to weaken West Point's defenses. He also continued selling army goods for personal profit, a needless risk that could have led to the revelation of his greater deception.

The next difficulty was establishing a meeting with Major John André. Away from the advice of his wife, Arnold took risks with the steps he took and the messages he sent. One, sent thought a double agent, failed to arouse suspicion due to the ineptness of the American general who read it.[25] Another message sent by Arnold to André suggested forwarding their plot by the capture of a British officer who could later be exchanged. André refused this method due to the risk of hanging as a spy if all did not go according to Arnold's plan. Possibly, he worried that his imprisonment and execution was precisely Arnold's plan.[26] André insisted on meeting under a flag of truce and in uniform, perhaps pretending to discuss a prisoner exchange, but Arnold knew he had raised too many suspicions to openly meet with a British officer no matter what the ruse.[27]

At the same time, Arnold and André were negotiating arrangements to meet, Peggy was traveling to join her husband at West Point with their young son in tow. Possibly, the fact that Peggy was there gave André a greater feeling of safety regarding his dealings with her husband. Arnold chose the home of loyalist Beverly Robinson as his lodgings near West Point. This was an appropriate residence for his wife and son, as well as being conveniently placed at enough distance from the forts to allow their escape should that become necessary. Upon Peggy's arrival, she charmed her husband's aides, helping to reduce their suspicion of his activities, and added her own touch to the West Point community. The home was made comfortable, and Peggy held dinners for her husband's staff. One, Major David Franks, who had also served Arnold in Philadelphia, was so attentive to Peggy's needs that he earned the nickname 'The Nurse'.[28]

When Arnold learned that General Washington was going to be at West Point, he may have felt his stars were aligning. Despite support that Washington had given him, Arnold might have prepared to turn over the commander-in-chief, not seeming to consider, or not caring, that he was likely to be hanged as a traitor. Conversely, Arnold may only have mentioned Washington's presence to warn André of increased security since an attack could likely not be formulated so quickly. If it could, it would indeed be a prize for the British, given that Washington traveled with General Henry Knox, Marquis de Lafayette, and Colonel Alexander Hamilton. After the fact, Washington admitted that he did not believe Arnold hoped the attack might happen while he was at West Point.[29]

Arnold may not have known about Major Benjamin Tallmadge's position as Washington's chief spymaster when he wrote to him regarding 'John Anderson', a poorly conceived code name for John André. Supposedly, Tallmadge was to bring John Anderson to the Robinson House should their paths cross. Major André approached West Point onboard the *HMS Vulture*, sailing up the Hudson. He met with Arnold after two failed attempts on 21 September 1780. Arnold turned over documents detailing West Point's defenses.[30] Peggy, back at the Robinson house, maintained a calm atmosphere and attempted to dismiss the concerns of her husband's aids when they expressed that something suspicious was afoot.

While Arnold and André met, the *Vulture* was forced to move downriver due to American artillery, leaving André stranded in dangerous territory. Historian D.A.B. Ronald hypothesizes that this may have been Arnold's plan when he insisted upon meeting terms. Perhaps, he schemed for André's capture.[31] On the other hand, it is possible that André simply made a series of errors that led to his capture. Historian Kenneth Daigler stated, 'his low opinion of his enemies could explain some of the sloppiness in his actions'.[32]

General Clinton had given André orders not to accept incriminating documents. André was to memorize vital information. He was also not to enter American territory or wear anything except his uniform. André failed on all three counts. Whether by scheme or happenstance, André was captured on 23 September 1780, dressed in common clothes to ease his passage through rebel territory. André still might have been taken by his captors to Arnold, giving the trio of conspirators an opportunity to escape together. However, their plot unraveled. The incriminating papers were forwarded to Washington, while André was sent to West Point. Tallmadge, possibly the first to realize what had occurred, countermanded the order and took possession of André before he could be reunited with either of the Arnolds.

Benedict Arnold received word of André's capture and successfully fled to the *Vulture*, taking the men who rowed him out as prisoner and making use of André's intended path of escape.[33] His wife was left behind to fend for herself as General Washington approached. Peggy remained in her bedroom, where her husband had whispered the urgent, damning news of André's capture before he fled. Did Peggy worry what would happen to André, now imprisoned as a spy? Was her only concern that her husband would escape? As she fretted with her six-month-old baby at her breast, she formulated her own plan and Washington's men began arriving at the Robinson house for breakfast. She bided her time while they ate and left to join Arnold at West Point. Of course, he was not there, and Washington was shocked by the poor state of the forts.

Alexander Hamilton wrote to John Laurens that Benedict Arnold's treason 'seems to have originated with Arnold himself, and to have been long premeditated. The first overture is traced back to some time in January last. It was conveyed in a letter to Colonel Robinson, the substance of which was, that the ingratitude he had experienced from his country, concurring with other causes, had entirely changed his principles; that he now only sought to restore himself in the favour of his king by some signal of his repentance and would be happy to open a correspondence with Sir Henry Clinton for that purpose.'[34] What Hamilton and most of his peers failed to deeply consider was that Arnold's wife, the beautiful socialite, Peggy Shippen, had been involved. They never could have conceived that it might have been her who had been the mastermind behind her husband's defection.

After their tour of West Point, Hamilton and other of General Washington's men approached Peggy, still abed in her room. The isolated river home that was intended to ease escape held Peggy trapped with the top officers of the Continental army. She was hysterical, or at least made a show of being so affected in the mind that none of the gentlemen dared doubt her sincerity. She raved, 'General Arnold will never return, he is gone; he is gone for ever, there, there, there the spirits have carried up there,' reported one witness. She also claimed a hot iron was held to her forehead and that the officers were there to kill her child. She was believed to be a 'poor distressed, unhappy, frantic and miserable lady.'[35]

Peggy's innocence was reaffirmed by her husband, once he was well away and took the time to secure her safety as well as his own. In a letter to Washington, Arnold confessed but insisted that 'Mrs Arnold is as good and innocent as an angel, and is incapable of doing wrong'.[36] Peggy was given leave by General Washington to return to Philadelphia on 27 September 1780, apparently having come under little or no suspicion.

Arnold's letter to Washington made no mention of Major John André, and Washington was adamant that he would hang as a spy. Having been captured out of uniform with incriminating information on him, André could only plead to be treated as an officer and shot instead. He wrote to Washington on the day before his death, 'I trust that the request I make of your Excellency at this serious period, and which is to soften my last moments, will not be rejected. Sympathy towards a soldier will surely induce your Excellency, and military tribunal to adapt the mode of my death to the feelings of a man of honour. Let me hope, Sir, that if aught in my character impresses you with esteem towards me, if aught in my misfortune marks me as the victim of policy and not resentment, I shall experience the operation of these feelings in your breast by being informed that I am not to die on a Gibbet.'[37]

André had little hope of being exchanged unless the British offered up Benedict Arnold in his stead. An anonymous letter later identified as Alexander Hamilton's stated, 'Arnold appears to have been the guilty author of the mischief; and ought properly to be the victim, as there is good reason to believe he meditated a double treachery, and had arranged the interview in such a manner, that if discovered in the first instance, he might have it in his power to sacrifice Major André to his own safety.'[38]

General Clinton, knowing few spies would offer their services if trade to the enemy might be their fate, could not consider such an exchange.

One must wonder what Peggy thought as her husband fled, forevermore an infamous traitor, and one who was her friend, if not more, awaited his execution. Was her concern only for herself and infant son or did she mourn the fate of one or both the men with whom she had plotted? She must have been shocked that neither Washington nor any of his aides seemed to suspect her. Had her hysteric fit been legitimate or a clever distraction? Later in life, she wrote, 'I have frequently in the course of every day a confusion in my head resembling what I can suppose would be the sensations of anybody extremely drunk, and very desirous of concealing their situation.'[39] Had Peggy truly gone mad with the stress of unsuccessful treason, or did she play on the low eighteenth-century expectations of her gender when she flailed half-dressed in front of Washington's men? The next day, she appeared healed and claimed not to remember her fit at all. As Peggy put on what was likely a carefully planned bit of theater, John André arrived at West Point under guard and wondering if his charm and intellect would get him out of his dire circumstances. There is no evidence that the two met on this occasion.

As Jacob and Case noted, 'In an era when female intelligence and talents were often dismissed, women held one advantage: They were rarely suspected of elaborate crimes'.[40] Washington allowed Peggy to be transported to Philadelphia with 'every reason to believe she is innocent'. Lafayette concurred, 'We are certain she knew nothing of the plot', and Hamilton wrote to his fiancé, Elizabeth Schuyler, 'Her sufferings were so eloquent that I wished myself her brother to have a right to become her defender'. She had thoroughly fooled them all. Hysteria forgotten, Peggy requested of one of her husband's reeling former officers, 'You will be so obliging as to receive any monies which may be due to General Arnold and transmit the same to me'.[41]

Only days after Peggy left with her son for Philadelphia, Major John André was hanged on 2 October 1780. Hamilton was among those Americans struck by the young officer's death. He wrote to his fiancé, Elizabeth Schuyler, 'Poor André suffers to-day ... Everything that is amiable in fortitude, in delicate sentiments and accomplished manners pleads for him; but hard-hearted policy calls for a sacrifice'.[42] André's plea to Washington for a more honorable manner of death was denied. He had given no testimony to incriminate anyone besides himself. His last words were, 'All I request of you, gentlemen, is that you will bear witness to the world that I died like a brave man. It will be but a momentary pang'.[43] A monument to André was later erected in Westminster Abbey where his remains were reinterred.

Peggy's choice to return to her family in Philadelphia rather than immediately join her husband was additional evidence for those who wished to believe she was innocent. It was easy for her contemporaries to continue 'cursing Arnold and pitying his wife', as John Jay wrote.[44] She could have had several other motives for selecting Philadelphia at that time. Perhaps she was angry with Arnold for failing to fulfill their plot or heartbroken over André's demise. It could have been as simple as wishing to see her family or secure certain possessions, such as the £200 that had been sent by André to cover expenses but had arrived in Philadelphia after Peggy's departure for West Point.[45]

Her party was preceded by the news of her husband's treason, making some hesitant to provide needed food and lodging. Theodosia Prevost, who would later marry the controversial Aaron Burr, was a remarkable exception. She was at this time married to British officer Jacques Marcus Prevost but had friends on both sides of the war, including Burr with whom she was having an affair. Burr claimed later that Theodosia had confided in him that Peggy had confessed her involvement in the treasonous plot. When the account was published in 1836, after Burr's death, the Shippen family denounced it.[46] Just as news of her husband's turn had preceded her, by the time Peggy arrived in Philadelphia, the testimony of Washington, Lafayette, and Hamilton had been spread far and wide. Few believed her guilty with their endorsements, if it had crossed their minds at all to think she might have been involved anyway. They had hanged Arnold's effigy, using a paper-mâché model that had previously been used to honor him. However, few denounced Peggy alongside her husband.

Also arriving at approximately the same time as Peggy was the news of Major John André's hanging. His plea to be shot having been rejected. Clinton's offer to trade him for any prisoner held (besides Arnold) was also denied. Unknown is the extent of Peggy's mourning, but the news must have increased her fear for her own future and that of her husband and young son. There remains no documented incident of her ever speaking of André again. In the meantime, Arnold was demanding payment from the British, though he had provided them with nothing and caused them the loss of a valuable officer. He received £6300.[47] He was also given a command as brigadier general, but he remained untrusted by his new peers.

Joseph Reed, who had led the Philadelphia investigation into Arnold's illegal business dealings, was one who saw through Peggy's theatrics of innocence. And he had evidence. While confiscating and investigating Arnold's possessions, he found a letter from André to Peggy. It was dated August 1779 and spoke of their memories during his time in Philadelphia. Reed insisted that this letter, though it was innocent in its content, was too much of a coincidence coming from the executed British spy.[48] Reed and others called for Peggy's exile while her family defended her innocence and pled for her to be allowed to remain. Her father was at the forefront of this fight, vowing that his daughter would not write to her husband and that she would turn over anything received from him. On 27 October 1780, Peggy's brother-in-law, Neddy Burd wrote, 'The Council seemed for a considerable time disposed to favor our request, but at length have ordered her away'.[49] It is impossible to know whether Peggy had planned on remaining separated from her husband or if she had a desire to join him. The choice was taken from her, and she was forced to leave Philadelphia within a fortnight of the council's ruling.

Peggy joined her husband in New York, where she was more welcomed by her fellow loyalists than he had been. The man who had been an American hero was now disdained by both sides. If Peggy mourned John André or regretted the treason they had concocted, she could not allow it to show. Arnold now wore a British brigadier general coat and was tasked with forming a loyalist regiment. He was not popular with his new peers, but some were friendly and saw his choice as a sign of the end of the bloody war. Some appreciated his presence, remembering his reputation as a general with bravery that had rarely been displayed by his former foes. Perhaps, with Arnold on their side, they could win this drawn-out engagement and return to their homes.

Soon after reuniting with her husband, Peggy was pregnant again, and she lived a more private life than she had enjoyed in Philadelphia. Those days of flirting with handsome young men must have seemed so far away, but Peggy was only twenty years old. She was part of New York society, but things would never be the same as they had been before her fateful meeting with John André.

While Peggy attempted to live a quiet life free of scandal, the Americans had not forgotten about her husband. A spy was sent to join Arnold's new regiment with the assignment to arrange an abduction. Had Washington approved an assassination, his false defector, John Champe, had ample opportunity once he had successfully befriended Arnold in New York. However, an abduction was more complicated, and the right opportunity never presented itself before Arnold was dispatched south.[50]

Arnold led his first British operation in December 1780, taking Richmond and sending Virginia governor, Thomas Jefferson, literally running for his life. He had moderate success in this role, but came, once again, under suspicion for underhanded business dealings. More seriously, some believed Arnold guilty of poisoning Major General William Phillips when he died in May 1781.[51] Before he returned to New York, Arnold advised Cornwallis to move up the James River to what he considered a more secure location than Yorktown, but this suggestion was ignored.

Arnold was back in New York in time for the couple to welcome their second son on 28 August 1781. Peggy was still in bed recuperating with little James Robertson when his father was given another mission. Alone with her small children and still recovering from childbirth, Peggy received news that her grandfather, Edward Shippen, had died and freed his enslaved servants in his will.

The British surrendered at Yorktown on 19 October 1781. After betraying their country, the Arnolds found themselves on the losing side. As they packed to leave for London, a city Peggy had never visited, she must have wondered if she would ever see her family again. They sailed on 8 December 1781.[52] The Arnolds were not alone. Thousands of loyalists and African Americans fled the new country that was less than welcoming to them.

Peggy was well received in London. Called the 'Fair American', she found her place in society, and she may have felt a bit like she did in her old Philadelphia days, if not entirely vindicated in the decisions she had made.[53] The Arnolds were presented to King George and Queen Charlotte. They were rewarded generously for their service, even if General Arnold had not provided the British with the victorious engagement for which they had hoped. A pension paid to Peggy separate from the money paid to her husband is further evidence of her active involvement with the treachery that had left André dead.[54]

They took a residence in Portman Square and enjoyed relative popularity. If nothing else, the American turncoats were a novelty of whom people liked to have a story to share with friends. Peggy was better received, once again, than her husband. Of him, one wrote, 'To George a rebel, to the Congress traitor, Pray, what can make the name of Arnold greater?'[55]

Peggy saved the generous pension Clinton had approved for her while her husband struggled with life after the war. She had her own troubles, giving birth to a daughter, Margaret, who lived only six months in 1783. After everything Peggy had been through, losing this namesake daughter must have been a blow. A son, George, born in 1784, also died after two months. The Arnolds' relationship remained close enough that another child was born in 1785. Sophia Matilda thrived and served as a balm to her grieving mother.

The Arnolds made friends with the English and American exiles alike. At least one witness claims to have seen them at the monument to John André. But Peggy seems to have strived for an uncomplicated life, and the most commonly documented comments about her during this time of her life relate to her notable beauty.

Shortly after Sophia's birth, Arnold, along with Richard, his oldest son from his first marriage, departed for Canada, leaving Peggy in London. Arnold purchased the *Lord Middlebrook*, a ship he hoped would make him successful in trade as he had been before the war – a lifetime ago. Peggy settled into a smaller home with her young children, while her husband took his Atlantic voyage. One wonders what she thought of her situation and the path that had taken her there.

In Canada, Arnold set up a shop, purchased land, and built another ship. However, Peggy was tormented by rumors that his ship had been lost at sea. Such was eighteenth-century communication that one might wonder for months if a loved one had safely reached a destination. She wrote to her father, 'I am still in the most unhappy state of suspense respecting the general, not having heard from him since the account of his ships being lost'.[56] In addition to fears that she might be a widow, Peggy endured creditors who came to her regarding her husband's debts. Although she had casual friends in England, it was to her father that she confided her personal concerns. Writing to her 'dear papa', Peggy unburdened herself. 'Separated from and anxious for the fate of the best of husbands, torn from almost everybody that is dear to me, harassed with an expensive and troublesome lawsuit, having all the general's business to transact, and feeling that I am in a strange country, without a creature near me that is really interested in my fate, you will not wonder if I am unhappy.'[57]

Peggy eventually received word of her husband's safety, and he returned to London in 1786 to collect his family. Was Peggy excited to return to North America the following year? Arnold was proud of what he had built in Canada and looked forward to sharing it with his wife, whom he had named another new ship after. Departing on the *Peggy* in 1787, the Arnolds were also expecting another child.

In St John, New Brunswick, Peggy made a comfortable home for her family, bringing furnishings from London and her indomitable spirit. Arnold collected his entire family at their new home, including his spinster sister, Hannah, and his older children. It is unknown at what point after her arrival that Peggy learned of another child her husband had sired. One must wonder after all she had suffered at his side, how Peggy felt to discover that Arnold had fathered a child with a woman in St John during his first trip to Canada. At just the point when their life seemed to be turning around, Arnold's affair drove a wedge between him and his wife. Two months after arriving in St John, Peggy gave birth to another son, named George like the son who had died, a common practice at the time. Had Peggy already learned of her husband's infidelity? One can imagine how much it might change her state of mind as she recovered from childbirth, depending upon when this realization was made.

Once recovered, Peggy managed her household and assisted her husband with his business with two goals in mind. She wished to visit her family in Philadelphia and she wished to return to England. 'I am much gratified by your earnest solicitations for me to visit, and hope to accomplish so desirable an event in the fall. Yet my pleasure will not be unaccompanied by pain; as when I leave you, I shall probably bid you adieu forever. Many disagreeable and some favorable circumstances will, I imagine fix me forever in England,' she wrote in June 1788. Whatever Peggy may have wished otherwise, her choices had made England her home. Partly because she was dependent upon the pension she earned for her contribution during the war. 'While his majesty's bounty is continued to me, it is necessary I should reside in his dominions'.[58] The longed-for trip to Philadelphia was made in December 1789.

Both Peggy and Philadelphia had changed during the years of her absence. Congress and the political tension that went with them had moved to New York, but Peggy might have been more interested in other changes taking place. The leveling of streets and loss of familiar faces of people who had fled the city after the war left it a different place than the one Peggy had left. Most shocking to Peggy was the news that her mother was dying. Peggy was welcomed heartily by her family, especially her siblings who had all named their firstborn daughters after her. The townspeople's reaction was more predictably mixed, and Peggy left feeling unfulfilled. 'I had hoped that by paying my beloved friends a last visit, I should insure to myself some portion of it, but I find it far otherwise'.[59]

She returned to chilly Canada wishing she could go home, which she was now certain was England. Arnold's ongoing business problems, including a warehouse fire, raised concerns about the family's future. Holding an auction of their household goods to raise funds, they returned to England where Peggy did not feel as many cold shoulders turned her way. Despite some continued trouble – it seemed Benedict Arnold would always be in some sort of trouble – Peggy was glad to be home in London. She stood by Arnold's side as he struggled to succeed in business and put himself in the center of disputes. In one case, he challenged the Earl of Lauderdale to a duel for a comment Arnold found insulting. Peggy feared for her husband's life and reputation almost constantly, a long-suffering wife indeed.

In early 1794, the restless Arnold left his pregnant wife for the Caribbean on another quest for riches. Peggy was forced to move to less expensive lodgings once again and managed the children's education as she prepared to give birth with her husband at sea. On 25 June 1794, Peggy gave birth to her final child and named him William Fitch Arnold, the name chosen in honor of another American loyalist exile. Her husband did not return until a year later, having little to show for the time besides adventurous stories and thousands of acres of 'waste lands of the crown in Upper Canada'.[60]

It is difficult to guess Peggy's feelings when Benedict Arnold died on 14 June 1801. He had been irrational, unsuccessful, and unfaithful, but she had stood by him, mostly uncomplainingly. Being a widow had its own challenges, but Peggy addressed them head-on. Peggy's key concern was her finances. Her husband had created a complicated web of business contracts and debts that Peggy was responsible for unwinding as executor of his estate.[61] The fact that Arnold had named his wife executor is evidence of her intellect and his trust in her, as few eighteenth-century wives were selected for this role that was typically reserved for men. Peggy had five children besides Arnold's older sons and illegitimate son in Canada, who he had not left out of his will. One can only imagine what Peggy thought of her husband of twenty-two years including his fourteen-year-old bastard in his will while she scrambled to ensure her own children's futures. She refers to him in letters to her sons simply as 'the Boy', though she knew his name was John Sage. 'The Boy who is with you ought to be taught, by his own labor, to procure his own livelihood; he ought never to have been brought up with any other ideas'.[62]

Peggy's children were not raised in the type of lifestyle their mother had enjoyed in Philadelphia. Peggy wrote that her daughter Sophia had 'little chance of her marrying, having but a moderate share of beauty and no money'.[63] Her sons each entered the military and gained favorable positions with the help of Peggy's connections. Her passion for securing their future is clear in her letters. 'I am making every exertion to keep up as much as possible the respectability of the family, and am determined, while it is in my power to prevent it, that the fortunes of my children shall not be marred by the change in our situation.'[64]

Taking the role as head of her household in a way her sixteen-year-old self could never have imagined necessary, Peggy was proud of herself. She wrote, 'I believe I may without vanity say that there are few women that could have so far conquered as I have done'.[65] Another letter bemoaned the situation in which her husband had left her, 'I am convinced that my present misfortunes have not been in consequence of any imprudence of my own; and your dear Father's motives were so laudable, being actuated by his anxiety to provide for his Children, that we must admire them, though we lament the effect.'[66]

Unfortunately, Peggy's health was failing, and healthcare of the dawn of the nineteenth century was not able to help her. She wrote to her sons on 10 June 1802 of 'having been for some months past so afflicted with a severe nervous complaint', but that was simply what she chose to tell her sons.[67] Peggy likely suffered from uterine cancer. In a 27 July 1803 letter, she confessed to her sons, 'I am sorry to inform you that I have great cause of alarm respecting my own health; and fear that my dear Children will soon lose their other protector ... For the last ten weeks I have been entirely precluded from the use of animal food, wine, beer, or any other thing that can enrich the blood – and have been almost entirely confined to a recumbent posture. This has lowered me, and rendered me very uncomfortable, and does not appear to have abated any of the unfavorable symptoms of the disease.'[68]

With her finances desperate and her health failing, Peggy frequently encouraged her sons to determine the location and quality of the frontier lands in Canada that were part of their inheritance. In the hope that they would be valuable enough to cover Arnold's myriad of debts and give relief to the family, Peggy clung to the idea that exploration and use of these lands could solve all their problems. Letters written between her husband's death and her own became increasingly fervent about locating the Canada lands, but in this hope, Peggy was disappointed.

In a November 1803 letter to her father, Peggy spoke again of her health, 'I have lately been much worse, in consequence of a very large tumor having formed which broke and discharged an immense quantity'.[69] She would eventually depend upon opium for her pain, though her mind remained sharp. She died on 24 August 1804 and was buried next to her husband. According to family lore, a lock of John André's hair was found among her belongings.

Chapter 7

Deborah Sampson Gannett

It cannot be denied that this romantic girl exhibited something of the same spirit as Joan of Arc.

– Elizabeth Ellet

One of seven children of a poor family, Deborah Sampson was indentured to a farm family as a child to ease her mother's burden. Her father had abandoned the family, leaving his wife and children to struggle in a world not designed for families without a male representative and protector. In her position as servant in the home of Jeremiah and Susannah Thomas, Deborah was provided with necessities but not educated.[1] Deborah demonstrated ambition in teaching herself to read. At eighteen, her indenture ended, and Deborah was free to plot her own future.

Some legends regarding Deborah's story have her joining the army with the sons of the Thomas family as soon as she was freed from service and able to do so. However, her enlistment date of 20 May 1782 does not support this idea. She was twenty-three years old when she donned men's clothing and signed up as Robert Shurtliff.[2] She may have felt some familial connection to the Thomas boys, but it is unlikely that she went to the fighting front with or because of them. However, when performing farm work with the ten Thomas boys, Deborah may have begun wearing men's clothes and begun wondering what other parts of the world might be opened to her if she kept them on.[3]

According to historian Alfred F. Young, what Deborah did gain from her relationship with the Thomas boys was access to books. As a servant, her education was hands-on instruction in running a household. However, Deborah wanted to read and learn, and she did so by burying herself in whatever books she could get her hands on to the extent that Jeremiah Thomas accused her of 'always hammering upon some book', wishing that she would not 'spend so much time in scrabbling over paper'.[4] Deborah may have viewed reading and learning as a way to escape to other worlds or grasp at a better future for herself. It was not a typical pastime for girls of her station, but nothing could deter her.

It was uncommon for single, unmarried women to live alone at this time, but it is likely that is what Deborah did after she turned eighteen. In the midst of the Revolutionary War, many women took up duties that they might not have otherwise. Deborah worked as a spinner and weaver, skills she may have learned while serving the Thomases, although weaving was not a standard household chore. The boycott of British goods had increased the demand for American cloth, so Deborah may have found increased opportunities in this area. She also spent time teaching, a job that must have brought joy to the underprivileged girl with a love of learning. This may have also been a position more available to her due to the war, since young men were typically preferred as teachers, especially for older children.[5]

Women had many reasons to go to war. Those who had nowhere to go when their fathers or husbands enlisted might choose to go with them. Large numbers of women were camp followers, cooking, cleaning, and nursing men within the army camp just as they did at home. For some women, this provided an income and way of life, even if they were not connected to a particular soldier. Deborah Sampson had no male provider or protector, and she made a different choice, one that offered greater pay, freedom, and anonymity than typical women's work. When she took advantage of her tall, robust build and dressed as a man to enlist in the Continental Army, Deborah crossed a line that most were afraid to approach. She was not the only woman to do so, but she did succeed in keeping her identity hidden for longer than any other known example of women fighting in the Revolutionary War. Maybe she felt it was her calling. Perhaps she saw it as an opportunity to travel and have experiences that she would never have otherwise. Whether patriotism or some other motive drove Deborah, she soon entered a world normally closed to eighteenth-century women.

Linda Grant DePauw proposes that 'a few hundred' women might have 'fought with the Continental line'. In addition, a 'much larger number – the entire able-bodied adult female population at some times in some places – participated in local defensive combat operations'.[6] We can only guess how many other women took up arms the way Deborah did and never revealed their secret.

A soldier's life was dangerous. If one was not injured or killed in combat, they still had the unsanitary camp conditions to deal with. High casualties can be attributed to disease, cold, and heat rather than any British weapon. Reasons women might disguise themselves in order to fight were numerous, despite the risks. Those who were enslaved or indentured servants might see it as a path to freedom, especially if they were light-complexioned enough to claim Caucasian ancestry once away from those who knew of their origins. Women might attempt to leave behind a shameful past or hide a premarital pregnancy. Like Deborah, they might hope to escape poverty or the insecurity of being a single woman in a nation at war. Some fled abusive husbands or parents, and, just as their male counterparts did, some women wanted to join the war effort due to passionate patriotism.

Whatever was Deborah's inspiration, in April 1782 she enlisted in the army, claiming to be Timothy Thayer. Discovered and in fear of prosecution, she fled her native Middleborough, Massachusetts.[7] Whether she had intended to honor her enlistment or whether she, like many others, was hoping to slip away with her signing bounty in hand, is unknown. But when she enlisted a second time on 20 May 1782, this time as Robert Shurtliff, a name common enough in the area to allow Deborah to remain anonymous, she accepted a bounty of £60 and joined new recruits at Worcester for muster.[8] The American victory at Yorktown had taken place the previous October, but three-year recruits were still being signed on in the case that a treaty did not follow as expected. After all, it was not the first American victory of the war and news took weeks to cross the Atlantic. The Continental Army could not yet rest.

One might wonder how Deborah avoided detection during her seventeen months of service. She would have lived in close quarters with other soldiers and enjoyed little privacy. Her hair was likely cut short, though it need not have been. Many soldiers of the day had hair long enough to be tied back into a queue. She also did not need to worry about her lack of facial hair, since she had claimed to be only eighteen years old. At five feet seven inches, she was taller than most men and any other lack of manliness could be ascribed to youth.

The army Deborah joined in 1782 was better supplied and organized than it had been in 1776, although its future remained uncertain. The British continued to hold New York City, so the Hudson River Valley required protection. With this in mind, 'Robert Shurtliff' was placed in the Light Infantry Company of the Fourth Massachusetts Regiment. As Alfred F. Young has said, 'the attributes Sampson needed to maintain her deception – to be alert, quick, and street smart – were the very ones that made her an ideal choice for the light infantry.'[9] The area around West Point at which she was posted was infamous for chaos and deception of cowboys and skinners and shifting loyalties that had led to the capture of Major John André in 1780. Therefore, although she served during a less active point in the war, Deborah was sure to see action that could cost her life. If she died as Robert Shurtliff, would anyone know her complete story?

Even women not in disguise have not had their stories told in full. Instead, we have legends like that of Molly Pitcher, a conglomeration of women romanticized into a single story. We will never know how many women stepped up 'to load, or aim, or fire a field piece after her gunner husband fainted from heat, or collapsed from a wound, or died as a result of a direct hit'.[10] Even this legendary woman's original function is not entirely accurate, as water was more likely brought to soldiers for swabbing out their cannon than for drinking.[11]

Deborah's service involved scouting and small skirmishes rather than large battles or sieges. In this type of action, Deborah had to be as vigilant as a soldier as she was as a woman concealing her identity. A comprehensive record of her time in the army does not exist, so it is difficult to know exactly what Deborah did while in uniform. What is known is that she did see military action and was wounded at least once. Conflicting accounts make clear little more than that Deborah was wounded, likely near Tarrytown, New York. A musket ball lodged in her thigh made Deborah fear discovery enough that she later claimed to have considered killing herself.[12] Unwilling to take such a drastic step, she fled from the camp hospital to tend her own wound before any undressing could occur. Evidence exists that she suffered at least one more wound, possibly in the shoulder. Since she received a disabled veteran pension, it seems likely that Deborah was involved in dangerous active duty and that she was injured at least once. One story of a musket ball that could not be removed from her body also supports this idea, although it is possible that she was only shot once in either the thigh or the shoulder, not both.

Folklore and legend regarding Deborah as Robert Shurtliff abound. Various accounts put her in skirmishes at locations that she was never near on dates that were outside her enlistment period. An early, highly inaccurate biography claims that Deborah led a troop to capture a group of loyalist soldiers and even seduced a Tory's daughter along the way. Discerning the truth in the hyperbole surrounding Deborah's story is an unfortunate circumstance of her outstanding experience.

Another verified portion of Deborah's story is that she joined the staff of General John Paterson and served as a 'waiter' during the winter of 1783.[13] In this position, she would have performed many tasks with which she was familiar as a servant in the Thomas home. Her skill in housekeeping and service duties must have been noted in camp, enabling her to move into the safer role in the general's 'family'. She was safer from both enemy fire and discovery in this role, until she fell ill during a mission to Philadelphia.[14]

Sent to put down a mutiny that had ended before they arrived, General Paterson's brigade, which included Deborah, found themselves battling smallpox and measles that raged through the city instead. It is likely that Deborah contracted one of these diseases and was severely ill to the point that she was moved from her bed to a pile of corpses. Dr Barnabas Binney is credited with saving her by removing her from the macabre situation after noticing signs of life.[15] Cutting her clothes away in order to give treatment, Dr Binney discovered Robert Shurtliff's secret. He is credited with keeping it to himself rather than seeing her dishonored. It is also possible that Binney did tell General Paterson, and that he also decided to protect Deborah until her anticipated discharge occurred. Given the camaraderie of military units and the fact that complete disbandment of the army was close at hand, this is not an unreasonable theory. Whether Binney kept the secret himself or General Paterson decided to do so, Deborah was enabled to remain Robert Shurtliff for a few more months before receiving her honorable discharge after the peace treaty was settled between the new United States and Great Britain.[16]

Most women did not join the fight at the front the way Deborah did, but they attended to the wounded and dying left behind. When Benedict Arnold, soon after turning traitor to the British, attacked New London, Connecticut, the soldiers under his command slaughtered Americans, even those in the act of surrendering. One of these was the Fort Griswold commander, Lieutenant Colonel William Ledyard, who was killed with his own sword after surrendering it.[17] In the wake of this vicious attack, courageous women sorted through the butchered bodies to find those still living.

One woman, Anna Warner (later Bailey), found her uncle, badly wounded and loaded onto a cart with dead bodies. She brought his wife and child to him so that he could see them before he died.[18] Frances Ledyard, who may have been the sister or another relative of the fort's commander, also tended to those left behind, giving them small comforts of sympathy, drink, and what nursing she could provide.[19]

Other women, such as Rachel and Grace Martin, sisters-in-law staying with their mother-in-law while the men were away fighting, temporarily took a page from Deborah Sampson's book. Hearing that a British messenger was in the area, they disguised themselves in their husbands' clothes and took the courier's party by surprise. They obtained the British correspondence and quickly forwarded it to General Nathanael Greene. In need of a place to stay that night, the British party made their way to Mrs Martin's house, never suspecting that the young women serving them were the rebel men who had attacked them on the road.[20]

At least two other women attempted Deborah's scheme but were discovered. Their fate, though Deborah could not have known it, was what she feared. One, who attempted to enlist in Elizabethtown, Pennsylvania, was discovered during a physical exam and forced to walk through the town to a drummed out 'Whore's March'.[21] Sally St Clair was killed in the Battle of Savannah, and 'Samuel Gay' was discharged for 'being a woman, dressed in mens cloths'.[22] The number of young men serving in the army made it particularly easy for a woman's smooth skin or high voice to be overlooked by those not expecting a woman to be in uniform.

Deborah was honorably discharged by General Henry Knox, who would soon become Washington's Secretary of War, on 25 October 1783.[23] This must have been an emotional time for Deborah as she left a life behind that she had no realistic way of recapturing during peacetime. What were her options? Her secret had been revealed to at least one person, so continuing her life as Robert Shurtliff was a dangerous path leading to an uncertain end. She would go back to being Deborah Sampson, but her future remained in a fog. The army had given her life a purpose, but it had come to an end.

Hamilton Grange – Home built by Alexander and Elizabeth Hamilton in New York City.

Elizabeth Schuyler Hamilton – Portrait by Ralph Earl, 1787, Museum of the City of New York. (*Public Domain*)

Independence Hall –
Philadelphia, Pennsylvania.
The Pennsylvania State
House became known as
Independence Hall after its
use by the Second Continental
Congress to vote on the
Declaration of Independence.
It was used by the fledgling
federal government until they
moved to Washington City in
1800.

Assembly Room – Independence Hall, Philadelphia, where the vote on American independence took
place on 2 July 1776 and Declaration of Independence was approved on 4 July 1776.

Betsy Ross House – House on Arch Street in Philadelphia, believed to have been the residence of Elizabeth 'Betsy' Ross.

Site of First President's House – Philadelphia. An outline of the home where presidents George Washington and John Adams lived before the federal government moved to Washington City in 1800.

George Washington's Mount Vernon – Virginia on the Potomac River.

Old Tomb at Mount Vernon – George and Martha Washington were originally laid to rest here before later being moved to the current public tomb on Mount Vernon grounds.

Replica of Martha Washington's Wedding Dress and Shoes – On display at Mount Vernon.

James Madison's Montpelier – Home of James and Dolley Madison in Orange County, Virginia.

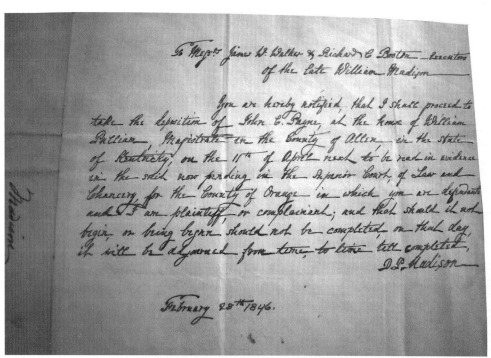

Dolley Madison Letter – Letter written by Dolley Madison in 1846 on display at the James Madison Museum in Orange County, Virginia.

Boston Castle – Yorkshire, England, built by the Earl of Effingham and named in support of the American colonists in 1773. (*Sharon Bennett Connolly*)

City of Washington from Beyond the Navy Yard by George Cooke, 1833. White House Historical Association. (*Public Domain*)

Sybil Ludington Stamp – Issued by the US Post Office in 1975 for the Bicentennial of American Independence, Smithsonian National Postal Museum.

Margaret Shippen Arnold – Portrait by Daniel Gardner, circa 1783-9, child pictured is believed to be Peggy's daughter Sophia, Philadelphia History Museum. (*Public Domain*)

Dolley Todd House – Philadelphia, Pennsylvania, where Dolley Payne Todd lived with her first husband.

James and Dolley Madison – Statue at Montpelier.

Mercy Otis Warren –
Portrait by John Singleton
Copley, 1763, Boston
Museum of Fine Arts,
(*Public Domain*)

Culper Spy Ring Code – Written by Benjamin Talmadge, page shows 355=lady, *George Washington Papers, Series 4*, 1783, Library of Congress, loc.gov/item/mgw434918/

HISTORY

OF THE

RISE, PROGRESS AND TERMINATION

OF THE

AMERICAN REVOLUTION.

INTERSPERSED WITH

Biographical, Political and Moral Obfervations.

IN THREE VOLUMES.

BY MRS. MERCY (OTIS) WARREN,

OF PLYMOUTH, (MASS.)

............Troubled on every fide............
perplexed, but not in despair; persecuted, but not forsaken;
cast down, but not destroyed.   *ST. PAUL.*

O God! thy arm was here............
And not to us, but to thy arm alone,
Ascribe we all.   *SHAKESPEARE.*

VOL. I.

BOSTON :

PRINTED BY MANNING AND LORING,

FOR E. LARKIN, No. 47, CORNHILL.

....
1805.

Mercy's History – Title page of *History of the Rise, Progress and Termination of the American Revolution: interspersed with Biographical, Political and Moral Observations* by Mercy Otis Warren, Library of Congress. (*Public Domain*)

Deborah Sampson Gannett – Engraving published by Herman Mann in *The Female Review*, 1797, Library of Congress, loc.gov/item/2002725275/ (*Public Domain*)

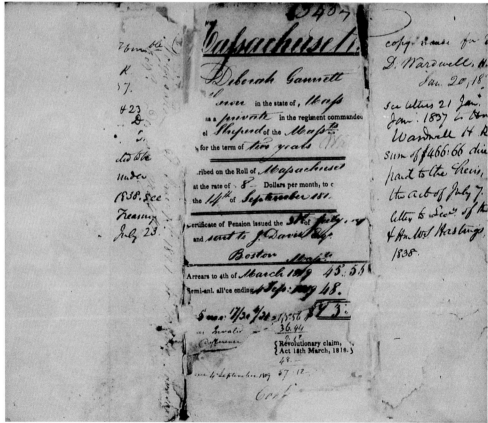

Revolutionary War Pension of Deborah Sampson Gannett – National Archives, catalog.archives.gov/id/54636851 (*Public Domain*)

Abigail Adams – Portrait by Benjamin Blyth, 1766. (*Public Domain*)

Abigail Adams Letter – Written to John Adams in March 1776. A portion of the text reads, 'I long to hear that you have declared an independency – and by the way in the new Code of Laws which I suppose it will be necessary for you to make I desire you would Remember the Ladies, and be more generous and favourable to them than your ancestors. Do not put such unlimited power into the hands of the Husbands. Remember all Men would be tyrants if they could.' Adams Family Papers, Massachusetts Historical Society.

Photo Credit: Samantha Wilcoxson unless otherwise noted.

Boston Massacre by Paul Revere – This engraving served as propaganda for the Sons of Liberty, portraying the British soldiers as aggressors and the colonists as innocent bystanders. *The bloody massacre perpetrated in King Street Boston on March 5th 1770 by a party of the 29th Regt.*, 1770. Library of Congress, loc.gov/pictures/item/2008661777/ (*Public Domain*)

Boston Massacre by Alonzo Chappel – This engraving portrays a less biased version of events than the more popular Paul Revere engraving. National Archives, catalog.archives.gov/id/513326 (*Public Domain*)

Washington Monument – Modern Washington DC. Dolley Madison and Elizabeth Hamilton supported the building of the Washington Monument in their widowhoods and were present for the laying of the cornerstone in 1848. Its construction was delayed by the American Civil War. It was completed on 6 December 1884.

Wedding of George Washington and Martha Custis – *Life of George Washington--The citizen* painted by Stearns; lith. by Régnier, imp. Lemercier, Paris, 1854, Library of Congress, loc.gov/item/98501405/ (*Public Domain*)

The White House – The earliest known photo of the President's House by John Plumbe Jr, 1846, Library of Congress, loc.gov/item/2004664421/ (*Public Domain*)

Dolley Madison Daguerreotype – by Matthew Brady, 1848, Library of Congress, loc.gov/resource/cph.3g06776/ (*Public Domain*)

Deborah's actions immediately following her discharge are unknown, though she may have lived with relatives in Stoughton, Massachusetts, because that is where she married Benjamin Gannett Jr on 7 April 1785.[24] Their first son, Earl Bradford Gannett, was born on 8 November 1785. Did Deborah choose to get married because she felt she had few other paths open to her, or was she in love with Benjamin Gannett? Was she eager or reluctant to leave her life as Robert Shurtliff behind? Whatever her motives or emotions, for the remainder of her life, she would be Deborah Gannett.

The Gannett's owned a small farm, and Deborah would have worked hard to raise crops, livestock, and the three children that she and Benjamin had by the end of 1790, having added two daughters, Polly and Patience, to their little brood. Deborah also adopted an orphaned baby, Susanna Shephard, in 1796.[25] In addition, the Gannett household included Patience Payson, a servant who was also something of an adopted family member. She remained with the family her entire life and was buried with the Gannetts when she died.[26] Deborah took some teaching and spinning work as she had done when she was younger to supplement what the farm produced. She also decided to go public about her experiences as Robert Shurtliff.

Keeping the secret of her identity had been vital during Deborah's time in the army, but now she was ready to speak openly about it. Several motives have been attributed to Deborah for this decision. Was she tired of rural life and looking to regain some of the excitement of her days as a soldier? Did the family need the money that Deborah anticipated her story might earn? Perhaps the truth is, as it often is, a combination of things.

At least one facet was financial, since the first step Deborah took was petitioning for her backpay as a soldier in 1792. She was required to provide proof of her service, which meant her secret was exposed to those she had served with, if they had not known already. By all accounts, she had served as a faithful, vigilant soldier, and she was awarded £34 in back pay.[27]

Deborah also started working with the man who would write the biography that provides modern historians with almost as many questions as answers. Herman Mann was not a historian or a writer, and he created a sensationalized version of Deborah's life in *The Female Review* that seems more calculated to entertain than inform. However, Deborah was involved in the creation of the first version, so, at least until later edits and additions were made, Mann must have portrayed Deborah in a way of which she approved, regardless of its level of accuracy. Their partnership was lasting and led to a lecture tour beginning in 1802.

In the first such tour made by an American woman, Deborah presented herself in Boston and then throughout New England, speaking about her experiences in a speech written by Herman Mann. She was eager to earn money and to gain support for her pension petition to congress which had thus far failed. However, the tour also forced her to leave behind her three children for a year, a difficult task for mothers of any era. Deborah must have felt strongly about the work she was undertaking to make such a sacrifice in a day when travel was difficult and slow.

Deborah's own journal written during her 1802 tour does not provide evidence of a passion for the work or excitement for sharing her story. On the contrary, she tracks her minor illnesses and expenses with equal precision. The trip seems to be a chore taken on only for the income it would provide.[28]

At each stop on her journey, Deborah would speak about her time in the army. Depending on the venue, she also might share songs sung by troops in camp and offer a demonstration of the presenting of arms and maneuvers in full uniform. Each night saw her transform from a rural housewife into a skilled soldier. Attendants were charged 25¢ each.[29] One wonders what early nineteenth-century audiences thought of this woman soldier before them, but Deborah seemed to feel she was well received. We can possibly forgive her for claiming that she served under General Alexander Hamilton at Yorktown. During her New York City performance, she may have believed she would be more successful if she claimed a connection with the famous New Yorker. Deborah, of course, did not enter the army until after the surrender of the British at Yorktown.

Did Deborah make audiences uncomfortable with her casual dismissal of firm gender lines or was she seen as an oddity that could be entertaining without being threatening? Perhaps, to some, she was an inspiration. In the changing world of the early 1800s, she was undoubtedly rejected and admired and everything in between. How would it have felt for Deborah to return home after her year of travels? Did she relish her return to normal life or regret the expectations that returned her to the domestic sphere?

When she reapplied for her federal pension, she had a supporter of prominence to ensure this petition's success. Paul Revere himself wrote on her behalf, 'I have been induced to enquire her situation, and Character, since she quitted the Male habit, and Soldiers uniform; for the more decent apparel of her own Sex; & Since she has been married and become a Mother. -- Humanity, & Justice obliges me to say, that every person with whom I have conversed about Her, and it is not a few, speak of Her as a woman of handsom talents, good Morals, a dutifull Wife and an affectionate parent.' He went on to encourage, 'I have no doubt your humanity will prompt you to do all in Your power to git her some releif; I think her case much more deserving than hundreds to whom Congress have been generous.'[30] Congress's generosity was needed. Despite the earnings of her tour, Deborah's finances were precarious, and Revere also lent her money. She was awarded $4 per month on 11 March 1805.[31] She went on to plead for two decades of backpay on her pension, either because of her family's desperate need for cash or because she truly felt that the US government owed her. However, her participation in a year-long lecture tour and weapon demonstrations brings into question the physical disability she claimed was caused by her time as a soldier.

Margaret Corbin shared Deborah's status as a wounded female Revolutionary War soldier. She had enlisted under her own name alongside her husband, John. She was wounded and he killed at Fort Washington. After she had recovered, Margaret served with the Invalid Corps at West Point, where she was later buried. Margaret also received a government pension.[32]

Deborah died on 29 April 1827 without a grand funeral or recognition of her contribution to society. Even her grave was unmarked until decades later after her husband and son had both passed away.[33] For all her striving for fame and fortune, Deborah Sampson Gannett died poor and obscure.

Chapter 8

Abigail Smith Adams

You are really brave, my dear, you are an Heroine.
— John Adams

Abigail Adams is a renowned letter writer, making her one of the most studied and admired of the women of the American Revolution. As her husband once observed, 'My wife must write!' Abigail wrote to her sister, Mary Cranch, 'My letters to you are first thoughts without corrections'.[1] Her writing, therefore, gives historians an unpolished and honest look at the life of women of this era. It is also a genuine record of Abigail's personality and character, which would be impossible to obtain through any other source.

Two centuries of historians have attempted to paint different pictures of Abigail Adams, and the one thing that is often agreed upon is that Abigail is a character full of contradictions. Portrayals of her as a politician or feminist fail to understand Abigail's own mindset and acceptance of the role she played in her own society. Her priorities were the management of her home and proper raising of her children, and, though she enjoyed discussing politics especially with her highly political husband, she would not have described herself as a political activist. In her own words, 'I believe nature has assigned to each sex its particular duties and sphere of action, and to act well your part, "there all the honor lies"'.[2] Abigail insisted, 'However brilliant a woman's tallents may be, she ought never to shine at the expence of her Husband'.[3] While Abigail had called upon John to 'Remember the Ladies', she also wrote to him, 'Regard us then as Beings placed by providence under your protection and in immitation of the Supreem Being make use of that power only for our happiness'.[4] A reading of their letters also reveals that while John and Abigail came to their political opinions while apart, they often arrived at the same conclusions.

Neither was Abigail a submissive, angelic wife. Her letters, which she never intended for publication, reveal a woman with opinions and complaints about daily life and even her famous spouse. On the other hand, reflecting on marriage to John, Abigail wrote, 'After half a century, I can say. My choice would be the same if I again had youth and opportunity to make it'.[5]

When John Adams was elected as America's second president, Abigail worried about living up to Martha Washington's example as First Lady. Martha had defined the role, and Abigail did not excel at fitting into well-defined roles. As a minister's daughter, young Abigail had been trained in typical domestic arts, but she had also spent hours in her father's library, learning about topics such as philosophy and literature that were normally considered outside women's realm. She maintained this fine balance between traditional eighteenth-century woman and her hunger for knowledge throughout her life.

The first recorded meeting of Abigail and John Adams occurred when she was fifteen years old and he was courting a Quincy cousin. They did not seem to seriously consider each other until three years later when John's friend, Richard Cranch, began courting Abigail's older sister, Mary.[6] Sharing a love of learning and streaks of stubbornness, Abigail and John soon decided to marry, as did Mary and Richard.

As a New England housewife, Abigail had some unique challenges. The shallow, rocky Massachusetts soil made farming a challenge and caused many families to divide land between fields, grazing, orchards, and woods. Access to forest land was incredibly valuable due to the necessity of heating a home through the frigid New England winter. Abigail was used to all these varied duties but was now responsible for them herself.

On the other hand, the Adams homestead's proximity to Boston meant that Abigail could purchase some home goods, such as cloth, soap, and candles, rather than taking the time to make them herself. With only one servant borrowed from John's mother when they first married, Abigail was a busy, young wife.[7] She was soon also a mother, when a daughter, also named Abigail, was born in July 1765. She was called Nabby, as her mother had been when she was a girl. Despite the work and her obligation to her husband, Abigail enjoyed married life and wrote to her sister, Mary Cranch, 'I desire to be very thankful that I can do as I please now!!!'[8]

At about the same time, the Stamp Act was enacted, placing John and Abigail on a road they had no idea they were traveling. As a lawyer, John was a part of discussions regarding parliament's actions from the beginning. What were the colonist's rights as British subjects, and what could they do to see them recognized? These were questions John strove to answer without thoughts of independence at this stage. When the colonists' destructive protests ensured that nobody wanted the position of stamp distributor, John worried that his practice, which required the stamped paper, would be insufficient to support his family.[9]

With the repeal of the Stamp Act in 1766, the Adamses enjoyed a brief period of calm and normality, although John was away from home approximately a week each month attending court. Of great significance to Abigail at this time was the ability to visit her sister, Mary, who had moved to Salem. The sisters had always been close and struggled with separation. 'Tis a hard thing to be weaned from any thing we Love ... I think of you ten times where I used to once', Abigail wrote.[10] On a trip to Salem to visit the much-missed sister Mary, John and Abigail had their portraits done by Benjamin Blyth, giving us our first glimpse of twenty-two-year-old Abigail with pinned back hair and dark eyes that give away little of her feisty personality.

Abigail welcomed her first son into the world on 14 July 1767. Proud as both father and mother undoubtedly were, they could have had little notion that they were smiling down at future US President, John Quincy Adams. As she had done with Nabby, Abigail nursed John Quincy for a year before beginning to feed him cornmeal mixed with water.[11] Caring for her young children, who faced a high mortality rate in the eighteenth century, was Abigail's consuming responsibility as her family grew.

In March 1768, Mary and Abigail were reunited as both of their husband's careers took them to Boston.[12] Due to the land leveling and filling in of swamp area that has occurred since the eighteenth century, Boston appeared much different to Abigail than it does today. At that time, Boston could only be reached by boat or over one narrow pass at Roxbury. Practically an island, Boston was home to approximately 16,000 residents in six square miles heavily focused on North End. Abigail's large white house was close to local government buildings and Faneuil Hall.

Life was different in Boston compared to Braintree. Abigail had only a small city garden, which meant she visited the nearby market most days to purchase items that she would have previously made or grown herself. This would have freed up some of her time for activities that were common in the city, such as visiting friends, reading books and newspapers, and shopping.

While living in Boston, Abigail gave birth to a daughter named Susanna. It was a challenge for her to care for this sickly child in addition to young Nabby and John Quincy. Poor Susanna survived only a year, but Abigail's grief was assuaged with the knowledge that she was pregnant again. Most families of this era lost at least one child in infancy, and Abigail would have leaned upon her faith to cope. She believed that God had a greater plan than she could see and that she would one day be reunited with Susanna in heaven.

About a month after Susanna's death, the Boston Massacre drew John back into politics, and the Adams family's period of normalcy came to an end. From their home, Abigail could hear the sound of the rising mob and the shots that rang out leaving five dead. The very next day, John's services were called upon to provide the British soldiers with a defense. Valuing the right to legal counsel and fair trial over his blossoming reputation as a leading patriot, John took the case with Abigail's full support.[13]

The people of Boston soon demonstrated that they believed in John's patriotism and integrity even as he stood as defense for British soldiers by electing him to the Massachusetts legislature in June 1770. Abigail had just given birth to their second son, Charles, and she would have been thankful to be in the city where she had her sister and friends close at hand as she looked toward a future that would pull John away from home with greater frequency. Her fears were not so much for herself, but she did fear for John, knowing he could be labeled a traitor to the British crown. John wrote, 'That excellent Lady, who has always encouraged me, burst into a flood of Tears, but said she was very sensible of all the Danger to her and to our Children as well as to me, but she thought I had done as I ought, she was very willing to share in all that was to come and place her trust in Providence.'[14]

Exhausted and ill from the stress of the Boston Massacre trials, John wrote, 'Farewell Politicks' in his diary and moved the family back to Braintree.[15] There, Abigail gave birth to another son, Thomas, and the family enjoyed a country respite until moving back to Boston in November 1772.

When Britain passed the Tea Act in 1773, creating a monopoly for the British East India Company, Boston responded. First, colonists requested that ships leave with their cargoes intact. When that failed, tea was dumped into the harbor. Abigail fully supported the boycotts of British goods and the treatment of the tea. She was also grateful that clearer heads had ensured that nothing on the ship besides tea was damaged. It sent an untarnished message that this was not random destruction.

Believing that radicalism was limited to Boston and that the remainder of the colonies would be compliant if Boston were dealt with quickly and harshly, Britain passed the Boston Port Bill, effectively shutting down the city's economy. The colonies did not react as anticipated. The retaliation served to unite the colonies as they sent aid to Boston and were appalled by the arrival of British troops. From their perspective in Boston, the possibility of war and independence seemed closer than to residents of other colonies, or even Massachusetts outside of the city. The most radical patriots were centered in Boston, as were the bulk of British troops in America. John and Abigail likely saw what was on the horizon long before many others who would become the founders of the United States.

In the center of it all, Abigail supported the Sons of Liberty but believed the British would continue to make an example of Boston. When she wrote to Mercy Otis Warren, she asked the older woman for advice on raising a family but also discussed the politics of the day. The women shared a worldview that included an intellectual interest in politics and education even as they maintained that a woman's first responsibility was to her family. Their closeness to the rising rebellion and like-mindedness made the two close confidants throughout the revolution. Abigail believed, just as her male counterparts did at this point, that American colonists were being deprived of their rights as British citizens. While some of the most radical patriots were speaking of independence, most colonists could see little besides deadly defeat at the conclusion of a war against the British. It was thought more prudent to obtain correction of the rights violations that were occurring and restoration of their full standing as British subjects. Abigail was prophetic when she wrote to Mercy, 'Altho the mind is shocked at the Thought of sheding Humane Blood, more Especially the Blood of our Countrymen, and a civil War is of all Wars, the most dreadfull Such is the present Spirit that prevails, that if once they are made desperate Many, very Many of our Heroes will spend their lives in the cause, With the Speach of Cato in their Mouths, "What a pitty it is, that we can dye but once to save our Country."'[16]

As history was happening in Boston, Abigail also had daily life to attend, and much of her duties were made more difficult by the presence of British troops, the shortage of supplies, and the boycotting of British goods. Even in town, women turned to homemade goods as those in the country did. Thankfully, Abigail had the experience and skills to cope with this better than those who had lived in the city their entire lives.

After John was selected to be a Massachusetts delegate to the Continental Congress in June 1774, Abigail and the children once again returned to Braintree. With more work to do but fewer concerns about shortages or violence, Abigail managed the household and farm while John, along with his cousin Samuel Adams, was in Philadelphia. She was proud of her husband yet missed him terribly. They were a close couple separating at a difficult time. Within a matter of days, she was writing, 'The great distance between us, makes the time appear very long to me. It seems already a month since you left me. The great anxiety I feel for my Country, for you and for our family renders the day tedious, and the night unpleasent.'[17]

Throughout John's absence, Abigail depended on letters. The process of writing was a comfort to her, and receiving John's replies reassured her of his health and kept her up-to-date on the news of the day – or at least recent news since letters might take weeks to travel the 300 miles from Philadelphia to Braintree. She also was able to supply him with information about what was really happening and what people were saying in nearby Boston.

Besides managing the farm, Abigail had to make decisions on her own that John would normally make. Her letters were peppered with appeals for his advice and guidance, but she did not always hear back in time to depend on his reply. Over the years of the Revolution, Abigail was forced to grow confident in her own decision making. One of the first was regarding schooling for John Quincy. In 1774, the precocious seven year old was ready for school, but none in Braintree was considered adequate. Abigail chose to hire a tutor, so that her son could begin learning things she was incapable of teaching him, such as Greek and Latin.[18]

In her darker moments, when Abigail was overwhelmed with her duties and missing her husband, she poured out her heart in letters to John. In September 1774, she wrote, 'I had rather give a dollar for a letter by the post, tho the consequence should be that I Eat but one meal a day for these 3 weeks to come'.[19] A month later, she wrote, 'My Much Loved Friend, I dare not express to you at 300 hundred miles distance how ardently I long for your return. I have some very miserly Wishes; and cannot consent to your spending one hour in Town till at least I have had you 12.'[20] He had been in Philadelphia for ten weeks, and Abigail had little way of knowing the length of absences they would soon endure. John returned home in December and was there when war broke out in April 1775 at Lexington and Concord outside Boston. Friends of the Adamses, Paul Revere and William Dawes, rode through the night to alert colonists to be prepared for the coming British regulars.

Abigail had reason once again to be thankful her family had moved out of Boston as it became occupied by British troops under siege by colonial militiamen. She took in refugees from the city and militiamen as they traveled through Braintree, creating a chaotic scene at the Adams farm. Little John Quincy was found marching alongside drilling soldiers in his parents' field.[21] Abigail had to worry about what she might do if the British raided Braintree for supplies. What if she was forced to take the children and run? John wrote to 'fly to the Woods with our Children' should an attack come.[22]

When the British attacked Charlestown, north of Boston, Abigail, with seven-year-old John Quincy at her side, could hear the guns and see smoke from Penn's Hill. She soon learned that one of the Charlestown casualties was Joseph Warren and had to break the terrible news to John that one of his friends had fallen. 'My bursting Heart must find vent at my pen. I have just heard that our dear Friend Dr. Warren is no more but fell gloriously fighting for his Country – saying better to die honourably in the field than ignominiously hang upon the Gallows. Great is our Loss. He has distinguished himself in every engagement, by his courage and fortitude, by animating the Soldiers and leading them on by his own example.'[23] She must have wondered if the same would be required of her husband before the war was over. The American defeat in Charlestown became known as the Battle of Bunker Hill, although much of the fighting took place on nearby Breed's Hill. John continued in Philadelphia while Abigail wondered what the next British move would be.

As the Continental Congress slowly deliberated, Boston suffered under its occupiers, and refuges who were able paid up to $40 for passes out of the city.[24] Abigail found herself taking in more people in need as they streamed out of the city. She struggled with one tenant who refused to offer space to refugees or listen to Abigail in her husband's absence.[25] By the summer of 1775, the Continental Army led by George Washington reached Cambridge, assuaging the fears of colonists in the Boston area. Abigail had the opportunity to meet General Washington and concurred with John's positive opinion of him.

Abigail settled back into an odd existence where skirmishes could occasionally be heard in the distance, but most of life went on as normal, or as normal as it could be in John's extended absence, with the farm and her children her greatest concerns. When John was able to come home for only three weeks at the end of summer, Abigail wrote to Mercy Otis Warren, 'I find I am obliged to summon all my patriotism to feel willing to part with him again. You will readily believe me when I say that I make no small sacrifice to the publick.'[26]

Soon after John's departure, Braintree was struck by an outbreak of dysentery. Abigail contracted and quickly overcame the disease, but she feared for the lives of her little Thomas and her aged mother. She was forced to care for many patients in both households when only recently recovered herself. Thomas recovered, but Abigail's relief was mingled with grief when her mother, Elizabeth Smith, died on 1 October 1775. Abigail was almost inconsolable over the loss of her mother and had to settle for letters to John as comfort. 'Have pitty upon me, have pitty upon me o! thou my beloved for the Hand of God presseth me soar ... How can I tell you (o my bursting Heart) that my Dear Mother has Left me, this day about 5 oclock she left this world for an infinitely better ... At times I almost am ready to faint under this severe and heavy Stroke, seperated from thee who used to be a comfortar towards me in affliction, but blessed be God, his Ear is not heavy that he cannot hear, but he has bid us call upon him in time of Trouble.'[27]

The dysentery epidemic waned as winter arrived. War had not been officially declared as armies settled into their winter camps, and many wondered what the future held as 1775 came to a close. Congress continued to discuss possibilities of reconciliation, but from her perspective close to the heart of the burgeoning rebellion, Abigail had become convinced that a full battle for independence would become necessary. She wrote to John that congress should give up their pleas to Britain and instead, 'a reconciliation betwen our, no longer parent State, but tyrant State, and these Colonies. – Let us seperate, they are unworthy to be our Breathren. Let us renounce them and instead of suplications as formorly for their prosperity and happiness, Let us beseach the almighty to blast their counsels and bring to Nought all their devices.'[28]

Many colonists began to agree with Abigail when *Common Sense* by Thomas Paine was published in January 1776. It was the first widespread public call for independence rather than reconciliation with England. Paine boldly rejected the very idea of a monarchy and expressed surprised dismay that Americans would consider pledging their loyalty to a corrupt king. After years of level-headed minds working toward conciliation, Paine argued, 'Everything that is right or reasonable pleads for separation. The blood of the slain, the weeping voice of nature cries, 'TIS TIME TO PART. Even the distance at which the Almighty has placed England and America is a strong and natural proof that the authority of the one over the other was never the design of Heaven.'[29] And people listened. *Common Sense* was printed and distributed far and wide, uniting colonists behind the idea of an independent nation. Abigail, who received a copy of *Common Sense* from John shortly after its publication, agreed with Paine and was grateful for the pamphlet's ability to spur people, especially congress, to action.

When Abigail was kept awake by cannon fire in March 1776, she did not realize that she was hearing cannons that had been moved all the way from Fort Ticonderoga to Dorchester Heights for the Continental Army to turn them on the British in Boston.[30] However, she knew exactly what was happening when she watched from Penn's Hill as dozens of British ships sailed out of Boston Harbor, abandoning the city at last. She was unhesitant in her words to John, 'I long to hear that you have declared an independancy'.[31]

Tied to her passion for independence were Abigail's thoughts on women's rights, which are often remembered today, if not always within their proper context. Possibly the most famous quote by Abigail Adams was written to her husband as congress debated the form of the new government. 'I desire you would Remember the Ladies, and be more generous and favourable to them than your ancestors. Do not put such unlimited power into the hands of the Husbands. Remember all Men would be tyrants if they could.' These lines have been cited to laud Abigail as an early feminist, but they must be interpreted with Abigail's worldview in mind. It is also important to note that she closed out the letter with 'Regard us then as Beings placed by providence under your protection and in immitation of the Supreem Being make use of that power only for our happiness.'[32]

Abigail did believe that girls should be offered greater educational opportunities. Evidence of this is that she had her own daughter, Nabby, receive tutoring in Latin, a subject normally reserved for boys in the eighteenth century. Abigail also believed that wives should have legal rights and protection in the case of abusive or neglectful spouses. Women had no legal voice or property of their own, which could leave them in a desperate situation. While Abigail believed in Biblical marriage and gender roles that placed a woman in the home with her children, she also saw the great need to protect women in bad marriages. She strove for a future where women would be educated and given rights that would enable them to be the best wives and mothers. Our modern idea of feminism, or even women's suffrage, would have been a radically unfamiliar idea to Abigail Adams.

Abigail's 'Remember the Ladies' letter to John also stated, 'I have sometimes been ready to think that the passion for Liberty cannot be Eaquelly Strong in the Breasts of those who have been accustomed to deprive their fellow Creatures of theirs. Of this I am certain that it is not founded upon that generous and christian principal of doing to others as we would that others should do unto us.'[33] From the beginning of the Revolution, she saw that slavery would be an issue in uniting the colonies and doubted the patriotism of Southerners. Abigail's parents had owned two slaves during her childhood, but she had become a bold abolitionist as her passion as a patriot was ignited. In 1774, she had written John, 'I wish most sincerely there was not a Slave in the province. It allways appeard a most iniquitous Scheme to me – fight ourselfs for what we are daily robbing and plundering from those who have as good a right to freedom as we have.'[34] Her feelings that all people of every color should be free was also not universally held, and many who agreed with her were willing to put that discussion off for another day.

Independence would mean a new form of government. The constitutional republic seems a natural choice today, but it was not considered so at the time. A republican form of government was favored by Abigail but not widely popular. For colonies that had long lived under a monarchy, a republic seemed unstable and inadequate.

As Bostonians flooded back into the city during the summer of 1776, smallpox broke out. Abigail decided that it was time for her and the children to be inoculated as John had endured years earlier. She was not alone. Her sisters and their families joined her in Boston for the weeks that the process demanded. It was here that Abigail received word from John that the Declaration of Independence had been signed, and she attended a reading of the document on 18 July.[35] She shared the experience with John, 'I went with the Multitude into Kings Street to hear the proclamation for independance read and proclamed... great attention was given to every word. As soon as he ended, the cry from the Belcona, was God Save our American States and then 3 cheers which rended the air, the Bells rang, the privateers fired, the forts and Batteries, the cannon were discharged, the platoons followed and every face appeard joyfull. Mr. Bowdoin then gave a Sentiment, Stability and perpetuity to American independance. After dinner the kings arms were taken down from the State House and every vestage of him from every place in which it appeard and burnt in King Street. Thus ends royall Authority in this State, and all the people shall say Amen.'[36] After taking time out to celebrate, Abigail returned to the family's preparations for smallpox inoculation.

Inoculation was a difficult choice for a parent to make in the eighteenth century. The choice to purposely infect one's child with what was intended to be a mild case of a disease was not to be taken lightly. The science was not perfected, and some children became severely ill and died. Abigail must have felt fear and guilt when Nabby grew increasingly ill, as did Charles after going through his third attempt at inoculation.[37] His case grew severe enough that Abigail warned John that he might die, and she must have hoped that her husband's grief would not be blamed on her. She spent weeks caring for her children and praying for their recovery. Those prayers were finally answered, and the family returned to Braintree in the autumn and were joined by John.

John was home only long enough for Abigail to become pregnant. They were both thrilled to be expecting another child. Married women of the eighteenth century often had a child approximately every other year, but Abigail's youngest, Thomas, would be five years old by the time the baby was born. They also both hoped that John would be home more regularly by then. In the meantime, John rejoined congress, this time in Baltimore. Facing pregnancy, wartime shortages and inflation, and management of farm and children alone, Abigail became depressed. She had reason to wonder if the sacrifice her family was making would prove worthwhile. However, she did not become concerned about childbirth until she realized that John would not be able to be present. This caused her to fear the specter of death that came for so many women in the eighteenth-century childbed.

In mid-July, Abigail fell ill and stopped feeling the familiar movements of her unborn child. She gave birth to a stillborn daughter a week later.[38] Abigail shared deep, personal moments with John through writing, even writing to him as she labored to deliver their daughter. 'I must lay my pen down this moment, to bear what I cannot fly from – and now I have endured it'.[39] Abigail longed for another daughter, but instead had lost her as she had little Susanna. The distance that continued to separate John and Abigail augmented their grief.

War action increased in 1777, providing a distraction from their great sorrow. John faced the work of congress – the endless struggle to supply the army, wooing allies, and developing a united government amid thirteen previously unconnected colonies. Abigail faced the struggle at home – fear of invasion, working the farm, and raising the children. As the couple observed their thirteenth wedding anniversary apart, Abigail wrote, 'This day dearest of Friends compleats 13 years since we were solemly united in wedlock; 3 years of the time we have been cruelly seperated. I have patiently as I could endured it with the Belief that you were serving your Country, and rendering your fellow creatures essential Benefits. May future Generations rise up and call you Blessed, and the present behave worthy of the blessings you are Labouring to secure to them, and I shall have less reason to regreat the deprivation of my own perticuliar felicity.'[40]

During John's following trip home, he received news that he had been elected Commissioner to France. Abigail was in anguish at the prospect, but she still believed in the cause enough to let him go. It was too expensive for the entire family to travel to Paris, but it was determined that John Quincy, at age ten, was old enough to join his father for the educational value of the trip. They left on 13 February 1778.[41] Upon their departure, Abigail wrote to friend John Thaxter, 'my Hands and my Heart have both been full. My whole Time has been taken up in prepareing my dearest Friend, and Master John for their Voyage ... And now cannot you immagine me seated by my fire side Bereft of my better Half, and added to that a Limb lopt of to heighten the anguish.[42] Abigail was an affectionate mother, but on multiple occasions, she accepted separations from her children for the advancement of their education. After John Quincy left with his father, Abigail wrote, 'It is a very dificult task my dear son for a tender parent to bring their mind to part with a child of your years into a distant Land, nor could I have acquiesced in such a seperation under any other care than that of the most Excellent parent and Guardian who accompanied you. You have arrived at years capable of improving under the advantages you will be like to have if you do but properly attend to them.[43]

Her anxiety was not only due to separation, but the dangers that father and son faced during a risky ocean crossing. Abigail had no way of knowing when or if she would see her husband or son again. Shortly after John's departure for France, false rumors of Ben Franklin's assassination caused Abigail's fears for the safety of her husband and eldest son to increase to an agonizing level. Within months, she was writing, 'I wish a thousand times I had gone with him'.[44]

She wrote to one her husband considered a friend and fellow politician, James Lovell. Some historians have insinuated that Abigail had inappropriate correspondence with Lovell, she being a middle-aged, married woman and he no less attached. However, as Edith Gelles points out, Abigail had few to turn to for news while John and John Quincy were overseas.[45] While Lovell's letters did at times cross the lines of propriety, Abigail would have been desperate for information during the long months without any communication from John.

This was not Abigail's first correspondence with James Lovell. Their letter-writing had begun in August 1777 with a letter from Lovell that included a map he had drawn which he believed Abigail would find interesting. The two were acquainted through John, so this was not improper, but his proclaimed 'affectionate esteem' would have raised an eyebrow. It likely struck Abigail as too familiar. She responded uncertainly, 'I cannot describe to you the distress and agitation which the reception of your Letter threw me into'. Abigail seemed to decide that the safest course was a reference to her husband. 'I thought it would announce to me the sickness or death of all my earthly happiness'.[46]

If Abigail found James Lovell's letters uncomfortably flirtatious, she still appreciated that he was one of few connections who responded to her requests for information and cared about the sacrifices she was making while John was away. She begged him, 'When ever any perticulars arrive with regard to this black affair I must beg of you to acquaint me with them'.

The price Abigail paid for insider information was Lovell's increasing familiarity. 'How do you do, Lovely Portia, these very cold Days? Mistake me not willfully; I said Days', he once wrote.[47] James also assisted Abigail with receiving shipments of goods from John, which sometimes arrived from Europe in Philadelphia. It is difficult to know if Abigail enjoyed these flirtations while her husband was away for months at a time, or if she endured them due to the help that she needed from the rakish congressman. In her letters, she never reaches the depths of impropriety that Lovell does when he claims, 'I suspect I shall covet to be in the Arms of Portia's' or 'how dearly I would love thee!' On the contrary, Abigail calls James a 'flatterer' and 'wicked man', and at times went long stretches without writing to him at all.[48] Eventually, Lovell accepted true friendship with Abigail rather than pursuing a flirtation, as reflected in their letters which became more genuine and caring over the years.

Abigail appears to be an innocent victim of Lovell's early attention, but this relationship spotlights how difficult it must have been for Abigail to go such long stretches of time with John away. James was friends with John and they had similar personalities. Both were blunt but witty, acerbic but with a hidden sensitive side. Exchanging correspondence with James when it was not possible to do so with John might have been a comfort to Abigail.

Close companions and a love match, John and Abigail would not have the time together that they had enjoyed as newlyweds until late middle-age. Abigail resisted those who might usurp John's place, but he could not deny the call of country at the cost of his family life. Abigail also had surprise visitors during John's time in France. Although she lived a simple life, she was also the wife of the Commissioner to France. When French allies began arriving in Boston, they were quick to visit Mrs Adams. She savored the news and enjoyed learning about the French.

Knowing John's absence would be extended, the decision had been made to lease out the farm. With that responsibility lifted and the children getting older, Abigail's daily life was considerably eased. In fact, with Nabby spending time in Boston for school or sent to Mercy Otis

Warren for home education, Abigail's lonesomeness increased until her niece, Louisa, was sent to her. She was two years old and the daughter of Abigail's brother, William. Abigail might not have more children of her own, but Louisa was a welcome substitute.

As the anniversary of John's departure came and went, Abigail struggled with depression, exacerbated by the lack of communication. John's letters were few and unfulfilling when they arrived due to the time required to cross the ocean and his fear that they would be intercepted. Therefore, Abigail did not feel comforted or informed by John's missives.

On 2 August 1779, Abigail's joy was exquisite when she was surprised by the arrival of John and John Quincy in Braintree. She had no idea that John had been attempting to get home since February, and she hoped that he was home to stay. However, that was not to be. Less than three months passed before John was requested to return to France as a treaty negotiator. John would not consider exposing Abigail to the dangers of crossing the Atlantic. He did, however, decide to take John Quincy and nine-year-old Charles. They departed on 13 November 1779.[49] Preparing for another separation of unknown length, Abigail comforted herself with the belief that peace must come soon.

In the meantime, she occupied herself with becoming a skilled money manager. Abigail found that she enjoyed negotiating land deals and finding buyers for the goods that John sent from France. She had competently run the farm, but these duties she enjoyed. As paper money's value continued to fall, Abigail depended upon French goods that enabled her to barter for her household needs.

Abigail had other relationships that helped her endure eighteenth-century single motherhood. Key among them were her sisters, Mary, three years older, and Elizabeth, six years younger. Besides their collective upbringing, the women shared the unique experience of living through a Revolution, the trials and joys of married life, and the loss of their adult daughters to illness.[50] The Puritan faith was a deeply engrained part of their characters, and it gave them strength, or at least resignation, to cope with the difficulties they faced. Their honest, detailed letters give historians an intimate look into the women's lives. During Mary's time living in Germantown, Abigail wrote to her, 'When ever I receive a Letter from you it seems to give new Springs to my nerves, and a brisker circulation to my Blood, tis a kind of pleasing pain that I feel'.[51] For much of the time that John Adams was absent from home serving his nation, Abigail and her older sister Mary were neighbors in Braintree, Massachusetts. This gave Abigail a close confidant and friend when she most needed one. Their letters indicate a deep devotion to one another and like-minded personalities. Abigail was crushed when Mary died in 1811.

But in 1780, the war dragged on. Peace, which John had traveled to Paris to negotiate, seemed as far away as ever when an unanticipated blow struck. In September 1780, Benedict Arnold fled to the British after it was discovered that he had attempted to turn over West Point. The treason had been uncovered by a series of coincidences and accidental successes on behalf of the Americans, and it challenged the confidence of the Continental Army.

Fighting moved south in 1781, and Abigail might have missed the days when gunfire in the near distance made her fearful and her nights sleepless but she had been able to see what was happening from the top of Penn's Hill. News of surrender on 19 October 1781 must have given Abigail mixed feelings – joy at victory blended with the knowledge that John's work as treaty negotiator would only now begin in earnest.

Just as Abigail was making decisions on her own at home, John was forced by circumstances to do the same in Europe. Abigail learned only after the fact that her boys attended school in Holland and later that John Quincy traveled to St Petersburg as secretary to America's Minister to Russia, Francis Dana.[52] Charles, on the other hand, grew homesick and John decided to send him home. When Charles arrived home in January 1782, Abigail had received little news of her husband and sons for much of the previous year.

Abigail comforted herself during John's lengthening absence with land purchases in Vermont. Perhaps she enjoyed the business side of this endeavor, or maybe she believed that she and John would someday escape it all and live on the frontier. Whatever her motive, she purchased hundreds of acres of land that she would never see.

Abigail was losing patience with her 'widowhood' and begged John to come home.[53] They had sacrificed enough years of their life for the sake of liberty, especially when it did not always seem appreciated by their fellow countrymen. In their letters, both John and Abigail bemoaned their lost years together. In May 1782, John firmly stated, 'I must go to you or you must come to me. I cannot live, in this horrid Solitude'.[54] But the couple could not agree on the best course to take through painfully slow post and uncertain news of peace.

Another consequence of John's patriotism was his absence as his children came of age to begin courting. It was through letters that Abigail introduced John to Royall Tyler in 1782. John's reply was that of a typical father, 'My child is too young for such thoughts ... I don't like this method of Courting Mothers'.[55] Nabby was sixteen years old, the same age Abigail had been when she and John became a couple. There was little John could do about the budding romance, and he gave reluctant approval by letter for the couple to be engaged in 1784. However, his wife and daughter had already decided to join John in Europe. Nabby could marry Royall upon her return, whenever that might be.[56]

Abigail turned to her younger sister once she had accepted that the way for her to be with her husband was to go to him in Europe, rather than wait for him to come home. She arranged to leave her sons, Charles and Thomas, with Elizabeth to continue their education under the tutelage of Elizabeth's husband.[57] The boys were ten and twelve years old at the time, and it was a difficult separation for Abigail. Elizabeth, understanding this, wrote to Abigail with reassuring news about the children's education, physical health, and affectionate treatment within the family.

Abigail had many decisions to make before she could undertake a voyage of indefinite length. Louisa, who thought of Abigail more like a mother than an aunt, did not wish to be returned to her family. Abigail and her daughter finally set sail on 20 June 1784.[58]

Abigail had long feared the hardships of an ocean voyage, and her experience aboard the *Active* still managed to disappoint her. She wrote to her sisters about the terrible food, lack of privacy, and filthy conditions. Once she overcame her seasickness, Abigail took it upon herself to see to the ship's cleanliness, recognizing that none of the crew appeared to consider it a task worth attending to. She also decided to offer the cook some lessons, unpacking some of her dishes to make up for the ship's inadequacies.[59]

Abigail and Nabby arrived in London on 21 July 1784. It was a city unlike any that mother or daughter had ever seen, dwarfing Boston with a population approximately fifty times greater, so they were thankful to see the familiar faces of cousins, Isaac Smith Jr and Charles Storer, soon after arrival.[60] They shared a few whirlwind days of sightseeing and visiting before John Quincy arrived to help escort Abigail and Nabby across the channel. Abigail would have struggled to recognize her little boy in the strapping seventeen year old before her. He had traveled throughout Europe and to the court of Russia, making him a sophisticated intellectual for his years. John Quincy would follow in his father's footsteps and spend years serving the United States in foreign posts.

Finally, on 7 August 1784, after almost five years apart, John and Abigail Adams were reunited at London's Adelphi Hotel.[61] Abigail later wrote to her sister, Mary, 'But you know my dear sister, that poets and painters wisely draw a veil over those Scenes which surpass the pen of the one and the pencil of the other. We were indeed a very very happy family once more.'[62] However happy the reunion, it was certainly rushed as John and John Quincy escorted the women to Paris the following day.

Paris was small and crowded compared to sprawling London, and Abigail was concerned about the language barrier. She found Paris dirty and claimed Boston was 'much superior in my eyes'.[63] The family rented a house outside of the city, where Abigail had to quickly accustom herself to being an ambassador's wife rather than that of a simple farmer. Parisian culture disappointed Abigail. She valued hard work, piety, and education, none of which appeared to be important to the residents of Paris.

Despite her joy over reunion with John, Abigail was quickly homesick. Arrangements were made to send John Quincy home to complete his education at Harvard, and Abigail longed for the entire family to go. In May 1785, they were all preparing to leave France, but John, Abigail, and Nabby traveled back across the Channel while John Quincy made his ocean voyage. John had been named the first US ambassador to England.[64]

It was no Boston, but Abigail greatly preferred London to Paris. She felt she had more in common with the English, despite the recently ended war. The Adamses rented a house in Grosvenor Square. Due to John's position, Abigail faced presentation to King George alongside his queen and princesses. Even in relatively simple court dress, Abigail felt overdressed, and she found the royal family unimpressive. Abigail found it difficult to live under constant scrutiny of the public and press. She was agitated by negative reports, especially those that demeaned her husband who had sacrificed so much and worked so hard. They were also ridiculed for living meagerly compared to what was expected of foreign dignitaries and government officials.[65]

Nabby also struggled with unhappiness in London. Lonely and no more impressed with the European obsession with pleasure and entertainment than her parents, Nabby had few duties to occupy her time and no close friends. She also had few letters from her fiancé, and she began to see the deficiencies in his character that her parents had seen in him all along. As Abigail had admitted, Royall 'has good qualities, indeed he has but he ever was his own enemy'.[66] The engagement broken, Nabby became interested in Colonel William Smith, a former aide-de-camp of Washington's who was also stationed in London. They became engaged in February 1785.[67]

With all three of her boys an ocean away at Harvard, Abigail faced separation from her only daughter as the wedding day approached. Nabby was married in June and gave birth to her first son the following April. Since her husband was forced to travel soon after the birth, Nabby and her son stayed with her parents. Abigail must have been thrilled to have them with her, despite an ailment that sidelined her during the spring of 1786.[68] That summer, Abigail temporarily added Polly Jefferson to her household. The girl was on her way to join her father in Paris, and Abigail enjoyed having a young girl to spend time with. Back home, John Quincy was graduating from Harvard.[69]

Abigail's life in London was markedly different from life in Braintree. She attended the theatre and was both entertained and offended by it. She also decided to dig into her family tree, hoping to prove that a signer of the Magna Carta the first Earl of Winchester, Saar de Quincy, was an ancestor.[70] As she explored England outside of London, she became aware of the great divide between the rich and impoverished. Abigail wrote her sister, Elizabeth Shaw, 'The Noble and the wealthy, fare sumptuously every day, poverty hunger and Nakedness is the Lot, and portion of the needy pesantry, who are the inhabitants of the County Towns and villages, by whom the Earth is manured, and the Harvest gatherd in.' The well-off were not quite so extravagantly rich in America, neither were the poor so miserably destitute. 'When I reflect upon the advantages which the people of America possess, over the most polished of other Nations, the ease with which property is obtain, the plenty which is so equally distributed, their personal Liberty, and Security of

Life and property, I feel gratefull to Heaven, who marked out my Lot in that happy land.'[71]

By the time they left England in April 1788, Abigail was looking forward to returning home. She had enjoyed seeing more of the world but was thankful to be an American. Her only regret was that Nabby would be returning to New York with her husband. Abigail would finally have to let her daughter go.

The return to Braintree included a new, larger home that still seemed small and provincial compared to their European lodgings. Abigail set to work renovating the home and furnishing it with furniture from Europe. She also soon began adding on more rooms, surprised to find the larger home inadequate for their needs. Abigail had become more sophisticated in England than she cared to admit. They named their new home Peacefield.

Before they could settle, John was elected to be George Washington's vice-president, and they began looking for a house in New York City. This was pleasing to Abigail, despite the inconvenience, because she would be closer to Nabby, who had recently given birth to a second son. She also brought her niece, Louisa. Since the Adams and Washington families were expected to welcome guests, Abigail followed Martha's lead and planned weekly events, somewhat like royal drawing rooms she had attended in London. She enjoyed these levees no more than the First Lady, but it was important that the leaders of the new country be accessible to those they represented. Later, when Abigail became First Lady, she wrote to Martha for advice and expressed her desire to emulate that great lady's example.[72]

Many of the people gathered in New York City had opinions on the developing a new form of government. Those who had been unified in fighting the British became divided in what should replace monarchical rule. Abigail was a firm Federalist and supported centralized government to the extent that she abandoned old friends who disagreed, such as Mercy Otis Warren. Abigail was not one to agree to disagree.

Abigail grew to love her estate just outside the city and was disappointed when the government moved to Philadelphia. It would take her away from Nabby and her growing family and require another inconvenient and expensive move. Charles was also in New York, but Thomas went with his parents as did niece Louisa.

Abigail did not like Philadelphia, from its unhealthy air to its European style love of entertainment. The city was also the center of the growing chasm between political partisanship. Exhibiting her profound political acumen, Abigail noted, 'I firmly believe if I live Ten years longer, I shall see a devision of the Southern & Northern States'.[73] Abigail and John decided to go to Quincy, as their neighborhood of Braintree had been renamed, over the summer, in spite of the inconvenience of moving the household. Doing so meant that the Adamses avoided the yellow fever outbreaks that seemed to plague Philadelphia each summer for reasons that no one in the eighteenth century understood.

During John's second term as vice-president, Abigail chose not to join him in Philadelphia. John missed her so much that he threatened to resign, but Abigail was used to him saying such things. She turned her attention to the farms in hopes of paying off the debt they had incurred while living in Philadelphia on John's painfully low government salary.

In September 1794, John Quincy left once again for Europe after being named American Minister to Holland, taking his younger brother, Thomas, along.[74] Abigail was proud of her intellectual son but also uncertain about him following his father into politics. It had robbed John and Abigail of wealth and time together. What price would their son pay?

Abigail had more to manage with John Quincy away. He had been managing the family's Boston property. In addition, Abigail found herself taking over the Shaw farm, when Elizabeth's husband, John, died suddenly. Abigail's sister did not share her skill or tenacity and soon remarried to ease her burden. Elizabeth also sent her daughter, Betsey, to Abigail, hoping the girl would behave better in the care of her aunt.[75]

When closely held rumors of Washington's retirement were whispered early in 1795, John and Abigail began to discuss whether he would be elected America's second president. While John felt he was entitled to the job, Abigail did not desire it for him. She had not enjoyed her time in the public eye and felt John had earned his retirement as had Washington. John was caught, not for the first time, between his political ambitions and his desires for a peaceful family life. They wondered if Thomas Jefferson or John Jay might be elected in John's stead. Abigail wanted her husband home, but she felt he was infinitely more qualified to lead the country than either Jefferson or Jay. When the results were announced, Abigail worried about John's ability to fill the shoes of the popular Washington and how poorly she would compare to the friendly Martha. She had reason to be glad that Thomas Jefferson was John's vice-president and hoped they would demonstrate to their peers how leaders of opposing factions could work together for the greater good of their country.

In March 1796, John Adams was inaugurated as the second president of the United States. During that same month, his wife had to turn away a Quincy tax collector because she lacked the cash to cover property taxes on their farms.[76] Politics has not always paid well, and inflation had been skyrocketing throughout the 1790s. Before Abigail could join her husband in Philadelphia, she had to ensure that their lands would be properly managed in her absence. Money was tight and demanded wages were high. She did not arrive in the city until May. She had no idea how they would manage to entertain and live in the style established by the Washingtons without private wealth to supplement John's government salary.

The high point of John's popularity as president was quickly followed by the lowest. Revealing French attempts at bribery in the XYZ Affair momentarily quieted his pro-French foes and gave credence to what the Federalists had been saying for years. However, the Alien and Sedition Acts, which allowed for the arrest of anti-government publishers and increased naturalization requirements, were heavily criticized as going against everything for which America stood. Abigail's support of her husband never wavered.

The Adamses may have been called monarchists by their political opponents, but Abigail demonstrated otherwise when she objected to a celebration of George Washington's birthday in Philadelphia on 22 February 1798. Not only was the event reminiscent of the birthday parties that had been held for their absent English kings, but she felt it was an insult to the current president, her beloved John.[77] Abigail, in this case, agreed with the Republicans that Independence Day on 4 July was a more appropriate national holiday.

In August 1798, the Adamses travelled to Quincy in the midst of a heatwave to attend to their property. Abigail became ill and was bedridden for three months. The family feared for her life, and John especially wondered how he could possibly manage without her. By November, she had recovered enough for John to return to his duties in Philadelphia, but she was not well enough to travel with him. Therefore, the couple found themselves enduring another lengthy separation. Abigail spent the time recuperating and worrying over her children's futures.

She had stepped in and taken over the arrangements for Nabby's sons, sending them to her sister, Elizabeth, as Abigail had done with her own sons.[78] It was one of those sons who was causing Abigail concern at this point. Charles, who had been so charming and full of potential, had turned to drink and let his finances fall apart. Meanwhile, the return of Thomas from Europe after more than four years gave Abigail both joy and sadness as she compared this refined young man to his dissipated brother. She admitted to having only 'faint hopes' for Charles.[79]

For John's final winter in office, Abigail had recovered her health and was eager to join him. She preferred to be at his side and would enjoy the government's last months in Philadelphia before the move to the new capital city.

Abigail had been concerned for her daughter throughout Nabby's marriage to William Smith, who would suddenly be absent from the household for months at a time, leaving Nabby without the resources to support herself.[80] Their bright moment had been during the federal government's residence in New York. Nabby lived in the city with her young family and the Adamses moved there for John to serve as George Washington's vice-president. While managing the duties of First Lady, Abigail worried about her daughter and would often encourage Nabby to move in with them.

During this same time, Charles was losing his battle with alcoholism. Abigail stopped to visit him on her way to the new capital city in October 1800 and found him deteriorating quickly. He died on 30 November, and Abigail wrote to her sister, Mary, 'I know my much loved Sister that you will mingle in my sorrow, and weep with me over the Grave of a poor unhappy child who cannot now add an other pang to those which have peirced my Heart for Several years past; cut off in the midst of his days, his years are numberd and finished; I hope my Supplications to heaven for him, that he might find mercy from his maker, may not have been in vain ... he was beloved, in spight of his errors, and all spoke with grief and Sorrow for his habits.'[81] Charles' wife and two daughters soon moved in with John and Abigail.

Forced to move on after the death of her son, Abigail journeyed to Washington City, as it was called at that time, and put her homemaking skills to their most difficult test in making the partially completed presidential mansion livable. It was too large for John and Abigail to furnish or heat properly, and much of it remained under construction. The same could be said of most of the city. It was nothing like the bustling, affluent city of Philadelphia. Looking at the rustic beginnings of the new federal city, it is no wonder Abigail wrote, 'I have lived to witness changes, such as I could never have imagined'.[82]

Martha Washington never lived in the city named for her husband, so Abigail got to set some precedents of her own, such as the tradition of opening the White House to visitors on New Year's Day.[83] Abigail did not have to endure the literal swamp that was Washington City for long. John lost the election of 1800, and they were happy to return to Quincy after what they both regarded as a lifetime of service to an ungrateful public. The public would be sorry, Abigail thought, when the party of Jefferson and Burr brought the country to its ruin. In March 1801, the Adamses were settled in Quincy, for good this time.

By the end of summer, John Quincy returned from Europe with a wife and child in tow. He had been gone for seven years, and his proud mother basked in his presence. Peacefield became a bustling center of family and friends as children, grandchildren, and extended family were revolving visitors. In 1805, Thomas and his new wife came to live with John and Abigail, much pleasing his mother who had long been trying to tempt him back to Quincy.[84]

For a few years, John and Abigail enjoyed being surrounded by their family, living peacefully on their farm as they had longed to do for many years. As they aged and were influenced by John Quincy as he joined domestic public life, they become more moderate in their political views, no longer considering themselves Federalists or the Republicans evil incarnate. In their final years, John and Abigail made peace with those they had quarreled with, including Mercy Otis Warren and Thomas Jefferson.[85]

The idyllic arrangement of the family all gathered in Quincy came to an end when John Quincy was named ambassador to Russia by President Madison in 1809. When he left, Abigail was certain she had laid eyes on him for the last time. She was comforted by the grandchildren left in her care and the presence of Thomas's family until a greater tragedy struck. Nabby was diagnosed with breast cancer, and the difficult decision was made to operate. At that time, that meant an excruciatingly painful ordeal without anesthetic. It was a step only taken in extreme circumstances and under the recommendation of Dr Benjamin Rush. Recovery was not guaranteed and would take several painful months. Afterwards, Nabby briefly seemed to improve before it was discovered that cancer had spread throughout her body in a way incurable with early nineteenth-century medicine.

In 1811, when she feared that her daughter was dying, Abigail insisted that John Quincy return from St Petersburg. When that failed, she was not afraid to recruit help. She wrote to President James Madison and requested that he officially order John Quincy home from St Petersburg.[86] Madison promptly acquiesced, but travel from Russia was difficult, not to mention the work that had sent him there, and John Quincy did not return to America until 1817 after completing negotiations for the treaty ending the War of 1812 and serving as ambassador to Britain.

In the meantime, Abigail suffered another blow when her sister Mary and brother-in-law Richard Cranch died within days of each other in October 1811.[87] Mary had long been Abigail's confidant, in person or through letters. She was closer only to John and her own children. Her grief was tempered by the fact that Richard and Mary had lived a long, happy life and gone to God together.

In 1813, John was at Abigail's side when Nabby returned to her parent's home as a comfortable place to die. Accompanied by her children, Caroline and John, Nabby suffered from breast cancer to the extent that she had to be carried from the coach into the house.[88] She was forty-nine years old. Abigail, at age sixty-eight, was forced to watch her daughter and close confidant die. She called upon her deep, abiding faith to see her through. To John Quincy, she wrote, 'I fear I shall have one of the most distressing and trying scenes of my Life to go through'. Nabby died three weeks later, and Abigail again wrote to her oldest son, 'To me the loss is irreparable'.[89] The statement is uncharacteristically hopeless for the faithful woman who had endured so much.

After her daughter's death, Abigail expressed grief as she never had before, though she had lost many loved ones before Nabby, including two infant daughters. However, she was greatly comforted by Nabby's daughter, Caroline, eighteen years old at the time of her mother's death. When she wrote to friends, she not only warned them that grief assailed her to the point of aging her features, but she shared with them her joy that Caroline was with her and such a 'dear representative of her mother'.[90]

When Abigail's younger sister, Elizabeth, died in April 1815, she again fervently wished for John Quincy to come home. She was worried that she would never see him again. Instead, John Quincy arranged for his sons, George and John, to join the rest of his family in London, and Abigail was forced to see them off.[91] John Quincy returned to the United States with his family until 6 August 1817, when he arrived to take up his post as Secretary of State under President Monroe.[92]

After enjoying just over a year of having John Quincy and his family near, Abigail fell ill with typhoid fever. Although she was almost seventy-four, her recovery was expected since she still led such an active life. Family and friends alike were shocked when she died on 28 October 1818 after only a few days of illness. Abigail was surrounded by family, just as she wished. Crushed by her death, John said to John Quincy, 'The separation cannot be so long as twenty separations heretofore'.[93]

Their final separation ended on 4 July 1826, when John (and Thomas Jefferson) died on the fiftieth anniversary of the Declaration of Independence. He, unlike Abigail, had lived long enough to see their son, John Quincy, elected to the presidency in 1824.

Chapter 9

Elizabeth Schuyler Hamilton

My good, my tender, my fond, my excellent Betsy.
— Alexander Hamilton

An entry in the Philip Schuyler family Bible reads, 'Elizabeth. Born 9 August 1757. Lord do according to thy will with her'.[1] Known during her childhood as Betsy, most who know of her at all today know Elizabeth Schuyler Hamilton as the demure, devoted Eliza from *Hamilton* the musical. As with most pop culture portrayals of historical figures, some of this representation is correct. However, there is much more to Eliza including the half-century that she outlived her husband and became one of America's first female activists.

Before becoming an activist or the wife of America's first secretary of the treasury, Eliza Schuyler was the daughter of General Philip Schuyler, who joined Generals Montgomery and Arnold in the attempt to make Canada part of the American Revolution. While not formally educated, Eliza benefited from vast experiences living in northern New York. Her mother, Catherine Van Rensselaer Schuyler, raised Eliza and her sisters to maintain a large estate, entertain society's top names, and take joy in charitable deeds. This last lesson certainly took root in Eliza, who was involved in philanthropic work throughout her long life.

As children, the Schuyler girls would accompany their mother to take food and goods to those in their neighborhood who were in need. They would also spend time visiting and extending invitations to their own home. They were taught to offer kindness and friendship along with charity, not condescension.[2] During the war, her family hosted many men whose names are now a part of history, including some British. General Schuyler was a gentleman, and his wife, Catherine, 'lively' and 'affable' according to one visitor.[3]

Catherine Schuyler proved her own courage matched that of her husband several times during the war. 'A general's wife should not know fear,' she insisted when the British approached her Saratoga home.[4] The death of Jane McCrea, who had been scalped by Native Americans, had left most of her Saratoga neighbors skittish, and they lacked the stamina to risk being present when the British arrived. While others fled the area, Catherine remained until she had set the Schuyler fields to torch rather than leave the valuable grain to the enemy. Only then did Catherine flee to Albany with what few valuables she had been able to salvage. British officers spent the night before the Battle of Saratoga at the Schuyler's summer home, but they were surrounded by burned fields thanks to Catherine's quick and fearless actions. Neither Catherine nor those officers could have anticipated that they would soon meet.

When Generals Burgoyne and Riedesel was taken captive at Saratoga, General Schuyler sent them to stay with his own family in Albany. One of the officers escorting them was a young Alexander Hamilton, and this may have been the first time he and Eliza met.[5] Frederika Charlotte Riedesel also accompanied her husband and was struck by Schuyler's kindness toward his enemies. Burgoyne praised Schuyler to parliament, 'That gentleman conducted me to a very elegant house, and, to my great surprise, presented me to Mrs Schuyler and her family. In that house I remained during my whole stay in Albany, with a table of more than twenty covers for me and my friends, and every other demonstration of hospitality.'[6]

The family to whom Burgoyne referred included twenty-year-old Eliza, and one might imagine what the young woman thought as the party of British prisoners was escorted up their drive. She and her sisters would have had to make room in their home for the British generals and their entourage and help their mother serve and entertain them, all while knowing that these were some of those her father was risking his life to fight!

Of course, the Schuylers also hosted American officers and diplomats. Eliza dined with American generals and learned how to play backgammon from Benjamin Franklin.[7] The lonely men must have been charmed by the Schuyler sisters, of whom there were five, not only three as the musical indicates. Eliza also had three brothers, who are entirely left out of *Hamilton*, which includes only the three eldest sisters, Angelica, Eliza, and Peggy. It was through her father's service that Eliza became acquainted with the controversial man who became her husband.

According to historian, Ron Chernow, Eliza met Alexander for the first time in November 1777 when he stopped at the Schuyler home after a tense meeting with General Horatio Gates.[8] Did Eliza think about the handsome, young officer after his departure? Alexander at that time was twenty-two years old, slim, auburn-haired, and charming. Did Alexander think of her? She was two years younger with dark hair and eyes, and he may have been just as interested in the fact that her father was both affluent and a respected general in the Continental Army. Their paths would soon cross again.

Eliza accompanied her mother to the Continental Army camp in Morristown early in 1780. It was a brutal winter, but she found herself warmed by the attentions of Colonel Alexander Hamilton. One historian describes him as 'young, handsome, brilliant, with the complexion of a girl and the distinguished air of a man of the world'.[9] Eliza herself later listed his admirable qualities: 'Elasticity of his mind. Variety of his knowledge. Playfulness of his wit. Excellence of his heart'.[10] Despite Hamilton's obscure heritage and lack of wealth, General Schuyler welcomed him to court his daughter. Though he lacked many things, Hamilton was a close aide to General Washington and had already begun making a name for himself with his fiery combination of courage, intellect, and patriotism for his adopted country.[11] General Schuyler's acceptance of Hamilton is clear in a letter written upon the couple's engagement. 'You cannot, my dear sir, be more happy at the connexion you have made with my family than I am. Until the child of a parent has made a judicious choice, his heart is in continual anxiety; but this anxiety was removed the moment I discovered on whom she had placed her affections.'[12]

Eliza did not spend all of her time in Morristown charming Alexander. She also joined Mrs Washington in sewing, knitting, and mending as the women attempted to make up for the stingy congress in keeping the soldiers clothed and warm. She would later describe the kind, unpretentious Martha as 'my ideal of a true woman'.[13] One can see the influence of women like Martha Washington on the woman that Eliza Schuyler would become.

When Eliza married Alexander on 14 December 1780, one described her as 'a charming woman, who joins to the graces all the candor and simplicity of an American wife'.[14] Eliza's husband and father spent many hours discussing America's future and together agreed that a strong centralized government would be needed. Having both served in a military that suffered from disjointed, unorganized orders and desperate lack of resources, they had good reasons for believing some decisions could not reasonably be retained at the state level. Hamilton wrote in one letter, 'The fundamental defect is a want of power in Congress'.[15]

The Hamiltons resided with the army where Alexander served as General Washington's aide-de-camp. Eliza had been trained to manage a large estate, but here she lived more simply and frugally, her husband's income being in no way equal to her father's. Alexander's mind was always at work, a fact that sometimes left him depressed by his surroundings. He once wrote to his closest friend, John Laurens, 'I hate congress – I hate the army – I hate the world – I hate myself. The whole is a mass of fools and knaves'.[16] Eliza centered him and surrounded him with unconditional love.

When Alexander left Washington's service and the couple moved to her parent's home in Albany, Eliza must have wondered what her future would look like at the side of this fiery man. He had been passed over for positions as envoy to France and minister to Russia, but he was not panicked.[17] Instead, he spent the time studying in the Schuyler library and preparing for a career in law after the war.[18]

The war came in full to the Schuyler home on 7 August 1781. In an attempt to kidnap General Schuyler, his home was attacked by a loyalist group, but the family had received warning. They barred themselves upstairs with weapons at the windows when they realized the youngest member of the family had been left in a crib downstairs. The two oldest daughters, Angelica and Eliza, were pregnant, so middle daughter, Peggy, ran downstairs, ignoring her father's orders to the contrary. She not only saved the infant, Catherine, but Peggy, pretending to be a household servant, informed the invaders that the master of the house was not present, rather he had gone to alarm the town.[19] According to lore, Peggy even scarcely evaded a thrown tomahawk as she rushed back up the stairs. General Schuyler was, of course, still upstairs, but the belief that reinforcements were on the way and their target was absent discouraged the attackers. General Schuyler joined in the ruse, shouting out the window to his nonexistent help, 'Come on, my brave fellows; surround the house, and secure the villains who are plundering.'[20]

Not long after the thwarted attack, the Schuylers hosted another young man who was studying to become a lawyer. Aaron Burr came recommended by General McDougall as 'a soldier, an officer, and a worthy citizen'.[21] Eliza would have no way of knowing at the time the profound impact this young man would have on her later in life.

Freedom was in the air in more ways than one in the late eighteenth century. Women, too, were grasping at liberty as is evinced by the Schuyler daughters' marriages. Of the five girls, only obedient Eliza married at the family home with her parents' blessing. The other four eloped, although at the time of Eliza's wedding only Angelica, the eldest, had.

Alexander was at Yorktown, finally commanding troops as he had wished to do for several years, on 17 October 1781 when a British officer presented a white handkerchief in surrender.[22] As soon as possible, he raced toward Albany where he lay bedridden for weeks from illness and exhaustion. He had pushed himself, and his horses, to the brink in order to be present when Eliza gave birth to a son, Philip, on 22 January 1782. Her mother had given birth to her last child only months earlier.

The war won and the real work of creating a successful government underway, Alexander went to Philadelphia and Eliza followed soon after with little Philip in tow. A member of congress with a head full of ideas, Alexander was somewhat adrift after the death of John Laurens, but he soon formed an attachment with the bookish James Madison. It was a connection doomed not to last. In the beginning, though, Hamilton and Madison worked together to create a viable government system and defend the new Constitution at a time when many Americans still considered themselves citizens of their particular state rather than of the United States.

On 25 November 1783, the British evacuated New York City, leaving it a disordered shadow of what it had been before their occupation in September 1776. However, it was soon on its way to recovery as Americans returned to the city in droves, including the young Hamilton family, who rented a house at 57 Wall Street.[23] Rejecting a position in the New York Assembly, Alexander opened his law practice.

Eliza was busy at home, giving birth to a daughter, Angelica, on 25 September 1784, and a son, Alexander, on 16 May 1786. With three little ones of their own, the Hamiltons also took in Fanny Antill, when the young girl's parents died in quick succession.[24] On 14 April 1788, Eliza gave birth to her third son, James, who would write family memoirs three-quarters of a century later. He attested to his mother's housekeeping skills, despite a much tighter budget than what she had been raised on. 'She was a skilful house-wife; expert at making sweetmeats and pastry; she made the undergarments for her children, was a great economist and most excellent manager'.[25] Even when Alexander was busy, which was often, Eliza would take the children to pew ninety-two at Trinity Church. She was the leader in faith in the family that her husband was not.[26]

In the meantime, Alexander had also joined the New York Society for Promoting the Manumission of Slaves. Though Eliza had grown up in a slave-owning home, she did not leave clear evidence of her thoughts on abolition. Many members of the Society owned slaves, a contradiction that spotlights the struggle the young country was dealing with. Even many who understood that slavery was inherently wrong were unsure how to abolish it. One plan suggested by Hamilton freed all New York slaves over forty-five years old and offered a gradual schedule of freedom for those that were younger.[27]

On 7 May 1789, Eliza attended America's first inaugural ball where she danced with the country's first president, George Washington. Her husband would be an important part of the precedents being set as Washington's secretary of the treasury. This position put Eliza among the top ranks of society. 'No one was better fitted for the part she was now called upon to perform. Accustomed to meeting in her father's house distinguished people from every country, trained by a careful mother to meet the demands made by large hospitality on the resources of a household, she added to this equipment an engaging personality.'[28]

Alexander was successful under Washington, and Eliza was doubly happy to have her sister, Angelica, visiting from Europe, where she had moved with her husband, John Barker Church. He was a member of parliament, but that had not reduced Angelica's American patriotism. Whispers of rumors began around this time of Alexander's infidelity, but one can only guess whether Eliza had any concerns on this topic. Some believed Angelica was his partner in crime, but Eliza left no evidence that she ever believed that to be true. She was heartbroken when Angelica returned to her family in England. 'My Very Dear beloved Angelia – I have seated my self to write to you, but my heart is so sadned by your Absence that it can scarsly dictate, my Eyes so filled with tears that I shall not be able to write you much but Remember Remember, my Dear sister of the Assurances of your returning to us, and do all you can to make your Absence short,' Eliza wrote shortly after Angelica's departure.[29]

Historian Ron Chernow writes, 'A man of irreproachable integrity, Hamilton severed all outside sources of income while in office, something that neither Washington nor Jefferson nor Madison dared to do.'[30] The salary for treasury secretary was significantly less than what Alexander earned as a lawyer, meaning Eliza had some creative housekeeping to do. She also received assistance from her parents, who would send shipments of goods but not so often as to hurt Alexander's pride. Eliza and the children also spent time at her parents' home in Albany while Alexander spent every waking hour at work.

In New York at her husband's side in March 1790, Eliza hosted a welcome dinner for Thomas Jefferson, who had returned from Paris to serve as Washington's secretary of state.[31] He had met Angelica while abroad and been charmed by her, so Jefferson and Eliza had that much in common. Henry Knox, with whom the Hamiltons were already well acquainted, was the final member of Washington's cabinet, serving as his secretary of war. The group was loosely connected, each with their own contributions to make to the building of a new government. Of this time, Eliza later wrote, 'I had little of private life in those days. Mrs Washington who, like myself, had a passionate love of home and domestic life, often complained of the "waste of time" she was compelled to endure.'[32] She and Martha were cut from the same cloth, taking their pleasure in the simple joys of friends and family and a welcoming home.

Aaron Burr came back into Eliza's life when he decided to run against her father for one of New York's seats in the US Senate in 1791.[33] Schuyler had recently voted in favor of Hamilton's plan for the national government to assume states' war debt, a scheme that did not enjoy universal popularity. Aaron Burr was seen as a more moderate choice, and he had the charisma to charm voters but was not afraid to turn his back on friends in order to advance his own ambitions.

The work of moving the household to 79 South Third Street in Philadelphia fell to Eliza, as the federal government left New York in an intermediate step to residence in Washington City. She, like other politicians' wives, arranged for the shipment or sale of furniture, fixtures, clothing, and everything else that a young family needed. Also in 1791, Eliza's oldest son, Philip, was determined old enough for boarding school.

She must have been both proud and sad to watch her nine-year-old ride off toward Trenton.[34] She still had four little ones at home (including the orphan Fanny) and more would follow. The busyness of the Hamilton household likely helped soothe the sorrow over Philip's absence.

Besides managing a growing household, Eliza was an attentive wife. She sometimes acted as Alexander's secretary, copying out papers and listening to his constant outpouring of ideas. When summer 1791 arrived, Eliza and the children left the city, which was considered an unhealthy place during the summer heat, for her parents' country home. She would have profound reason to wish she had not. She did not learn of her husband's relationship with Maria Reynolds until later. She stayed in Albany, encouraged by her husband, 'I cannot be happy without you. Yet I must not advise you to urge your return. The confirmation of your health is so essential to our happiness that I am willing to make as long a sacrifice as the season and your patience will permit.'[35] Sacrifice, indeed.

When Eliza returned to Philadelphia, she was blissfully unaware of the scandal that would soon erupt. All she knew was that her husband had been working all summer and had scarcely had time to miss her and the children. She became pregnant with their fifth child soon after returning to the city. Alexander's current passion, as far as she knew, was for American industrialization and modernization. If slavery could not be outlawed by politics, maybe it could be made uneconomical through mechanization, and war shortages had convinced him of the need for American industry. Unfortunately, Alexander was also caught up in a feud with Thomas Jefferson, who seemed to disagree with him on every issue, even accusing Hamilton of planning to replace the Constitution with a monarchy. Their sparring led to the creation of opposing political parties and Jefferson's resignation from office.

In the meantime, Alexander continued his affair with Maria Reynolds, paying her husband, James, to keep it quiet. With Hamilton and Jefferson regularly attacking each other in the newspapers, one must wonder how Alexander thought he would be able to keep his mistress a secret.

Eliza gave birth to John Church Hamilton on 22 August 1792. As she recovered, she did not realize that her husband was attempting to extract himself from a web of blackmail, deceit, and adultery. When James Reynolds was arrested for speculation and defrauding the government in November 1792, he and his associate, Jacob Clingman, threatened to name Alexander Hamilton as a partner in their scheme.[36]

Congressmen Frederick Muhlenberg, Abraham Venable, and James Monroe confronted Hamilton with the accusations of financial fraud on 15 December 1792.[37] They were astonished when he claimed innocence of any crime but guilt of his extramarital affair, revealing James Reynold's blackmail and his own helplessness to be rid of the scheming couple. They agreed to leave the private matter alone and dismissed plans to tell Washington of Reynold's accusations. However, Monroe had copies of the documents of the case made, and a set of those copies found their way to Thomas Jefferson. The possibility of revelation of his secrets hung heavy over Alexander Hamilton, but it is likely that Eliza still had no idea of what was going on outside her domestic circle.

Shortly after the beginning of Washington's second presidential term, the Jeffersonians in congress attempted to have Hamilton removed from office. They claimed he had misappropriated funds but had no proof of wrongdoing. The rumors the charges spurred were reward enough to his enemies who also began to spread whispers of the Reynolds affair.

A yellow fever epidemic struck Philadelphia during the summer of 1793. It is the source of James Hamilton's earliest recollection of his parents, 'both my father and mother were attacked by the disease at the same time. As soon as they were sufficiently recovered they set out for Albany ... but so great was the apprehension of contagion, that the family, when they arrived opposite to New York, were obliged to continue their journey on the west side of the river without going into the city.'[38] The Hamiltons recovered with the help of ministrations from Dr Edward Stevens, one of Alexander's few links to his West Indies roots.[39]

During the summer of 1794, Eliza was again at her parents' home in Albany, where the air was believed to be healthier. She was pregnant again, and baby Johnny fell ill. Alexander, as he almost always did, worked frantically in Philadelphia while she cared for the children. His letters express his dismay at being separated from his family, especially during his son's illness. He wrote paragraphs of medical advice to his wife and expected frequent reports. The baby recovered his health, but Eliza's pregnancy became difficult. Too late, Alexander rushed to be with her. Eliza suffered a miscarriage, nonetheless.[40] By the end of the year, Alexander decided to resign from his post as treasury secretary.

Alexander admitted that his family was his reason for resigning his cabinet position, 'To endulge my domestic happiness more freely was the principal motive for relinquishing an office in which it is said I have gained some glory, and the difficulties of which had just been subdued.'[41] The family returned to New York, where son James later remembered the happy home built by his parents, 'I distinctly recollect the scene at breakfast in the front room of the house on Broadway. My dear mother, seated as was her wont at the head of the table with a napkin in her lap, cutting slices of bread and spreading them with butter for the younger boys, who, standing at her side, read in turn a chapter in the Bible or a portion of Goldsmith's Rome.'[42]

Eliza was not only known for her kindness to family. Years earlier, upon hearing of the imprisonment of artist Ralph Earle for debt, she visited the jail in order to have her portrait painted. She then encouraged other ladies to do the same until Mr Earle had earned enough to secure his release.[43] This painting is the best-known likeness of Eliza that exists. She wears a white dress, powdered hair, and a simple black ribbon around her neck.

Rumors continued to circulate regarding her husband, but Eliza was likely happy that he was simply home. However, public office had left him with few resources to support his growing family. He was in debt with few assets, so he reclaimed his law career.

On 1 October 1795, the Hamiltons took in George Washington Lafayette, the son of the famous French general.[44] The young man could not be hosted by his namesake because President Washington feared that it would increase the ire of those already inflamed by the terms of the Jay Treaty. Washington was, however, beginning to plan to leave office, something that few expected him to do. Alexander was one of his few confidants and was the author of his Farewell Address. Acquiring proof of this service to America's first president was one of Eliza's quests after her husband's death. The papers, which had been left with a friend, Rufus King, were turned over only after Eliza took legal action. 'The whole or nearly all the "Address" was read to me by him as he wrote it and a greater part, if not all, was written by him in my presence,' she insisted.[45]

Hamilton's name was naturally included in conversations about who might be America's next president when Washington stepped down. Whether one was a supporter or detractor did not change the fact that

Alexander had been the second most important and powerful man in the country during Washington's two terms. Chernow writes that Hamilton looked to have those conversations quieted when his enemies threatened publication of Reynolds letters.[46] More than he wished to be president, Alexander Hamilton wished for his wife to remain ignorant of his affair.

Had Eliza truly remained in the dark about her husband's 1791 affair? According to John Adams, 'His fornications, adulteries and his incests were propagated far and wide'.[47] If any truth can be found in this enemy's words, how could Eliza have not known? If she did, she left no evidence indicating it, even when she outlived him by half a century. When James Callender wrote his *History of the United States for 1796*, he renewed accusations of financial speculation against Alexander, including copies of documents that Hamilton's enemies had presented to him back in 1791. Certain that James Monroe had betrayed her husband by handing over this evidence, Eliza never forgave him. For his part, Alexander furiously composed a rebuttal to Callender's accusations. Originally titled *Observations on Certain Documents Contained in No V & VI of 'The History of the United States for the Year 1796,' In Which the Charge of Speculation Against Alexander Hamilton, Late Secretary of the Treasury, Is Fully Refuted. Written by Himself*, it is remembered by history as *The Reynolds Pamphlet*.

As Chernow writes, 'Hamilton's strategy was simple: he was prepared to sacrifice his private reputation to preserve his public honor'.[48] We can only imagine what Eliza thought of this trade-off as she read these words from her husband's pen: 'The charge against me is a connection with one James Reynolds for purposes of improper pecuniary speculation. My real crime is an amorous connection with his wife, for a considerable time with his privity and connivance, if not originally brought on by a combination between the husband and wife with the design to extort money from me. This confession is not made without a blush … I had frequent meetings with her, most of them at my own house; Mrs. Hamilton with her children being absent on a visit to her father.[49] The words are buried among pages of Hamilton's defense of his financial activity, but they are the words that are burned into history and must have broken Eliza's heart.

Unless she, too, had decided that this form of humiliation was more tolerable than financial and legal scandal. Biographer Tilar Mazzeo believes this to be the case, even suggesting that Eliza helped concoct the false affair to cover for her husband's illegal financial activities.[51] Were this true, one might have hoped that Eliza would not have been left in poverty when her husband died. If he had been participating in financial schemes, he was not very good at them. It seems reasonable to assume that the most often accepted story – that of Alexander's sexual affair but financial purity – is accurate.

Which brings us back to Eliza, his devoted wife and, at that time, pregnant with his sixth child. Did she think back to the letters she had received from him during the summer of 1791? His insistence that 'my extreme anxiety for the restoration of your health will reconcile me to your staying longer', suddenly seemed devious rather than caring.[51] Eliza may have wondered how she could have missed the fact that the husband who normally hated to be separated from his family had urged her more than once not to hurry home.

She was undoubtedly crushed, but she had to decide how she was going to react to the scandal. Eliza chose to stand by her husband. Eighteenth-century wives had few legal rights, and societal expectations clearly defined their roles in the home. The infidelity of a woman was considered unacceptable, after all, it could lead to a man raising another man's children. However, infidelity of a husband was, if not acceptable, considered something a wife may have to tolerate. It sometimes reflected as poorly upon the wife if a husband strayed, for she might be blamed for not keeping him content. This was Eliza's world, and these attitudes may explain how she could forgive a tryst and publicly defend her husband as an eminent Founding Father, even long after his death.

Alexander's contemporaries were no less shocked than his wife. The general feeling of his friends can best be summarized with a statement by Noah Webster, who wondered why 'publish a history of his private intrigues, degrade himself in the estimation of all good men, and scandalize a family to clear himself of charges which no man believed'.[52] In fact, the admission did not clear him of the charges against him in the minds of his enemies. He had humiliated his wife but made little change in the opinions of his peers.

One couple made an effort to comfort Eliza and declare support for her husband in the midst of the Reynolds scandal. George and Martha Washington sent a wine cooler that Eliza treasured for the rest of her life. The accompanying note made no mention of current events, but bid

Alexander accept the gift 'as a token of my sincere regard and friendship for you'. The reminder that the Washingtons held the Hamiltons in 'high regard' and that George continued to consider Alexander a 'sincere friend' must have been an encouragement at a most difficult time.[53]

1797 began a happier year for Eliza. Her father, Philip Schuyler regained the seat in the senate that he had lost to Aaron Burr, and, even more exciting to the Hamiltons, Angelica Church moved back to New York.[54] With her return began renewed 'dark whispers' of Alexander's infidelities, possibly in reaction to his and Angelica's flirtatious relationship.[55] Still enduring the public attacks and private whispers of the affair, Eliza was distracted by the needs of her children. She gave birth to William Stephen Hamilton on 4 August 1797, and weeks later, fifteen-year-old Philip was on death's door. It is believed that he suffered from typhus, and Eliza had to be removed from his room as his pulse faded and he became comatose.[56] Alexander arrived, expecting to find Philip had passed, but the young man slowly recovered under the attentive care of his parents. This incident may have helped the couple heal as they focused on their shared love of their family.

Their brood gained another member after the early demise of Eliza's younger brother, John. His son, another Philip, was sent to live with the Hamiltons.[57] Eliza would have been fully occupied with her own six children and those that she had a habit of taking in, while her husband returned to politics, this time as General Hamilton as America prepared for possible war with France.

Eliza also began what would become a long career in activism, joining other women who were expanding their domestic spheres to include their broader community of people in need. She became a member of the Society for the Relief of Poor Widows with Small Children.[58] The Society worked to keep women out of the poorhouse and provide education for their children. Eliza had a passion for helping others, especially children, and, in doing so, she was helping to redefine the role of women as they entered the nineteenth century. Her involvement in charitable work increased dramatically later in life.

On 26 November 1799, a daughter, named Eliza for her mother, was born to the Hamiltons. It was a full household in which Alexander actively participated despite his heavy schedule. He often had the older boys, who were not away at school, accompany him at his work. As time progressed, he spent more time at home, an arrangement that must have pleased Eliza.

The death of George Washington just before the turn of the century was another blow to Alexander's ambitions. He had always had his critics but having such a presence in his corner had provided a significant level of protection and respect. The Federalists would fall apart in the wake of his loss. Soon, Thomas Jefferson, a man who made no secret of his animosity toward Alexander, became president and his political ambitions were at their end.

When the federal government moved to Philadelphia in December 1790, many had hoped that the dream of a city on the Potomac would never happen, making the temporary capital permanent. However, in 1800, Washington City was a reality, although Philadelphia got to keep the treasury mint. The election of 1800 hinted at America's future split with electoral votes for Jefferson versus Adams divided almost precisely by north versus south.

Exiled from politics, Hamilton decided to build a country home in what is now Harlem. The Grange, as Alexander named it after his family's ancestral estate in Scotland, still stands on land that the Hamiltons owned, though it has been moved twice as urban sprawl threatened to squeeze it out of existence. The yellow and white Federal-style home is modest compared to those of many other Founding Fathers, but the Hamiltons felt it was perfect. Eliza must have looked forward to a peaceful, country life that would be reminiscent of her youth in Albany.

Her parents were still assisting the no longer young couple. Hamilton had gained fame, but never riches. The Schuylers now sent timber for the new home in addition to the supply of food that they regularly sent from their farms. Increasingly vocal about his enemies' faults while frankly admitting his own, Alexander wrote to Richard Peters, 'A disappointed politician you know is very apt to take refuge in a Garden ... In this new situation, for which I am as little fitted as Jefferson to guide the helm of the UStates, I come to you as an Adept in rural science for instruction.'[59] Maybe he hoped that one day his own gardens would provide for his family and he could finally end his dependency on his in-laws. He built up his legal practice in order to cover the expense of the home and developing the land.

On 25 February 1801, Alexander Hamilton penned a letter that he knew would break his wife's heart beyond what she had already endured. 'Your

Sister Peggy has gradually grown worse & is now in a situation that her dissolution in the opinion of the Doctor is not likely to be long delayed'.[60] Peggy and Eliza were close in age and affection, therefore Eliza must have experienced the double sorrow of knowing that her sister was dying and that she would not be able to be with her in her last moments. She could only be comforted that Alexander, who was held in high esteem by the entire Schuyler family, was able to be present. When he wrote, 'Your Sister Peggy had a better night last night than for three weeks past and is much easier this morning. Yet her situation is such as only to authorise a glimmering of hope', on 9 March 1801, Eliza may have been tempted to trust in a miracle.[61] However, Alexander's 16 March 1801 letter brought the news she had been dreading. 'On Saturday, My Dear Eliza, your sister took leave of her sufferings and friends'.[62] Surrounded by a houseful of children, her husband and parents in Albany, Eliza grieved alone with no idea of the hardships that would soon assail her.

The Hamiltons' eldest son, Philip, was everything an early nineteenth-century firstborn son should be: handsome, intelligent, witty, with just enough rumor of sexual escapades to make him interesting. His proud parents gushed about his accomplishments and dismissed his 'naughty' side.[63] Philip was just as proud to be the son of Alexander Hamilton and challenged any who spoke negatively of him or his ideas. This led to a duel on 23 November 1801 with lawyer George Eaker, who shot Philip in the hip. He died after a night spent sandwiched in bed between his desperate parents. He was nineteen years old, and Eliza was pregnant with her eighth child. It is difficult to imagine Eliza's heartbreak in this situation. She had a choice to push Alexander away for his inability to protect their son or cling to him as one who shared her pain. When Eliza gave birth to a son on 2 June 1802, she named him Philip for his deceased older brother.

To make matters worse for the grieving mother, Eliza's daughter, Angelica, who had been close to Philip and was only two years younger, experienced a mental breakdown in the wake of his death from which she never fully recovered. Her parents were attentive, trying any suggested solution to restore her state of mind. For the remainder of her life, she spoke of Philip as if he had not died, a habit that could only have exacerbated her mother's pain.[64]

Eliza's husband also fell into depression following Philip's death, and she felt the burden of tending to her family's grief even as she suffered herself and managed a large household. She did have the benefit of Alexander's increased time at home. The Grange was nine miles from his law office in Manhattan, and he made the commute most weekdays rather than staying in the city in order to spend as much time as possible with Eliza and his children.

Just as peace was returning to Eliza's home, she received word of her mother's death on 7 March 1803. The loss of Catherine also caused a decline in Eliza's father's health. Eliza must have wondered what she would do without Philip Schuyler, who had so fervently supported the Hamiltons.[65] Her next loss, however, was not her father.

Alexander found it difficult to remain entirely disconnected from politics. When Aaron Burr ran for governor of New York, Hamilton vehemently opposed him. His decades-old accusations that Burr had no principles were gleefully rehashed by a muckraking media. When Burr lost the 1804 election, he placed the blame at Alexander's feet. On 18 June, Burr sent a letter demanding satisfaction. The ensuing negotiations inflamed animosity rather than quelling the situation. A duel was scheduled for 11 July 1804.[66]

These events were kept from Eliza, who must have thought that country life went on – and would go on – peacefully and contentedly. Alexander was determined to undertake the same dueling strategy that he had suggested, and that had led to the death of, his son. He 'resolved, if our interview is conducted in the usual manner, and it pleases God to give me the opportunity, to *reserve* and *throw away* my first fire, and I *have thoughts* even of *reserving* my second fire – and thus giving a double opportunity to Col Burr to pause and to reflect.'[67] Hamilton ordered his affairs for the sake of his wife and seven children, the youngest of whom was only two years old, and prepared to meet Burr in Weehawken, New Jersey. Alexander Hamilton took with him the dueling pistols that had been used by his son. He was shot in the hip, just as Philip had been.

Eliza was immediately sent for but was told only that her husband was in pain and suffering spasms.[68] She, of course, saw the truth when she entered the room where her husband lay dying in an eerie repetition of her son's death less than three years earlier. Angelica Church also arrived to comfort both her sister and the brother-in-law she adored. The next morning, Alexander lay paralyzed and fading. Eliza brought their seven children to him to say their farewells. He kissed two-year-old Philip when the boy was raised to his lips but could not bear to look long upon his children.[69] Before he died, Alexander requested last rites and reminded Eliza to be strong in her Christian faith. What strength was required of Eliza in these hours as she watched her husband slowly fade away and mourners crowd the room. When he passed away, she quietly cut a lock of his hair before bursting into inconsolable tears.[70]

Philip Schuyler wrote an emotive letter to his daughter after receiving news of Hamilton's death. 'If aught, under Heaven, could aggravate the affliction I experience, it is that, incapable of moving or being moved, I cannot fly to you to pour the balm of comfort into your afflicted bosom, to water it with my tears, and to receive yours on mine. In this distressing situation – under the pressure of this most severe calamity, let us seek consolation from that source where it can only be truly found, in humble resignation to the will of Heaven.'[71] He may not have been capable of going to her, but Eliza packed up her children and went to him in Albany to care for her ailing father and that they might mourn together. She soon mourned for her father as well. Philip Schuyler died on 18 November 1804, and Eliza must have wondered if she would spend the entirety of her life grieving for lost loved ones. She could not have known it then, but Eliza had much longer yet to live.

She comforted herself with the many letters Alexander had written her, sewing the pieces together when they began to crumble from age and constant handling.[72] Almost immediately, Eliza took up her campaign to see Alexander's name remembered honorably. 'Justice shall be done to the memory of my Hamilton', she is remembered stating many times throughout the fifty years after Alexander's death.[73] She tirelessly collected memories, letters, and papers related to her husband in the hope of having a comprehensive biography written that would secure his elevated place in history.

Only a few close friends realized the terrible financial situation Alexander had left to his wife. Gouverneur Morris, the friend who had consoled Eliza at Alexander's deathbed, arranged a secret fund where friends donated $80,000 and never told the Hamilton children of its existence.[74] Eliza's home and situation preserved through the generosity of friends, she had to decide how to move on without the man who had seemed larger than life.

Of course, life moves on after loss whether or not one wishes it to do so. Alexander Jr graduated shortly after his father's death, and Eliza struggled with the idea of him moving away from her to launch his career. It was a hardship she slowly learned to bear as the children completed their educations and sought to follow in their father's footsteps in quick succession.

Eliza forged ahead, creating a life of her own for the first time. In 1805, she joined the board of the New York Society for the Relief of Poor Widows with Small Children, joining the ranks of women in the early nineteenth century in branching out from their homes to help form and improve society through benevolence.[75] In March 1806, she was one of a group of women who formed the New York Orphan Asylum Society, as many of the small children of poor widows inevitably became orphans. Eliza perhaps also contemplated Alexander's youth as an underprivileged orphan and transferred some of her love for him to young people in need.[76]

Eliza led this organization from its formation in a small rented home in May 1806, and quickly realized more space was needed. A lottery grant from New York City Council raised $5,000 toward a new building with more space for children's quarters, as well as rooms for schooling, religious studies, and trade skill training.[77] In Eliza's lifetime, hundreds of children would receive housing, care, and education through the Orphan Asylum Society that she founded.

Her son, James, shared an anecdote of this time in his memoir. 'She found a little fellow in the arms of a fireman whose parents had been destroyed by the burning of their house. Being an orphan, she directed the fireman to take the little "McKavit" to the Orphan Asylum, on the Bloomingdale Road, giving him the means to hire a carriage to do so, and gave him her card.'[78] Many years later, Eliza found this young man a position at the Military Academy. When he was killed in the Mexican American War, he left all he had to the Orphan Asylum that had cared for him.[79] This organization exists to this day as the Graham Windham in Brooklyn.

In 1809, having learned a bit about politics from her late husband and knowing Jefferson was unsympathetic, Eliza petitioned the Madison administration for some share of the army pension that Alexander had declined.[80] She eventually received 450 acres and about $10,000. Three of Eliza's sons, Alexander, James, and John, served in the War of 1812, widely referred to as Mr Madison's War.[81] Eliza would later work with Dolley Madison on raising funds for the Washington Monument. Both elderly widows were present on 4 July 1848 when the cornerstone was finally laid. Did Eliza wonder as construction began what sort of monument would memorialize her husband? She still had hopes for, at least, a comprehensive biography, but the project was floundering in the hands of the man to whom she had entrusted Alexander's papers.

Throughout the years of America's Second War of Independence, another popular name for the War of 1812, Angelica Church's health was failing. She and Eliza had stood firmly by each other's sides through the Revolution, family scandals, and financial difficulties. Now, Eliza watched Angelica slowly fade away, suffering from what was likely tuberculosis. She died on 13 March 1814 and is buried on the opposite side of Trinity Church from Alexander. Angelica's death was another tragic reminder of the brevity and unpredictability of life, and Eliza renewed her efforts to see Alexander's biography written before it was too late, so she began the tedious work of reassembling his papers and looking for a new biographer. While her children began their own lives, spreading out from Washington City to the Illinois frontier, Eliza worked to protect Alexander's legacy and improve the lives of the less fortunate through her charitable work.

Her next project was a tuition-free school that would make education accessible to all children living in the relative wilderness surrounding Hamilton Grange. In 1818, when Eliza founded the Hamilton Free School near what is now West 187th and Broadway, it was the only school north of modern-day 155th Street.[82] Eliza was not involved in the day-to-day operations of the school but stayed engaged while focusing her efforts on the orphanage. The school provided free education until the building was destroyed by fire several years after Eliza's death.

Although the *Hamilton* musical claims Eliza spoke out against slavery, there is no historical record of her involvement in an abolitionist organization. If she held abolitionist beliefs, she may have expressed as much in her private correspondence, most of which has been destroyed.

On 8 May 1819, a forged duel challenge was received by Aaron Burr. It claimed to be from James Hamilton, 'Sir: Please to meet me with the weapon you choose, on the 15th May, where you murdered my father at 10 o'clock, with your second'.[83] An intermediary confirmed with James that the message was a forgery before events could escalate, but Eliza must have been horrified by the whisper of possibility that she might lose another son to a duel and to Aaron Burr, no less. She must also have been disappointed that, years after his death, rumors of Alexander still were bandied about from time to time.

Eliza tirelessly continued her work for poor women and orphans in New York City throughout most of the last fifty years of her life, petitioning the city for grants, increasing awareness of public needs, and personally overseeing the work of the orphan asylum for many of those years. 'She was a most earnest, energetic, and intelligent woman', wrote her son, James. 'Her engagements as a principal of the Widow's Society and Orphan Asylum were incessant. In support of these institutions she was constantly employed, and as I once playfully told her, "Mamma, you are a sturdy beggar." She replied, "My dear son, I cannot spare myself or others; my Maker has pointed out this duty to me, and has given me the ability and inclination to perform it."'[84]

The world of women's charity work of the early nineteenth century was one into which Eliza fit perfectly and helped define. She was able to extend her love for family and children to include those who needed her. As her children grew and had families of their own, she spent increasing time helping other women raise their children and serving as a substitute mother to those who had lost their own. Eliza not only was able to be a part of the raising of dozens of children, she had the connections necessary for the fundraising that was vital to any charitable organization.

She had connections with those who had resources but continued to struggle with the financial situation in which her husband had left her. In a letter to her son, James, dated 11 May 1827, Eliza reveals her continued need and her gratitude toward those who assisted her. 'My Dear Son: Your unremitting kindness and attentions, and in this last instance of providing for my comfort, demands my most ardent and affectionate thanks ... As all good acts are recorded in the habitation where your father now is, I have no doubt this one will be proclaimed to him, and have thus given him another motive to implore continued blessings upon you.'[85]

In 1833, Eliza was forced to sell the Grange, which Alexander had so proudly built and her friends had tried to save for her after his death. She simply could not afford the upkeep, so she moved into a townhouse in Manhattan, where she lived with her son, Alexander Jr, and daughter,

Eliza Holly, along with their families.[86] Eliza was seventy-six years old when she made this move, and she may have thought it would be her last. However, she moved once again nine years later, becoming a neighbor to Dolley Madison in Washington City. Her daughter, widowed by that time as well, lived with her in a house on H Street.[87] Here, she became a donor to the Washington Orphan Asylum that had been founded in part by Dolley Madison. Like Dolley, Eliza enjoyed participating in Washington society. One who knew both famous widows reflected, 'Mrs Hamilton, the widow of Alexander Hamilton, was in absolute contrast to Mrs Madison ... Her talents were many; illustrious names and a powerful family, the tenderest sympathy of a whole nation, and her own pitying loving nature blended with a rare sense of justice – all these she dedicated to the care of orphan children.'[88]

Before her move to Washington, however, Eliza went on one more adventure. She was seventy-nine years old in the spring of 1837 when she left on a steamboat to see the American West. Her son, William, had shaken off the Hamilton fame and moved to the frontier years earlier, and Eliza was determined to see him one more time. It was a dangerous and difficult undertaking, but Eliza embraced the experience, writing home about the wild beauty and difficulty of river navigation.[89] From the Erie Canal, a modern engineering wonder at that time, to the Mississippi River, Eliza added to her treasure trove of memories that few Americans of her day could claim to share. She may often be thought of as a sweet, submissive wife, but with this bold escapade, Eliza reveals a daring side that could keep pace with her fearless husband. It took her three weeks to reach the Wisconsin territory where William had established a settlement he originally called Hamilton's Diggings and later renamed Wiota.[90] The town still exists in modern-day Lafayette County. At the time of Eliza's visit, it was deep in largely undeveloped territory that would not become the state of Wisconsin until a decade later.

A few years after her western adventure, Eliza made the move to Washington City where she continued to welcome visitors to her small home when she was well into her nineties.[91] One visitor recalled her longing for Alexander decades after his death. 'She leaned back in her chair a long time with closed eyes, as if lost to all around her. There was a long silence, broken by the murmured words, "I am so tired. It is so long. I want to see Hamilton."'[92] One remembers seeing Eliza 'climb two fences in her short cut across the meadows rather than go on to the town where the carriage could meet her' when she was an 'old lady – past eighty'.[93] But those days finally came to an end, and Eliza slowed down considerably once she was living in Washington. Instead of climbing fences and wandering through meadows, she worked in her small garden and quietly reviewed memories of a fantastic life.

In his *Reminiscences*, James Hamilton remembers his mother's final moments on 9 November 1854. 'I took my seat at the bedside with my face to my mother's, holding the pulse of her right wrist with my right hand, and so continued about two hours, the pulse growing more feeble all the time. At length, about eleven o'clock, mother in a clear voice asked me to change the bedclothes at her feet, which I did, and then, intending to resume my place, I bowed my head down to see if there was any change in her countenance. She put her arm around my neck, pressed me to her, kissed me most affectionately; and said, "God bless you, you have been a good son;" the arm was relaxed, there was a slight hiccough, a slight discharge of dark-colored liquid from the sides of her mouth, and she was dead – her pulse and breath were gone ... She was a devout Christian, the best of wives, mothers, and women.' [94]

Chapter 10

Dolley Payne Todd Madison

Everybody loves Mrs Madison.
– Henry Clay, Speaker of the
House of Representatives

D olley Madison arrived in Washington City on 1 May 1801, long after the War for Independence had ended. She remains a woman of the American Revolution for her role in defining the position of First Lady, though it was not yet referred to as such, and for her experience during the War of 1812, also known as America's Second War for Independence. With the end of this war, the United States of America was accepted as a permanent fixture upon the globe, and Dolley's story serves as a fitting conclusion in the experience of revolutionary women.

The nation's capital was a rough new city, still under construction like the government it was built to house. It was a long way from the log cabin in which Dolley Payne had been born on 20 May 1768 in New Garden, North Carolina, a small Quaker community on the edge of what was then wilderness and is now Greensboro.[1] She was raised within the Society of Friends. Those dismissive of the rigorous religious group called them Quakers for their quivering behavior before a majestic God, and the Friends accepted and became better known by the nickname. Dolley did not live in New Garden for long. Her parents returned to Virginia within a year of Dolley's birth.[2]

Therefore, Dolley was a child through the events experienced by other revolutionary women and living within a community of pacifists. She was only seven when her cousin, Patrick Henry, declared, 'Give me liberty or give me death'.[3] She may, however, still have had an awareness of revolutionary events since much of her childhood was spent at or near Henry's Scotchtown plantation.

It is possible that Dolley's father owned or leased Scotchtown and sold it to Henry, but biographer Richard Côté suggests that Dolley's family were guests of Henry at Scotchtown from the time they returned from New Garden until they built a new home on land bought from another relative, William Coles, in September 1771.[4] This was only ten miles from Scotchtown, although Patrick Henry did not live there after the death of his wife, Sarah, in 1775. At the Coles Hill house, Dolley spent much of her formative childhood, learning the domestic arts and the strict religious training required of Quaker children. She particularly enjoyed needlepoint, but trouble with her eyesight made it more difficult as she became an adult.

Dolley's parents, like most Quakers, refused to bear arms or take sides in the Revolutionary War. They received accusations of cowardice and even treason but stayed true to their belief that it is always wrong to kill another human. These same principles, which valued every life as containing an Inner Light, led Dolley's parents to question the institution of slavery and way of life in their beloved Virginia. They were not the only ones. Many Quakers coordinated stops on the Underground Railroad to help slaves escape to freedom. By the time manumission of Virginian slaves became legal in 1782, Dolley's father, John Payne, had already freed all his enslaved workers, of whom he had owned approximately five.[5]

Unable to profitably run a large farm without enslaved labor, in 1783, the Payne family moved to Philadelphia, where John Payne decided to try his hand as a laundry starch merchant. The most sophisticated city in America at the time, it must have struck fifteen-year-old Dolley with awe. Friendly and intelligent, with dark hair and blue eyes, Dolley charmed many in Philadelphia in return. She had an un-Quakerlike worldliness that some said she inherited from her paternal grandmother, Anna Fleming. Less religiously strict as an Anglican, Dolley's grandmother enjoyed spoiling her and may have inspired the fashion sense that would serve Dolley well years later in Washington City.[6]

John Payne had noble intentions in seeking a way of life that did not depend upon slave labor, but Philadelphia provided its own challenges and misfortunes. Mary Payne, Dolley's mother, gave birth to her ninth child almost upon arrival, but the baby girl, named Philadelphia for the family's new home, died young. Their oldest child, Walter, was lost at sea the next year. To make matters worse, John's laundry starch scheme was not earning enough to support his large, grieving family. Dolley must have had conflicting emotions regarding the city she loved and the tribulation that struck her family once they moved there.

She was a popular, vivacious girl, described enthusiastically by Anthony Morris, 'She came upon our comparatively cold hearts in Philadelphia, suddenly and unexpectedly with all the delightful influences of a summer sun … she soon raised the mercury there in the thermometers of the Heart to fever heat.'[7] Dolley wrote to friends about both men's and women's fashions, fascinated with silks and buckles in a way that raised the eyebrows of her Quaker elders, but her circumstances did not allow her to indulge in wearing the styles she so admired.

In 1787, the Constitutional Convention met in Philadelphia, and nineteen-year-old Dolley would have watched the political leaders of the new country as they rushed about town. She likely saw the handsome, charismatic Alexander Hamilton and the quiet, bookish James Madison, among many others who were or would become some of the most famous names in American history. Dolley's attention, however, was on the young men of the city as she considered which might become her husband. She had a broad choice of suitors, but her father selected John Todd, a fellow Quaker. Todd was a lawyer five years Dolley's senior, who had long expressed interest in her. John Payne, failing in business and in poor health, may have pressured his daughter to wed Todd, but the couple's letters also indicate a love match. On 7 January 1790, she became Dolley Todd.[8]

By that time, John Payne's business had gone bankrupt causing his exile from their Quaker congregation. When the federal government moved to Philadelphia, Dolley's mother, Mary Payne, opened her home as a boarding house to support the family, a decision that would have a deep impact on her daughter's future. However, Dolley had no way of knowing that as she settled into married life and assisted her mother by frequently taking in her siblings.

She lived with her husband in a three-story brick home that still stands at the corner of Fourth and Walnut Streets in Philadelphia. Part of the first floor was used as John Todd's law offices and an extensive personal library. The couple soon welcomed two sons, John Payne Todd on 29 February 1792 and William Temple Todd in September 1793. Todd's business was successful, and their family was growing.

Had this idyllic situation continued, Dolley's name might not have become prominent in America's history. Tragically for the young wife,

Philadelphia's yellow fever epidemic of 1793 also entered into history at this point. The sickness sent government officials racing from the city for healthier air and left few households untouched, including the Todd house. John Todd sent Dolley away shortly after the birth of their second son, but he remained in the city to care for his father and a clerk in his office who had fallen ill. Approximately 5,000 Philadelphians died of yellow fever that summer, and Dolley lost both her husband and infant son on the same day, 24 October 1793.[9]

Dolley encountered difficulties with her brother-in-law concerning her inheritance from her husband and his parents, who had all died of yellow fever. Eventually, she was forced to employ the skills of a lawyer, Aaron Burr, to gain James Todd's cooperation. Burr assisted Dolley with the recording of her will, in which he was named guardian of two-year-old, John Payne Todd.[10] In Philadelphia serving as a senator from New York, Burr also introduced Dolley to his friend, Virginia senator James Madison.

When Burr asked Dolley if he could make the introduction, Madison's reputation had preceded him. Dolley wrote to friend Eliza Collins, 'Thou must come to me. Aaron Burr says that "the great little Madison" has asked to be brought to see me this evening'.[11] Eliza did come to be with Dolley as she welcomed the senators to her home.

James Madison did not have the charisma for which Aaron Burr was famous, but something about the quiet intellectual seventeen years her senior captivated the young widow. The man known as the Father of the Constitution undoubtedly gave her a sense of safety and security, which Dolley would have craved after the upheavals in her life. He was also a close advisor of President Washington, a great point in his favor. Madison was wealthy, but he was also a slave owner. He was not a Quaker, which meant that Dolley would no longer be counted among the Friends were she to marry him, but the social status she would gain as the wife of one of the Founding Fathers may have outweighed that concern. A niece wrote that Dolley had 'conquered the recluse bookworm Madison'.[12] Whatever her reasons, Dolley accepted James Madison's affections and the two were wed on 15 September 1794.

A year before Dolley's second marriage, her younger sister, Lucy, had eloped with George Steptoe Washington, nephew of the first president. The Payne sisters, who had been raised to be demure Quakers, suddenly found themselves at the center of the young country's political elite. In fact, the Madisons' wedding had been held at Harewood, George Steptoe Washington's estate.[13]

In an age when political and personal disagreements were not infrequently settled by duels or the threat of them (Aaron Burr killed Alexander Hamilton in a duel a decade later), James Madison was level-headed and conciliatory. He must have seemed a steady, peaceful choice compared to Dolley's late father. Avoiding confrontation, Madison took his new family back to Montpelier when John Adams was elected president.[14] Besides Dolley's young son, whom she called Payne, her sister, Anna, also joined them.

When Dolley first arrived at Montpelier, it was a comfortable eight-room home with a broad central passage common to Virginia homes. They immediately began an expansion project to create separate spaces for Madison's parents and his own new family. Ongoing building projects eventually transitioned Montpelier from the original house into the mansion that visitors see today.[15] British visitor Mary Bagot was reluctantly impressed. She wrote, 'The house is more comfortable and better furnished than any other I have been in in this horrid country'.[16]

The newlyweds enjoyed the Virginia countryside until it was time for James to take his place in Washington City as Thomas Jefferson's secretary of state. Upon arrival, the Madisons temporarily resided with Jefferson in the new presidential palace, which was not much of a palace in its drafty, unfinished state. Dolley continued to assist Jefferson with hosting after they had moved to their own quarters since he was a widower and his daughters remained home in Virginia.[17] In a new city lacking social structure, Dolley stepped forward to form it.

She called upon government officials, Washington City's few locals, and foreign visitors, setting precedents future First Ladies would follow even before her husband became president. Her niece, Mary Cutts, wrote, 'She was humble-minded, tolerant, and sincere, but with a desire to please, and a willingness to be pleased, which made her popular, and always a great friend and support to her husband'.[18] Not all First Ladies were as well suited to these duties as Dolley. When Louisa Adams, John Quincy's wife, lived in Washington, she made no secret of her disdain for the social requirements.

Dolley may have been taking some comfort in friends and social connections since she and James had no children. Although she had two children with her first husband, with James Dolley possibly experienced miscarriages but no full-term pregnancies. James was one of a dozen siblings but had no documented children of his own. (Bettye Kearse claims that her family descends from James Madison in her book, *The Other Madisons: The Lost History of a President's Black Family*.) Childbearing and raising a family were a large part of a woman's role in the early nineteenth century, but Dolley formed another role for herself, building a social network in the new US capital. She was stepping into a void left by Jefferson, who had no desire to create unity or transparency in government. The president was a widower and closed his house to visitors, foregoing the types of gatherings that his predecessors had regularly held, replacing them with politically geared dinners attended by carefully selected guests.

As historian Catherine Allgor has written, Dolley's 'actions demonstrated a clear plan to gently, subtly, make the Madison home the center of Washington life'.[19] The first Madison home in Washington was one of the row houses in a group known unimaginatively as the 'six buildings'. Next door lived Albert and Hannah Gallatin.[20] Gallatin had served in congress and was Jefferson's secretary of the treasury. After returning to Montpelier in the summer of 1801, the Madisons rented a brick house on F Street where they would remain through James's time as secretary of state.[21] It was this home that became famous for Dolley's welcoming hospitality and frequent social events.

Just like Martha Washington and Abigail Adams before her, Dolley was informally charged with creating an atmosphere that spoke of Republican glory without allowing it to become too monarchical. Americans took pride in their lack of royalty but did not want to appear provincial on the international stage. Martha and Abigail had favored more elite social gatherings and believed their husbands should be treated with something like the respect due to a king. Dolley transformed Washington City into something more uniquely American, opening her home to anyone who would like to come and encouraging political opponents to mix and mingle.

Unlike her predecessors, Dolley was young and eager to be the first to wear new fashions that sometimes scandalized women like Abigail

Adams. Dolley's portrait was even painted with her in a low-cut gown that would have raised Abigail's eyebrow. Other women in Washington followed Dolley's lead when she wore empire waist dresses, feathers in her hair, or her famous colorful turbans. Gone was the homespun that Martha Washington had worn to demonstrate her patriotism. Dolley was a trendsetter in the latest French fashions with her own distinctive additions to create something uniquely American. Danish minister Peder Pederson quoted Homer to describe her. 'She looks like a Goddess; she moves like a Queen'.[22]

Dolley faced one of her most challenging social troubles near the end of 1803 when the Merrys arrived from London. Anthony Merry was England's ambassador to the United States, and his wife, Elizabeth, accompanied him. Neither was prepared for the rusticity of Washington City or Thomas Jefferson's lack of etiquette. The President first offended the aristocratic couple by greeting them in his slippers, but he caused even greater offense just a few days later.

At a dinner at the President's house, which was not yet referred to as the White House, the Merrys reasonably expected to be honored as new ambassadors in the city. When Jefferson offered his arm to Dolley to go in to dinner, she whispered, 'Take Mrs Merry'.[23] She understood that this was an insult to the ambassador's wife, but Jefferson insisted. To make matters worse, he had invited representatives from France, a country with which England was at war. Jefferson, who had been a diplomat to France before serving as Washington's secretary of state undoubtedly knew the proper protocol and was purposely breaking it.

Madison escorted Mrs Merry, but Mr Merry was left by himself. Guests wondered at the intentional offense. The Spanish ambassador exclaimed, 'This will be the cause of war!'[24] A dinner a short time later at the Madison home went no better. Feeling obligated to follow the President's lead, the Merrys were again not treated as guests of honor, but Dolley attempted to soothe Mrs Merry's pride without speaking against the standard set by Jefferson. The two women settled into a friendly, if not close, relationship, that helped keep the incident from causing further harm. As it was, British and Spanish representatives began reaching out to Jefferson's Federalist opponents in response to his insulting behavior. He may have thought he was standing up for republican ideals, but he drove his enemies to unite against him.

Jefferson further strengthened America's ties with France when he approved the Louisiana Purchase, a transaction of questionable constitutionality that doubled the size of the United States while providing France with $15 million for land they believed America would soon claim anyway. The Republican president demonstrated the great power of the central government he had often lobbied against with the historic agreement, which he announced on 4 July 1803.

On 31 March 1804, Dolley attended a bittersweet event, the wedding of her sister, Anna to Richard Cutts. Dolley was almost a mother to Anna, and the women were very attached to one another. Dolley struggled with losing Anna to marriage, even as she was thankful for her happiness. Anna had been living with Dolley and James ever since their marriage. Her leaving was especially poignant since the couple had no children together. Dolley's son, Payne, was now twelve years old and was soon sent to school in Baltimore.

Just months later, Vice-President Aaron Burr killed Alexander Hamilton in a duel that created more scandal for the Jefferson presidency. Dolley must have been torn regarding this news. She considered Burr a friend and had once named him guardian for her son, but now he was charged with murdering the former secretary of the treasury. Worse was to come. In August 1804, Anthony Merry revealed that Burr had approached him with an offer 'to lend his assistance to his Majesty's Government in any Manner in which they may see fit to employ him, particularly in an endeavoring to effect a separation of the Western part of the United States from that which lies between the Atlantick and the Mountains.'[25] Burr's treason was shocking to his friends and colleagues, including the Madisons.

In 1805, Dolley was temporarily removed from Washington City's social scene when a large lump on her knee required treatment and rest. She went to Philadelphia, where the vibrant socialite was forced to endure the inactivity of bed rest. This time, however, caused Dolley and James to frequently write to each other and leave evidence of how close their relationship had grown. Dolley disliked being away from her husband. She missed him and worried about his health, although she was the one under a doctor's care. 'Never had I more extreme pain', she wrote her sister, even as she worried that she could not 'fly to aid him' when James complained of one of his frequent ailments.[26]

In a heartfelt letter to James, Dolley wrote, 'What a sad day! I found myself unable to sleep, from anxiety for thee, my dearest husband'. She closed the letter, 'Adieu, my beloved, our hearts understand each other – In fond affection thine...'[27] He responded in kind, 'let me know that I shall soon have you with me, which is most anxiously desired by your ever affectionate – James Madison'.[28]

If love for people made Dolley buoyant and charismatic, it also caused her to feel losses deeply. When two of her nieces, her mother, and one of her sisters died in quick succession, Dolley fell into a dark depression. She wrote to one of her closest friends, Eliza Collins Lee, 'Oh God! we must bow our heads to thy decrees however awful – we cannot change or avert them – Eliza, I cannot write – tho I wish to communicate every thing to you; when I trace the sad events that have occured to me, I feel as if I should die two.'[29]

Dolley's vivacious personality was an asset to her husband during the election season of 1808. His opponent, Charles Cotesworth Pickney, recognized her impact. 'I might have had a better chance had I faced Mr Madison alone'.[30] Mr Pickney knew a strong, influential woman when he saw one. His own mother, Eliza Lucas, had defied the odds when she discovered how to grow indigo and process it into valuable dye on her South Carolina plantation.

James Madison was inaugurated as America's fourth president on 4 March 1809, and Eliza Collins Lee expressed her certainty that the Madisons would serve the country well. 'I feel no small degree of exultation in knowing that the mind, temper, and manners of my Philadelphia Quaker friend, are peculiarly fitted for the station, where hospitality and graciousness of deportment, will appear conspicuously charming and conciliating.'[31]

James Madison was the first president to hold an inaugural ball on the evening of his swearing-in as president. Dolley was the ideal lady to organize and host such a function. She was an experienced Washingtonian by this time, and the party was so well attended that windows of the ballroom had to be broken in order to allow in fresh air.[32] Madison may have been the new president, but he was not the center of attention at his own ball when in competition with his gregarious wife and outgoing president, Thomas Jefferson. Scholarly pursuits were Madison's arena, not the ballroom, and that would serve him well as he took office.

The Madisons contracted Henry Latrobe to convert the presidential palace from the half-empty bachelor pad of Thomas Jefferson into something visitors would find more familiar today.[33] A parlor, decorated in sunshine yellow, was Dolley's favored room for entertaining. With Latrobe's assistance, she struck the perfect balance between aristocratic and republican. A larger drawing-room, called the Oval Room, was decorated with rich cream walls and crimson velvet curtains. Visitors were impressed and turned up in droves, just as they had at the Madisons' F Street house. Washington Irving described his visit, 'I was most graciously received; found a crowded collection of great and little men, of ugly old women and beautiful young ones, and in ten minutes was hand in glove with half the people in the assemblage'.[34]

It was during this time that the home that had been referred to as the president's palace and the executive mansion among other names was baptized with the name that stuck, the White House.[35] Another attraction that was uniquely Dolley was her pet macaw. The colorful bird was kept in a window of the White House where passers-by could observe its exotic plumage and quirky antics. The fact that the White House was quickly becoming a symbol of Americanism made it all the more heartbreaking when the British did their best to destroy it only a few years later.

In May 1809, a letter to Thomas Jefferson states, 'Mrs Madison cannot abide the smell of the paint; that may be on account of her pregnancy'.[36] No other evidence exists that Dolley was pregnant then (she would have been almost forty-one) or that she and James experienced any pregnancies together. This may be why Dolley's son, Payne, was too spoiled by them both. The cycle of paying his debts slowly bled the Madisons of thousands of dollars that eventually became too much of a burden for his mother to bear in her widowed years. During their time in Washington, they attempted to find positions that would tame him and help him mature, but each effort failed and Payne remained the charming but difficult wayward son.

On 10 January 1809, Dolley's sister, Lucy, became a widow when George Steptoe Washington died suddenly at age thirty-seven. Though grieving, Dolley was pleased to welcome Lucy and her three young sons into the White House. Having them around her likely soothed some of Dolley's anguish over her own son. Three years later, Dolley planned the first wedding ever held at the White House when Lucy married Supreme Court justice, Thomas Todd.[37]

'Mrs Madison's Wednesday nights' were the place to be in Washington City, and the casual nickname for her drawing-room events demonstrates the atmosphere she had created.[38] The fact that they were referred to as 'squeezes' is a good indication of how well attended they were. If Dolley was sometimes called the 'Queen of America,' her son, Payne, was 'America's Prince'.[39] In his late teens and early twenties during his step-father's administration, Payne served on diplomatic commissions and impressed people across the globe with his good looks, impeccable manners, and charisma. However, he also incurred astronomical amounts of debt that James and Dolley consistently covered for him. He was a socialite and spendthrift, just like his mother.

In the meantime, James had difficult foreign relations to cope with. Jefferson's Embargo Act had not had the desired effect, harming Americans more than the British it was meant to punish. England also continued pressing American sailors into service and seizing US cargo, practices that some saw as acts of war. The British used their ongoing war with France as an excuse, claiming that they were only ensuring that America was not aiding their enemy, but Madison had enough of these excuses. An estimated 3,000 Americans had been pressed into British navy service, and the British were boldly sending press gangs out within view of the American coast.[40] Some counselled the president to keep the peace, uncertain that war with Great Britain could be won a second time. However, this argument failed to credit the fact that the king was already treating the former colonies as if they were at war and daring them to do something about it.

War was declared on Great Britain on 1 June 1812. 'To have shrunk under such circumstances from manly resistance, would have been a degradation, blasting our best and proudest hopes: It would have struck us from the high rank, where the virtuous struggles of our fathers had placed us, and have betrayed the magnificent legacy which we hold in trust for future generations. It would have acknowledged that on the Element, which forms three forths of the globe we inhabit, and where all independent nations have equal and common rights, the American people were not an independent people, but colonists and vassals,' James Madison wrote.[41] In short, the Americans were fighting for independence again.

What did Dolley think of what was often referred to as Mr Madison's War? Was she worried that her bookish husband might himself take up arms? Dolley did her best to hide any fears she might have and show unwavering support for her husband. As always, she also saw it as her responsibility to maintain Washington social life. This role was second only to nursing her husband as the stress of war and leading the country was frequently a burden to his frail health. She cared for him while keeping up the image of a White House untroubled by the specter of war.

When it appeared that James might die in June of 1813, Dolley refused to permit anyone to see him as arguments ensued over who should replace him, the aged vice-president, Elbridge Gerry, an insufficient option in the eyes of many. People feared what might happen to the United States without Madison at the helm. French envoy Louis Sérurier spoke for the nation when he wrote that Madison's death would be 'a veritable national calamity'.[42] As Dolley nursed James, she must have been haunted by memories of her first husband's death of yellow fever. If James died, both Dolley and the country would suffer a tragic loss. When James seemed to be improving in July 1813, Dolley wrote to her friend, Hannah Gallatin, 'I attended his bed for nearly five weeks! even now, I watch over him, as I would an infant, so precarious is his convalescence'.[43]

Dolley was not alone in her gratitude for James' recovery. Jonathan Dayton expressed the thoughts of many when he wrote to James in July 1813. 'I almost tremble, sir, when I think of the contentions, divisions & disasters, to which your sudden removal at this critical period must have exposed us, & have frequently thanked Heaven for yet longer sparing your life to us, in it's goodness.'[44] Frail but no longer in danger of losing his life, James had to manage a war that was exposing the vulnerabilities in the United States' weak central government.

A significant difference between the Revolutionary War and this Second War of Independence quickly became evident. America no longer had a General George Washington. Madison and his congress struggled to agree upon how to make this war they had declared. Madison's party had fought Federalists like Alexander Hamilton over the issue of a standing army, and now the United States were at a distinct disadvantage that they did not have sufficient defense. British troops destroyed coastal towns at will, and failures in Canada ensured that the northern territory never became a part of the United States.

24 August 1814 is the day Dolley is best remembered for. On this sultry, late summer day, she used a spyglass to peer into the distance. She was looking for her husband to return, but it eventually became clear that the British forces would arrive first. Dolley had been packing irreplaceable documents and keepsakes, as James had requested. Knowing what a prize it would be to British conquerors, she also had the Gilbert Stuart painting of George Washington removed from the wall and loaded into Jacob Barker's cart. Dolley wrote to her sister, 'I insist on waiting until the large picture of Gen Washington is secured ... I must leave this house, or the retreating army will make me a prisoner in it, by filling up the road I am directed to take. When I shall again write you, or where I shall be tomorrow, I cannot tell!!' [45]

Not far ahead of the dust cloud stirred up by the marching troops, Dolley fled from Washington City. She had been so confident of Madison's return that dinner for forty was on the table for British troops to enjoy before they set the President's mansion to the torch.[46] Before that final destruction, looters broke into the abandoned mansion and stole many of the items that Dolley had not been able to carry away.[47] Her brave actions helped heal her husband's reputation which had been damaged by America's entrance into the war.

This dramatic rescue of Washington's portrait, ensuring that the British would not parade it as a great prize, earned Dolley great admiration. However, Paul Jennings, a fifteen-year-old enslaved personal servant of the Madisons, years later wrote, 'It has often been stated in print, that when Mrs Madison escaped from the White House, she cut out from the frame the large portrait of Washington (now in one of the parlors there), and carried it off. This is totally false'. According to Jennings, it was French servant, Jean-Pierre Sioussat, with the help of White House gardener, Thomas McGaw, who 'took it down and sent it off on a wagon, with some large silver urns and such other valuables as could be hastily got hold of'.[48] Of course, Dolley may have considered ordering servants to save the portrait the same thing as saving it herself. Whichever version of events is true, Washington's portrait was saved and Dolley's reputation benefited from that fact.

British Admiral Cockburn led his men to the greatest prize of the War of 1812. The White House stood dark and abandoned, and the victors took their places for dinner before setting the recently finished interior ablaze. Only the outer stone walls and some interior partitions survived. The flames of Washington City could be seen forty miles away.[49] The destruction was terminated abruptly when a storm raged through the area, lifting structures from their foundations and leaving British soldiers wondering if they had brought the wrath of God down on them with their actions.[50]

Dolley's feelings would have mirrored those of many Americans at that dismal moment. Had Mr Madison's War been lost? What would happen next? Washington City had not even been completed before it was burned and occupied. It was the lowest point since their fathers had fought in the Revolution.

Where was her husband?

Thankfully, Dolley did not wait long to be reunited, briefly, with James. It was enough to reassure her that he was safe, though he immediately returned to his duties, which now included reclaiming the nation's capital city. When Dolley went to a tavern, where she planned to wait for James, the proprietress demanded that she leave. Dolley had been chased from her home and now faced citizens angry with her husband's war. The mood of the public was evolving, however, and the destruction of Washington City caused Americans to unify the same way the siege of Boston had done decades earlier. Horrified by the senseless destruction of their capital city, the people began to bond together against the British once again. Within days, the Madisons returned to what was left of Washington as the British abandoned the capital and headed toward Baltimore.

Fort McHenry proved a stronger rival than the troops at Washington, and Francis Scott Key was inspired to write the Star Spangled Banner when a large American flag flew proudly over the fort after the British bombardment. American resolve grew into determination to avenge the humiliation in Washington. However, it was difficult to ignore the widespread concern that Great Britain might reconquer her former colonies, especially after their victories in Europe freed up troops and supplies. Could James Madison stand up to Lord Wellington?

Thomas Jefferson tried to encourage his friend and successor, 'Had Gl. Washington himself been now at the head of our affairs, the same event would probably have happened'.[51] James, with Dolley at his side, was determined to lead America to victory.

On 2 November 1814, just weeks after fleeing British troops, Dolley Madison opened the doors of her temporary home at the Washington City Octagon House for her drawing-room.[52] Although the White House would not be renovated until James Monroe became president, the Madisons demonstrated American perseverance and worked to unify the nation. They had their work cut out for them. New England states were considering seceding from the union, citing Madison's own logic from *The Federalist Papers* to justify their actions. They were weary of stifled trade, slavery, and the three-fifths compromise that gave enhanced power to the southern states.

Peace was declared on Christmas Eve 1814 with the signing of the Treaty of Ghent, though the news did not reach Washington until 14 February 1815, after the Battle of New Orleans had been fought and won by the Americans on 8 January 1815. America did not gain much in the treaty besides ending the impressment of sailors. More importantly, the United States had retained its independence when tested and would not be seriously challenged again. Celebrations broke out in the ash-strewn Washington City followed by fervent rebuilding.

War and the building of a new city had created another problem that led Dolley to publicly get involved in charitable work. Like Elizabeth Hamilton in New York, Dolley helped establish the Washington City Orphan Asylum. She served as the directress and was actively involved in the orphanage's operations.[53] Not only did this activity likely fill a gap left by Dolley's inability to have children in her second marriage, but many First Ladies followed her example of philanthropic work. Dolley encouraged and assisted with the education and care for the city's orphans in activities that were personally fulfilling and politically effective.

When James had completed his second term, Dolley received a letter from Eliza Collins Lee that echoed the sentiments she sent upon Dolley's rise to the position of First Lady. 'On this day eight years ago I wrote ... to congratulate you on the joyful event that placed you in the highest station our country can bestow ... How much greater cause have I to congratulate you, at this period for having filled it as to render yourself more enviable this day, than your successor, as it is more difficult to deserve the gratitude and thanks of the community than their congratulations – You have deservedly received it all.'[54] Dolley had achieved what the male politicians of the revolutionary era had failed to do. She had brought people together and encouraged the unity that George Washington had hoped that Americans would discover rather than breaking up into hostile political parties.

John Adams told James that he could have won a third term, 'Such is the State of Minds here, that had Mr. Madison been Candidate, he would probably have had the Votes of Massachusetts, and consequently of all New England.'[55] However, that was not Madison's plan. He followed Washington's example and retired after his second term to Montpelier in early 1817, leaving a rebuilt Washington City to the Monroe administration. It must have been a difficult move for Dolley to leave the city where she had been the center of society for sixteen years and settle at the plantation house where her mother-in-law still reigned as mistress. Would it be peaceful rest or boring isolation?

Dolley still had her son's spending habits to deal with. Rather than cutting him off, the Madisons continued to pay the debts that Payne managed to incur with astounding regularity. The $40,000 that was spent on the young man between 1813 and 1836 meant difficult circumstances for his parents.[56] Even with their consistent bailouts, Payne experienced debtors' prison more than once.

As those who had served before him had discovered, the presidency cost James more than it had paid. The dinners, décor, and clothing had cut into the Madisons' budget. In retirement at Montpelier, they experienced the same steady stream of guests that the Washingtons had reluctantly welcomed. Feeding and lodging all those visitors was another strain on their finances. Dolley enjoyed being the center of attention, but she could no longer afford it. In addition to these expenses, Montpelier's enslaved population had grown to more than the plantation could support, but James refused to consider sales that would break up the community. Although James and Dolley loved Montpelier, their finances also made it difficult for them to consider travel. For the remainder of James' life, they would leave on very few occasions.[57]

Their immobility was made more tolerable by their many esteemed visitors, such as General Lafayette in 1824.[58] Forty-four years had passed since Lafayette had first arrived in America as an enthusiastic nineteen-year-old offering his services to General Washington. He was still passionate for freedom, now on the part of America's enslaved population. James also struggled with the reality that slavery went against the pillars of liberty he had helped to build while his family and way of life was dependent upon the more than 100 people enslaved at Montpelier. He became a founding member of the American Colonization Society in 1816 with the goal of purchasing American slaves and transporting them to a new settlement in Liberia.[59] James left a bequest to the Society in his will but did not manumit any of his slaves.

One source of the Madisons' joy at Montpelier was their personal library. James was widely known as a scholar with a great love of books, but Dolley had also brought significant volumes into the marriage and was dedicated to personal improvement through reading. Dolley's sister, Mary, observed that their library was 'lined with bookcases' and 'the center so filled with them that there was only just room enough to pass among them. Books and pamphlets were piled up everywhere, on every available chair and table'.[60]

By 1836, James' health had been deteriorating for years, and he had prepared his 'Advice to my Country', painstakingly recorded by his wife, in the knowledge that his time for advising the nation he had helped create was running short.[61] In his final days, physicians contemplated forestalling death with medications that James declined. They had hoped he might die on 4 July, as Thomas Jefferson and John Adams had done in 1826 and James Monroe had in 1831. James died at Montpelier on 28 June 1836, after uttering, 'Nothing more than a change of mind'.[62]

In the midst of her great grief, Dolley wrote to her brother-in-law, 'I would write more, dear Richard, but have no power over my confused and oppressed mind to speak fully of the enduring goodness of my beloved husband. He left me many pledges of his confidence and love. Especially do I value all his writings.'[63] She had scarcely left his side throughout almost forty-two years of marriage and would have to create a new life for herself alone. However, Dolley was left in a situation many widows of her era suffered. She was land rich but cash poor. She also continued to bail her son out of debt regularly enough that his local creditors immediately looked to her when Payne defaulted.[64] She may have been a former First Lady and mistress of Montpelier, but that did not stop her neighbors from taking her to court.

Possibly because Dolley had lost everyone else who had been closest to her, she was ineffective in reining in Payne's bad behavior. Montpelier was not producing income like it once did. Mother's love blinding her to his many faults, Dolley called upon Payne to manage the estate. He had already cost his parents enough that Dolley's situation could be largely blamed on him, but he felt no impetus to repent.

Dolley's popularity did not fade with James' death. Returning to Washington in 1837, she used a congressional directory to track her visits and visitors.[65] When it was time for Samuel Morse to test his exciting new invention on 24 May 1844, Dolley was one of his guests when the first communication, 'What hath God wrought?' was sent. When asked if she would like to send a message, Dolley had Morse send 'Message from Mrs Madison. She sends her love to Mrs Wethered', a cousin who was at the other end of the line.[66] She was an honored guest at the inauguration of James Polk in 1845, the eleventh president of her lifetime, and she had met them all. She was a remnant of a past generation, a link to the Founding Fathers who were transitioning from mortal men into legends. She lived long enough to have her image captured by daguerreotype in addition to painted portraits. Her style changed, if her vanity had not. In the Matthew Brady photo, Dolley exposes much less skin than in her earlier sittings. Wrinkles and grey hair are carefully camouflaged and covered, but she still wears a fashionable white turban.

Rich in friends but not in cash, by 1844, Dolley was forced to admit that she could not afford to maintain Montpelier. The plantation and most of the Madison enslaved population were sold, and Dolley moved permanently to the row house she owned in Washington City. This is where she would remain until her death in 1849. Dolley had been struggling to compile her husband's papers but was overwhelmed by the job. When she was able to organize enough for sale, the amount raised was insufficient for her needs. She remained dependent upon the help of friends for the remainder of her days. Even former slave, Paul Jennings, whom Dolley had sold instead of manumitted as wished by James, wrote that he 'occasionally gave her small sums from my own pocket', after he had earned his freedom from Daniel Webster.[67]

Her impoverished position did not stop Dolley from being an honored guest at Washington events. She was more than a former First Lady, she was a symbol of the Revolution and America's birth. Along with Elizabeth Hamilton, she raised funds and laid the cornerstone for the Washington Monument.[68]

Some early historians have asserted that Dolley must have been uncomfortable with slavery, although she left no evidence that she had any abolitionist feelings. This assumption is based on her Quaker background and the fact that modern minds want her to have despised slavery. However, Dolley openly rejected the most restrictive Quaker teachings, does not seem to have been reluctant to marry one who would cause her to be exiled from the Society of Friends, and strived to strengthen the image of herself as a product of Virginia plantation society. As Holly Shulman points out, 'She must have hated the economic dislocation that was attendant on the Payne family's move to Philadelphia, and associated that experience with both leaving Virginia and her father freeing his slaves'.[69] Dolly never made any move to free the Madison slaves as her father had done, leaving the distinct impression that she did not disapprove of slavery as much as one might hope she did. Her brother, John, determined to do what his father had and moved to Illinois to farm without enslaved labor, but Dolley sold slaves to cover her living expenses, finding herself in a dire financial situation after her husband's death. When her slave, Ellen Stewart, attempted to escape in 1848, Dolley sold her to a slave dealer.[70] Paul Jennings, Madison's valet who later purchased his freedom, claimed that James wished for him to be freed upon his death, but Dolley sold him instead.[71] It seems that given examples of both abolitionist and plantation owners in her life, Dolley had made her choice.

Dolley died on 12 July 1849 after suffering a paralyzing stroke. Hundreds of people paid their respects in the largest funeral Washington City had ever seen, and it is believed that the first use of the term 'First Lady' was in the eulogy by President Zachery Taylor, America's twelfth president.[72] Whether or not this story is true, it is difficult to argue that any single woman defined the role of America's First Lady more than Dolley Madison.

Chapter 11

Revolutionary Women

Upon examining the biographies of illustrious men, you will generally find some female about them, in the relation of a wife, mother, or sister – to whose instigation a great part of their merit is to be ascribed.
                                                                    – John Adams

This selection of revolutionary women is incomplete, for it would be impossible to include the story of every woman who took part in the birth of the United States. Some names and stories are lost to history, while others remain household names. It is especially difficult to uncover individual personal stories of Native American women and women of color of this era. Their lives and actions not considered important enough at the time to document, there are few detailed biographical records of thousands of women who lived, loved, and died, just like their more famous counterparts. My hope is that this book has given women of the late eighteenth century a bit of the spotlight that has formerly shone only on America's Founding Fathers.

Mercy Otis Warren wrote, 'The narrow bounds, prescrib'd to female life, The gentle mistress, and the prudent wife: Maternal precepts, drawn from sacred truth, Shall warm the bosom of the list'ning youth; While the kind mother acts her little part, And stamps the tablet on the infant heart, Each fervent wish, I to my country lend, And thus subscribe, the patriot's faithful friend.'[1] In this dismissive recognition of the female's role in the revolution, she forgets that in simply writing these lines she is taking more than a 'little part' in history. She has left us some of the most complete first-hand observations of the period before, during, and after the War for Independence.

Abigail Adams also begged John to 'Be kind enough to burn this Letter. Tis wrote in great haste and a most incorrect Scrawl'.[2] She made similar requests to him and others on multiple occasions, but we are thankfully left with a rich first-hand history of the Revolution thanks to their disobedience.

Mercy's and Abigail's statements are profound examples of women underestimating their impact on a world where they raised and educated children, managed homes and businesses, and provided essential support to men who were fighting and creating policy. Would George Washington have been the man he was without Martha? Martha did destroy most of her letters, as did many women of the era, and how much poorer we are for that fact. Women throughout the ages have filled vital roles, even when they were not the same roles filled by men. That truth is demonstrated by no one better than the women in the pages of this book. I hope you have enjoyed seeing the history of the American Revolution through their eyes.

America is hail'd from sea to sea, Sits independent, glorious, and free ...
— Mercy Otis Warren

Acknowledgements

The writing community is fabulously supportive and inclusive. My fellow writers have offered their encouragement and assistance in so many ways since I started this project. Sharon Bennett Connolly has been a priceless friend from the beginning and even took photographs of Boston Castle in Yorkshire for me. Stephanie Churchill is my kindred spirit and my go-to when I need something read and critiqued because of her deep understanding of my reasons for writing. Paula Lofting is the energetic and fearless leader of our Historical Writers Forum. I don't know what I would do without the constant support of these amazing, brilliant women.

My children have survived hearing my daily historical fun facts and even found some of them interesting. I hope I have given them an example of devoting oneself to a career for which they have passion even if it means stepping outside of what most people think is reasonable or practical. No one has been a greater supporter of my writing than my husband, Duane. When covid caused us to share home office space, I was able to hear for myself how frequently he mentioned that his wife was a writer, and I realized that he was not only encouraging, he was actually proud of me. He accompanied me on my tour of Hamilton Grange, George Washington's Mount Vernon, James Madison's Montpelier, and many other places for research related to this book. He even endures my habit of explaining the importance of our James Madison souvenir glasses each time we have guests. I have taken my family to more historic sites than I can count, and they are always ready for an adventure. I cannot thank them enough, and I hope they know I love them fiercely.

Finally, I would like to thank Pen & Sword for reaching out to this historical novelist and offering me an opportunity I would not have thought to seek for myself. It has been an amazing experience immersing myself in the lives of America's revolutionary women.

Samantha Wilcoxson
July 2022

Notes

Chapter 1: The American War for Independence

1. Warren, Mercy Otis and Cohen, Lester H., *History of the Rise, Progress and Termination of the American Revolution: interspersed with Biographical, Political and Moral Observations*, p. 27
2. Ibid, p. 53
3. Atkinson, Rick, *The British are Coming: The War for America, Lexington to Princeton, 1775–1777*, p. 4
4. Ronald, D.A.B., *The Life of John Andre: The Redcoat who Turned Benedict Arnold*, p. 96
5. Boston Castle, Yorkshire, castlesfortsbattles.co.uk/yorkshire/boston_castle. html.
6. Washington, George to Lieutenant Colonel Joseph Reed, 10 February 1776, *Founders Online*, founders.archives.gov/documents/Washington/03-03-02-0209.
7. Warren, Mercy Otis and Cohen, Lester H., *History of the Rise, Progress and Termination of the American Revolution: interspersed with Biographical, Political and Moral Observations*, p. 167
8. Jefferson, Thomas to Henry Lee, 8 May 1825, *Founders Online*, founders. archives.gov/documents/Jefferson/98-01-02-5212.

Chapter 2: Martha Dandridge Custis Washington

1. Brady, Patricia, *Martha Washington: An American Life*, p. 32
2. Fields, Joseph E., *Worthy Partner: The Papers of Martha Washington*
3. Kerber, Linda K., *Women of the Republic: Intellect and Ideology in Revolutionary America*, p. 193
4. Ibid, pp. 199–200
5. Brady, Patricia, *Martha Washington: An American Life*, p. 171
6. Ibid, p. 55
7. Chernow, Ron, *Washington: A Life*, p. 23
8. Brady, Patricia, *Martha Washington: An American Life*, p. 61
9. *George Washington's Mount Vernon* Replica of Martha Washington's Wedding Dress display
10. Ibid, mountvernon.org/library/digitalhistory/digital-encyclopedia/article/growth-of-mount-vernon
11. Ibid, mountvernon.org/the-estate-gardens/the-mansion/expansion-of-mount-vernons-mansion
12. Chernow, Ron, *Washington: A Life*, p. 56

13. Ibid, p. 6
14. Brady, Patricia, *Martha Washington: An American Life*, p. 75
15. *George Washington's Mount Vernon*, mountvernon.org/library/digitalhistory/digital-encyclopedia/article/growth-of-mount-vernon
16. Fields, Joseph E., *Worthy Partner: The Papers of Martha Washington*, pp. 152–3
17. Brady, Patricia, *Martha Washington: An American Life*, p. 88
18. *George Washington's Mount Vernon*, Mansion Tour
19. Ibid, mountvernon.org/video/view/351/
20. Ibid, mountvernon.org/the-estate-gardens/the-mansion/expansion-of-mount-vernons-mansion/
21. Brady, Patricia, *Martha Washington: An American Life*, pp. 89–92
22. *George Washington's Mount Vernon*, mountvernon.org/the-estate-gardens/location/spinning-house/
23. Chernow, Ron, *Washington: A Life*, p. 217
24. Fields, Joseph E., *Worthy Partner: The Papers of Martha Washington*, p. 164
25. Chernow, Ron, *Washington: A Life*, p. 230
26. Brady, Patricia, *Martha Washington: An American Life*, p. 111
27. Oberg, Barbara B., *Women in the American Revolution: Gender, Politics, and the Domestic World*, p. 135
28. Brady, Patricia, *Martha Washington: An American Life*, p. 112
29. Chernow, Ron, *Washington: A Life*, p. 285
30. Brady, Patricia, *Martha Washington: An American Life*, p. 115
31. Fields, Joseph E., *Worthy Partner: The Papers of Martha Washington*, p. 175–6
32. Chernow, Ron, *Washington: A Life*, p. 323
33. Brady, Patricia, *Martha Washington: An American Life*, p. 120
34. Chernow, Ron, *Washington: A Life*, p. 331
35. Oberg, Barbara B., *Women in the American Revolution: Gender, Politics, and the Domestic World*, p. 133
36. Ibid, p. 139
37. Kerber, Linda K., *Women of the Republic: Intellect and Ideology in Revolutionary America*, p. 102–3
38. Fields, Joseph E., *Worthy Partner: The Papers of Martha Washington*, p. 187
39. Brady, Patricia, *Martha Washington: An American Life*, p. 143
40. *George Washington's Mount Vernon*, mountvernon.org/the-estate-gardens/the-mansion/expansion-of-mount-vernons-mansion/
41. Fields, Joseph E., *Worthy Partner: The Papers of Martha Washington*, p. 193
42. Brady, Patricia, *Martha Washington: An American Life*, p. 148
43. Ibid, p. 150
44. Fields, Joseph E., *Worthy Partner: The Papers of Martha Washington*, p. 206
45. Ibid, p. 213
46. Ibid, p. 215
47. Ibid, p. 217
48. Ibid, p. 220
49. Ibid, p. 224
50. Brady, Patricia, *Martha Washington: An American Life*, p. 165
51. Ibid, p. 167

52. Ibid, p. 176
53. Chernow, Ron, *Washington: A Life*, p. 626
54. Fields, Joseph E., *Worthy Partner: The Papers of Martha Washington*, p. 226
55. Chernow, Ron, *Washington: A Life*, p. 678
56. Brady, Patricia, *Martha Washington: An American Life*, p. 199
57. Fields, Joseph E., *Worthy Partner: The Papers of Martha Washington*, p. 267
58. Ibid, p. 270
59. Brady, Patricia, *Martha Washington: An American Life*, p. 207
60. Chernow, Ron, *Washington: A Life*, p. 795
61. Ibid, p. 809
62. *George Washington's Mount Vernon*, Mansion Tour
63. Ibid.
64. Brady, Patricia, *Martha Washington: An American Life*, p. 224
65. Ibid, p. 225
66. Chernow, Ron, *Washington: A Life*, p. 815
67. Ibid, p. 816

Chapter 3: Agent 355

1. Nagy, John A., *George Washington's Secret Spy War: The Making of America's First Spymaster*, p. 131
2. Rose, Alexander, *Washington's Spies: The Story of America's First Spy Ring*, p. 5
3. Ibid, p. 44
4. Daigler, Kenneth A., *Spies, Patriots, and Traitors: American Intelligence in the Revolutionary War*, p. 15
5. Rose, Alexander, *Washington's Spies: The Story of America's First Spy Ring*, p. 121
6. Ford, Corey, *A Peculiar Service: A Narrative of Espionage in and around New York during the American Revolution*, p. 206
7. Rose, Alexander, *Washington's Spies: The Story of America's First Spy Ring*, p. 173
8. Pennypacker, Morton, *General Washington's Spies on Long Island and in New York*, p. 33
9. Daigler, Kenneth A., *Spies, Patriots, and Traitors: American Intelligence in the Revolutionary War*, p. 189
10. Ibid, p. 56
11. Atkinson, Rick, *The British are Coming: The War for America, Lexington to Princeton, 1775–1777*, p. 115
12. Ronald, D.A.B., *The Life of John Andre: The Redcoat who Turned Benedict Arnold*, p. 163
13. Diamant, Lincoln, *Revolutionary Women in the War for American Independence: A One-Volume Revised Edition of Elizabeth Ellet's 1848 Landmark Series*
14. Norton, Mary Beth, *Liberty's Daughters: The Revolutionary Experience of American Women, 1750–1800*, p. 175
15. Jacob, Mark and Case, Stephen H., *Treacherous Beauty: Peggy Shippen, the Woman behind Benedict Arnold's Plot to Betray America*, p. 230
16. Ford, Corey, *A Peculiar Service: A Narrative of Espionage in and around New York during the American Revolution*, p. xi

17. Nagy, John A., *George Washington's Secret Spy War: The Making of America's First Spymaster*, p. 135

18. Pennypacker, Morton, *General Washington's Spies on Long Island and in New York*, p. 114

19. Ibid, p. 121

20. Ibid, p. 184

21. Rose, Alexander, *Washington's Spies: The Story of America's First Spy Ring*, p. 173

22. Bleyer, Bill, "George Washington's Culper Spy Ring: Separating Fact from Fiction," *Journal of the American Revolution*, allthingsliberty.com/2021/06/george-washingtons-culper-spy-ring-separating-fact-from-fiction

Chapter 4: Sybil Ludington

1. Berkin, Carol, *Revolutionary Mothers: Women in the Struggle for America's Independence*, p. 139

2. Rose, Alexander, *Washington's Spies: The Story of America's First Spy Ring*, pp. 204–5

3. Johnson, Willis Fletcher, *Colonel Henry Ludington*, p. 90

4. Hunt, Paula D., "Sybil Ludington, the Female Paul Revere: The Making of a Revolutionary War Heroine," *The New England Quarterly*, p. 199

5. Ibid, p. 188

6. Ibid, pp. 197–8

7. Ibid, p. 204

8. Ibid, p. 205

9. "Women on Stamps: Sybil Ludington," Smithsonian National Postal Museum, postalmuseum.si.edu/exhibition/women-on-stamps-part-1-forming-the-nation-revolutionary-fighters/sybil-ludington

10. Berkin, Carol, *Revolutionary Mothers: Women in the Struggle for America's Independence*, p. 137

11. Miller, Marla R., Betsy Ross and the Making of America, pp. 361–2

12. Berkin, Carol, *Revolutionary Mothers: Women in the Struggle for America's Independence*, p. 21

13. Ibid, p. 44

14. Ibid, p. 48

15. Ibid, p. 93

16. Ibid, p. 95

17. Ibid, pp. 144–6

18. Lossing, Benson J, *Life and Times of Philip Schuyler VII*, pp. 249–53

19. Warren, Mercy Otis and Cohen, Lester H., *History of the Rise, Progress and Termination of the American Revolution: interspersed with Biographical, Political and Moral Observations*, p. 236

20. Berkin, Carol, *Revolutionary Mothers: Women in the Struggle for America's Independence*, p. 126

Chapter 5 – Mercy Otis Warren

1. Stuart, Nancy Rubin, *The Muse of the Revolution: The Secret Pen of Mercy Otis Warren and the Founding of a Nation*, p. 5

2. Warren, Mercy Otis and Cohen, Lester H., *History of the Rise, Progress and Termination of the American Revolution: interspersed with Biographical, Political and Moral Observations*, p. 29
3. Ibid, p. 28
4. Ibid, p. 32
5. Ibid, p. xvii
6. Stuart, Nancy Rubin, *The Muse of the Revolution: The Secret Pen of Mercy Otis Warren and the Founding of a Nation*, p. 33
7. Warren, Mercy Otis and Cohen, Lester H., *History of the Rise, Progress and Termination of the American Revolution: interspersed with Biographical, Political and Moral Observations*, p. 14
8. Ibid, p. 18
9. Ibid, p. 38
10. Stuart, Nancy Rubin, *The Muse of the Revolution: The Secret Pen of Mercy Otis Warren and the Founding of a Nation*, p. 41
11. Warren, Mercy Otis and Cohen, Lester H., *History of the Rise, Progress and Termination of the American Revolution: interspersed with Biographical, Political and Moral Observations*, p. 49
12. Stuart, Nancy Rubin, *The Muse of the Revolution: The Secret Pen of Mercy Otis Warren and the Founding of a Nation*, p. 43
13. Ibid, p. 47
14. Davies, Kate, *Catherine Macaulay and Mercy Otis Warren: The Revolutionary Atlantic and the Politics of Gender*, p. 133
15. Ibid, p. 134
16. Ibid, p. 135
17. Ibid, p. 139
18. Stuart, Nancy Rubin, *The Muse of the Revolution: The Secret Pen of Mercy Otis Warren and the Founding of a Nation*, p. 49
19. Ibid, p. 56
20. Mercy Otis Warren to Abigail Adams, 9 August 1774, *Founders Online*, founders.archives.gov/documents/Adams/04-01-02-0091
21. Davies, Kate, *Catherine Macaulay and Mercy Otis Warren: The Revolutionary Atlantic and the Politics of Gender*, p. 201
22. Warren, Mercy Otis and Cohen, Lester H., *History of the Rise, Progress and Termination of the American Revolution: interspersed with Biographical, Political and Moral Observations*
23. Mercy Otis Warren to Abigail Adams, 9 August 1774, *Founders Online*, founders.archives.gov/documents/Adams/04-01-02-0091
24. Stuart, Nancy Rubin, *The Muse of the Revolution: The Secret Pen of Mercy Otis Warren and the Founding of a Nation*, p. 65
25. Ibid, p. 73
26. Warren, Mercy Otis and Cohen, Lester H., *History of the Rise, Progress and Termination of the American Revolution: interspersed with Biographical, Political and Moral Observations*
27. Stuart, Nancy Rubin, *The Muse of the Revolution: The Secret Pen of Mercy Otis Warren and the Founding of a Nation*, p. 74

28. Ibid, p. 85
29. John Adams to Abigail Adams, 27 May 1776. *Founders Online*, founders. archives.gov/documents/Adams/04-01-02-0270
30. Stuart, Nancy Rubin, *The Muse of the Revolution: The Secret Pen of Mercy Otis Warren and the Founding of a Nation*, p. 112
31. James Warren to John Adams, 17 July 1776, *Founders Online*, founders.archives. gov/documents/Adams/06-04-02-0169
32. Stuart, Nancy Rubin, *The Muse of the Revolution: The Secret Pen of Mercy Otis Warren and the Founding of a Nation*, p. 125
33. Mercy Otis Warren to Abigail Adams, 19 January 1779, *Founders Online*, founders.archives.gov/documents/Adams/04-03-02-0124
34. Mercy Otis Warren to Abigail Adams, 15 March 1779, *Founders Online*, founders.archives.gov/documents/Adams/04-03-02-0150
35. Stuart, Nancy Rubin, *The Muse of the Revolution: The Secret Pen of Mercy Otis Warren and the Founding of a Nation*, p. 149
36. Warren, Mercy Otis and Cohen, Lester H., *History of the Rise, Progress and Termination of the American Revolution: interspersed with Biographical, Political and Moral Observations*, p. 45
37. Stuart, Nancy Rubin, *The Muse of the Revolution: The Secret Pen of Mercy Otis Warren and the Founding of a Nation*, p. 155
38. Massachusetts Historical Society, http://www.masshist.org/beehiveblog/2021/04/patriotic-fervor-or-a-quiet-life-the-siblings-of-the-otis-family-of-massachusetts/
39. Warren, Mercy Otis and Cohen, Lester H., *History of the Rise, Progress and Termination of the American Revolution: interspersed with Biographical, Political and Moral Observations*, p. 51
40. Ibid, p. 50
41. Davies, Kate, *Catherine Macaulay and Mercy Otis Warren: The Revolutionary Atlantic and the Politics of Gender*, p. 223
42. Ibid, p. 238
43. Stuart, Nancy Rubin, *The Muse of the Revolution: The Secret Pen of Mercy Otis Warren and the Founding of a Nation*, p. 181
44. Ibid, p. 184
45. Warren, Mercy Otis and Cohen, Lester H., *History of the Rise, Progress and Termination of the American Revolution: interspersed with Biographical, Political and Moral Observations*
46. Stuart, Nancy Rubin, *The Muse of the Revolution: The Secret Pen of Mercy Otis Warren and the Founding of a Nation*, p. 221
47. Warren, Mercy Otis and Cohen, Lester H., *History of the Rise, Progress and Termination of the American Revolution: interspersed with Biographical, Political and Moral Observations*, p. 284
48. Stuart, Nancy Rubin, *The Muse of the Revolution: The Secret Pen of Mercy Otis Warren and the Founding of a Nation*, p. 222
49. Ibid, p. 224
50. Withey, Lynne, *Dearest Friend: A Life of Abigail Adams*, p. 303
51. Mercy Otis Warren to Abigail Adams, 27 February 1797, *Founders Online*, founders.archives.gov/documents/Adams/04-11-02-0302

52. Stuart, Nancy Rubin, *The Muse of the Revolution: The Secret Pen of Mercy Otis Warren and the Founding of a Nation*, p. 238
53. Ibid, p. 240
54. Ibid, p. 245
55. Warren, Mercy Otis and Cohen, Lester H., *History of the Rise, Progress and Termination of the American Revolution: interspersed with Biographical, Political and Moral Observations*, p. 4
56. Ibid, p. 5
57. Stuart, Nancy Rubin, *The Muse of the Revolution: The Secret Pen of Mercy Otis Warren and the Founding of a Nation*, p. 255
58. Ibid, p. 258
59. Ibid, p. 262
60. Ibid, p. 264

Chapter 6: Margaret Shippen Arnold

1. Jacob, Mark and Case, Stephen H., *Treacherous Beauty: Peggy Shippen, the Woman behind Benedict Arnold's Plot to Betray America*, pp. 15–6
2. Ibid, p. 22
3. Ronald, D.A.B., *The Life of John Andre: The Redcoat who Turned Benedict Arnold*, p. xx
4. Ibid, p. 146
5. Jacob, Mark and Case, Stephen H., *Treacherous Beauty: Peggy Shippen, the Woman behind Benedict Arnold's Plot to Betray America*, p. 41
6. Ibid, p. 45
7. Ibid, p. 48
8. Ronald, D.A.B., *The Life of John Andre: The Redcoat who Turned Benedict Arnold*, p. 192
9. Ibid, p. 187
10. Daigler, Kenneth A., *Spies, Patriots, and Traitors: American Intelligence in the Revolutionary War*, p. 155
11. Jacob, Mark and Case, Stephen H., *Treacherous Beauty: Peggy Shippen, the Woman behind Benedict Arnold's Plot to Betray America*, p. 89
12. Daigler, Kenneth A., *Spies, Patriots, and Traitors: American Intelligence in the Revolutionary War*, pp. 155–6
13. Ibid, p. 157
14. Ronald, D.A.B., *The Life of John Andre: The Redcoat who Turned Benedict Arnold*, p. 193
15. Daigler, Kenneth A., *Spies, Patriots, and Traitors: American Intelligence in the Revolutionary War*, p. 159
16. Jacob, Mark and Case, Stephen H., *Treacherous Beauty: Peggy Shippen, the Woman behind Benedict Arnold's Plot to Betray America*, p. 108
17. Ibid, p. 126
18. Ibid, p. 90
19. Ronald, D.A.B., *The Life of John Andre: The Redcoat who Turned Benedict Arnold*, p. 195
20. Ibid, p. 197

21. Jacob, Mark and Case, Stephen H., *Treacherous Beauty: Peggy Shippen, the Woman behind Benedict Arnold's Plot to Betray America*, p. 92
22. Ronald, D.A.B., *The Life of John Andre: The Redcoat who Turned Benedict Arnold*, p. 198
23. Jacob, Mark and Case, Stephen H., *Treacherous Beauty: Peggy Shippen, the Woman behind Benedict Arnold's Plot to Betray America*, p. 124
24. Ibid, p. 127
25. Daigler, Kenneth A., *Spies, Patriots, and Traitors: American Intelligence in the Revolutionary War*, p. 163
26. Ronald, D.A.B., *The Life of John Andre: The Redcoat who Turned Benedict Arnold*, p. 208
27. Jacob, Mark and Case, Stephen H., *Treacherous Beauty: Peggy Shippen, the Woman behind Benedict Arnold's Plot to Betray America*, p. 135
28. Ibid, p. 138
29. Ibid, p. 140
30. Daigler, Kenneth A., *Spies, Patriots, and Traitors: American Intelligence in the Revolutionary War*, p. 165
31. Ronald, D.A.B., *The Life of John Andre: The Redcoat who Turned Benedict Arnold*, p. 227
32. Daigler, Kenneth A., *Spies, Patriots, and Traitors: American Intelligence in the Revolutionary War*, p. 153
33. Jacob, Mark and Case, Stephen H., *Treacherous Beauty: Peggy Shippen, the Woman behind Benedict Arnold's Plot to Betray America*, p. 157
34. Pennypacker, Morton, *General Washington's Spies on Long Island and in New York*, p. 125
35. Ronald, D.A.B., *The Life of John Andre: The Redcoat who Turned Benedict Arnold*, p. 241
36. Ibid, p. 242
37. Ibid, pp. 245–6
38. Ibid, p. 245
39. Jacob, Mark and Case, Stephen H., *Treacherous Beauty: Peggy Shippen, the Woman behind Benedict Arnold's Plot to Betray America*, p. 127
40. Ibid, p. 167
41. Ibid, p. 166
42. Humphreys, Mary Gay, *Catherine Schuyler: A Woman of the Revolution*, p. 184
43. Ronald, D.A.B., *The Life of John Andre: The Redcoat who Turned Benedict Arnold*, p. 246
44. Jacob, Mark and Case, Stephen H., *Treacherous Beauty: Peggy Shippen, the Woman behind Benedict Arnold's Plot to Betray America*, p. 168
45. Ibid, p. 180
46. Ibid, pp. 170–1
47. Ronald, D.A.B., *The Life of John Andre: The Redcoat who Turned Benedict Arnold*, p. 248
48. Jacob, Mark and Case, Stephen H., *Treacherous Beauty: Peggy Shippen, the Woman behind Benedict Arnold's Plot to Betray America*, p. 173
49. Ibid, p. 175

50. Ibid, pp. 190–1
51. Ibid, p. 192
52. Ibid, p. 195
53. Ronald, D.A.B., *The Life of John Andre: The Redcoat who Turned Benedict Arnold*, p. 249
54. Jacob, Mark and Case, Stephen H., *Treacherous Beauty: Peggy Shippen, the Woman behind Benedict Arnold's Plot to Betray America*, p. 196
55. Ibid, p. 197
56. Ibid, p. 202
57. Ibid, p. 203
58. Ibid, p. 205
59. Ibid, p. 207
60. Ibid, p. 218
61. Arnold, M., and Joyce D. Goodfriend. "Notes and Documents: The Widowhood of Margaret Shippen Arnold: Letters from England, 1801–1803." *The Pennsylvania Magazine of History and Biography*, vol. 115, no. 2, 1991, jstor.org/stable/20092605. p. 225
62. Ibid, p. 239
63. Jacob, Mark and Case, Stephen H., *Treacherous Beauty: Peggy Shippen, the Woman behind Benedict Arnold's Plot to Betray America*, p. 14
64. Arnold, M., and Joyce D. Goodfriend. "Notes and Documents: The Widowhood of Margaret Shippen Arnold: Letters from England, 1801–1803." *The Pennsylvania Magazine of History and Biography*, vol. 115, no. 2, 1991, jstor.org/stable/20092605. p. 228
65. Ibid, p. 226
66. Ibid, p. 235
67. Ibid, p. 236
68. Ibid, pp. 246–7
69. Jacob, Mark and Case, Stephen H., *Treacherous Beauty: Peggy Shippen, the Woman behind Benedict Arnold's Plot to Betray America*, p. 228

Chapter 7: Deborah Sampson Gannett
1. Young, Alfred F, Masquerade: The Life and Times of Deborah Sampson, Continental Soldier, p. 30
2. Ibid, p. 4
3. Kravits, Bennett, "A Certain Doubt: The Lost Voice of Deborah Samson in Revolutionary America," *Studies in Popular Culture*, vol 22, no 2 (October 1999), jstor.org/stable/41970372. p. 52
4. Young, Alfred F, Masquerade: The Life and Times of Deborah Sampson, Continental Soldier, p. 35
5. Ibid, p. 41
6. De Pauw, Linda Grant. "Women in Combat: The Revolutionary War Experience," *Armed Forces & Society*, vol 7, no 2, 1981, jstor.org/stable/45346224, p. 210
7. Young, Alfred F, Masquerade: The Life and Times of Deborah Sampson, Continental Soldier, p. 75

8. Ibid, p. 86
9. Ibid, p. 102
10. De Pauw, Linda Grant. "Women in Combat: The Revolutionary War Experience," *Armed Forces & Society*, vol 7, no 2, 1981, jstor.org/stable/45346224, p. 215
11. Ibid, p. 216
12. Young, Alfred F, Masquerade: The Life and Times of Deborah Sampson, Continental Soldier, p. 127
13. Ibid, p. 138
14. Ibid, p. 146
15. Ibid, p. 150
16. Ibid, p. 155
17. Diamant, Lincoln, *Revolutionary Women in the War for American Independence: A One-Volume Revised Edition of Elizabeth Ellet's 1848 Landmark Series*, p. 66
18. Ibid
19. Ibid, p. 69
20. Ibid, p. 174–5
21. Hiltner, Judith. "'She Bled in Secret': Deborah Sampson, Herman Mann and 'The Female Review.'" *Early American Literature*, vol 34, no 2, 1999, jstor.org/stable/25057161. p. 199
22. De Pauw, Linda Grant. "Women in Combat: The Revolutionary War Experience," *Armed Forces & Society*, vol 7, no 2, 1981, jstor.org/stable/45346224, p. 218
23. Young, Alfred F, Masquerade: The Life and Times of Deborah Sampson, Continental Soldier, p. 155
24. Ibid. p, 171
25. Ibid, p. 183
26. Ibid, p. 181
27. Ibid, p. 185
28. Gannett, Deborah Sampson, *Diary of Deborah Sampson Gannett in 1802*, Sharon Public Library, 1901. archive.org/details/diaryofdeborahsa00gann/mode/2up
29. Young, Alfred F, Masquerade: The Life and Times of Deborah Sampson, Continental Soldier, p. 207
30. Revere, Paul to Eustice, William, 20 February 1804, Massachusetts Historical Society, masshist.org/database/viewer.php?item_id=326&img_step=1&mode=transcript#page1
31. Young, Alfred F, Masquerade: The Life and Times of Deborah Sampson, Continental Soldier, pp. 228–9
32. De Pauw, Linda Grant. "Women in Combat: The Revolutionary War Experience," *Armed Forces & Society*, vol 7, no 2, 1981, jstor.org/stable/45346224, p. 219
33. Young, Alfred F, Masquerade: The Life and Times of Deborah Sampson, Continental Soldier, p. 265

Chapter 8: Abigail Smith Adams

1. Gelles, Edith B, *Portia: The World of Abigail Adams*, p. xvii
2. Ibid, p. 26

3. Withey, Lynne, *Dearest Friend: A Life of Abigail Adams*, p. 234
4. Abigail Adams to John Adams, 31 March 1776, *Founders Online*, founders. archives.gov/documents/Adams/04-01-02-0241
5. Gelles, Edith B, *Portia: The World of Abigail Adams*, p. 173
6. Withey, Lynne, *Dearest Friend: A Life of Abigail Adams*, pp. 13–4
7. Ibid, p. 21
8. Abigail Adams to Mary Smith Cranch, 15 July 1766, *Founders Online*, founders. archives.gov/documents/Adams/04-01-02-0043
9. Withey, Lynne, *Dearest Friend: A Life of Abigail Adams*, p. 27
10. Abigail Adams to Mary Smith Cranch, 13 October 1766, *Founders Online*, founders.archives.gov/documents/Adams/04-01-02-0045
11. Withey, Lynne, *Dearest Friend: A Life of Abigail Adams*, p. 29
12. Ibid, p. 32
13. Ibid, p. 37
14. John Adams Diary, 1770, *Founders Online*, founders.archives.gov/documents/ Adams/01-03-02-0016-0016
15. John Adams Diary 17, 16 April - 14 June 1771. *Adams Family Papers: An Electronic Archive*. Massachusetts Historical Society. http://www.masshist.org/ digitaladams/
16. Abigail Adams to Mercy Otis Warren, 5 December 1773, *Founders Online*, founders.archives.gov/documents/Adams/04-01-02-0065
17. Abigail Adams to John Adams, 19 August 1774, *Founders Online*, founders. archives.gov/documents/Adams/04-01-02-0093
18. Withey, Lynne, *Dearest Friend: A Life of Abigail Adams*, p. 61
19. Abigail Adams to John Adams, 14 September 1774, *Founders Online*, founders. archives.gov/documents/Adams/04-01-02-0099
20. Abigail Adams to John Adams, 16 October 1774, *Founders Online*, founders. archives.gov/documents/Adams/04-01-02-0116
21. Withey, Lynne, *Dearest Friend: A Life of Abigail Adams*, p. 65
22. John Adams to Abigail Adams, 2 May 1775, *Founders Online*, founders. archives.gov/documents/Adams/04-01-02-0128
23. Abigail Adams to John Adams, 18 June 1775, *Founders Online*, founders. archives.gov/documents/Adams/04-01-02-0150
24. Withey, Lynne, *Dearest Friend: A Life of Abigail Adams*, p. 67
25. Ibid, p. 68
26. Abigail Adams to Mercy Otis Warren, 27 August 1775, *Founders Online*, founders.archives.gov/documents/Adams/04-01-02-0178
27. Abigail Adams to John Adams, 1 October 1775, *Founders Online*, founders. archives.gov/documents/Adams/04-01-02-0189
28. Abigail Adams to John Adams, 12 November 1775, *Founders Online*, founders. archives.gov/documents/Adams/04-01-02-0214
29. Paine, Thomas, *Common Sense*, 1776, Project Guttenberg, gutenberg.org/ ebooks/147, p. 20
30. Withey, Lynne, *Dearest Friend: A Life of Abigail Adams*, p. 77
31. Abigail Adams to John Adams, 31 March 1776, *Founders Online*, founders. archives.gov/documents/Adams/04-01-02-0241

32. Ibid
33. Ibid
34. Abigail Adams to John Adams, 22 September 1774, *Founders Online,* founders. archives.gov/documents/Adams/04-01-02-0107
35. Withey, Lynne, *Dearest Friend: A Life of Abigail Adams,* p. 83
36. Abigail Adams to John Adams, 21 July 1776, *Founders Online,* founders. archives.gov/documents/Adams/04-02-02-0033
37. Withey, Lynne, *Dearest Friend: A Life of Abigail Adams,* p. 84
38. Ibid, p. 91
39. Abigail Adams to John Adams, 10 July 1777, *Founders Online,* founders. archives.gov/documents/Adams/04-02-02-0221
40. Abigail Adams to John Adams, 25 October 1777, *Founders Online,* founders. archives.gov/documents/Adams/04-02-02-0287
41. Withey, Lynne, *Dearest Friend: A Life of Abigail Adams,* p. 95
42. Abigail Adams to John Thaxter, 15 February 1778, *Founders Online,* founders. archives.gov/documents/Adams/04-02-02-0312
43. Abigail Adams to John Quincy Adams, 10 June 1778, *Founders Online,* founders.archives.gov/documents/Adams/04-03-02-0034
44. Abigail Adams to John Thaxter, 2 September 1778, *Founders Online,* founders. archives.gov/documents/Adams/04-03-02-0071
45. Gelles, Edith B, *Portia: The World of Abigail Adams,* p. 63
46. Ibid, p. 60
47. James Lovell to Abigail Adams, 13 January 1780, *Founders Online,* founders. archives.gov/documents/Adams/04-03-02-0200
48. Gelles, Edith B, *Portia: The World of Abigail Adams,* pp. 64–5
49. Withey, Lynne, *Dearest Friend: A Life of Abigail Adams,* p. 117
50. Gelles, Edith B, *Portia: The World of Abigail Adams,* p. 107
51. Ibid, p. 114
52. Withey, Lynne, *Dearest Friend: A Life of Abigail Adams,* pp. 129–30
53. Ibid, p. 135
54. John Adams to Abigail Adams, 14 May 1782, *Founders Online,* founders. archives.gov/documents/Adams/04-04-02-0216
55. Gelles, Edith B, *Portia: The World of Abigail Adams,* p. 74
56. Withey, Lynne, *Dearest Friend: A Life of Abigail Adams,* p. 151
57. Gelles, Edith B, *Portia: The World of Abigail Adams,* p. 117
58. Withey, Lynne, *Dearest Friend: A Life of Abigail Adams,* pp. 152–3
59. Ibid, pp. 155–6
60. Ibid, p. 158
61. Ibid, p. 159
62. Abigail Adams to Mary Smith Cranch, 9 December 1984, *Founders Online,* founders.archives.gov/documents/Adams/04-06-02-0006
63. Withey, Lynne, *Dearest Friend: A Life of Abigail Adams,* pp. 162–3
64. Ibid, pp. 172–3
65. Ibid, p. 180
66. Gelles, Edith B, *Portia: The World of Abigail Adams,* p. 85
67. Withey, Lynne, *Dearest Friend: A Life of Abigail Adams,* p. 186

68. Ibid, p. 196
69. Ibid, p. 197
70. Ibid, p. 198
71. Abigail Adams to Elizabeth Smith Shaw, 12 October 1787, *Founders Online*, founders.archives.gov/documents/Adams/04-08-02-0081
72. Abrams, Jeanne E., *First Ladies of the Republic*, p. 94
73. Withey, Lynne, *Dearest Friend: A Life of Abigail Adams*, p. 218
74. Ibid, p. 230
75. Ibid, p. 232
76. Ibid, p. 246
77. Abrams, Jeanne E., *First Ladies of the Republic*, p. 170
78. Withey, Lynne, *Dearest Friend: A Life of Abigail Adams*, p. 248
79. Ibid, pp. 259–60
80. Gelles, Edith B, *Portia: The World of Abigail Adams*, p. 154
81. Abigail Adams to Mary Smith Cranch, 8 December 1800, *Founders Online*, founders.archives.gov/documents/Adams/99-03-02-0807
82. Abrams, Jeanne E., *First Ladies of the Republic*, p. 5
83. Ibid, p. 191
84. Withey, Lynne, *Dearest Friend: A Life of Abigail Adams*, p. 291
85. Ibid, p. 304
86. Abrams, Jeanne E., *First Ladies of the Republic*, p. 139
87. Gelles, Edith B, *Portia: The World of Abigail Adams*, p. 163
88. Ibid, p. 150
89. Ibid, p. 168
90. Ibid, p. 171
91. Withey, Lynne, *Dearest Friend: A Life of Abigail Adams*, p. 308
92. Ibid, p. 311
93. Ibid, p. 315

Chapter 9: Elizabeth Schuyler Hamilton
1. Humphreys, Mary Gay, *Catherine Schuyler: A Woman of the Revolution*, p. 52
2. Ibid, p. 5
3. Lossing, Benson J, *Life and Times of Philip Schuyler VII*, p. 41
4. Humphreys, Mary Gay, *Catherine Schuyler: A Woman of the Revolution*, p. 154
5. Ibid, p. 179
6. Lossing, Benson J, *Life and Times of Philip Schuyler VII*, pp. 383–4
7. Chernow, Ron, *Alexander Hamilton*, p. 131
8. Ibid, p. 103
9. Humphreys, Mary Gay, *Catherine Schuyler: A Woman of the Revolution*, p. 172
10. Chernow, Ron, *Alexander Hamilton*, p. 132
11. Lossing, Benson J, *Life and Times of Philip Schuyler VII*, p. 404
12. Humphreys, Mary Gay, *Catherine Schuyler: A Woman of the Revolution*, pp. 180–1
13. Chernow, Ron, *Alexander Hamilton*, p. 131
14. Lossing, Benson J, *Life and Times of Philip Schuyler VII*, p. 432
15. Chernow, Ron, *Alexander Hamilton*, p. 138

16. Ibid, p. 140
17. Ibid, p. 150
18. Humphreys, Mary Gay, *Catherine Schuyler: A Woman of the Revolution*, p. 197
19. Chernow, Ron, *Alexander Hamilton*, p. 160
20. Lossing, Benson J, *Life and Times of Philip Schuyler VII*, pp. 419–20
21. Ibid, p. 422
22. Chernow, Ron, *Alexander Hamilton*, p. 164
23. Ibid, p. 185
24. Ibid, p. 203
25. Hamilton, James A., *Reminiscences of James A Hamilton*, p. 65
26. Chernow, Ron, *Alexander Hamilton*, p. 205
27. Ibid, p. 215
28. Humphreys, Mary Gay, *Catherine Schuyler: A Woman of the Revolution*, pp. 221–2
29. Elizabeth Hamilton to Angelica Church, 8 November 1789, *Founders Online*, founders.archives.gov/documents/Hamilton/01-05-02-0297-0002
30. Chernow, Ron, *Alexander Hamilton*, p. 287
31. Ibid, p. 320
32. Ibid, p. 335
33. Lossing, Benson J, *Life and Times of Philip Schuyler VII*, p. 452
34. Chernow, Ron, *Alexander Hamilton*, p. 336
35. Alexander Hamilton to Elizabeth Hamilton, 9 August 1791, *Founders Online*, founders.archives.gov/documents/Hamilton/01-09-02-0021
36. Chernow, Ron, *Alexander Hamilton*, p. 414
37. Ibid, p. 416
38. Hamilton, James A., *Reminiscences of James A Hamilton*, p. 1
39. Chernow, Ron, *Alexander Hamilton*, p. 450
40. Ibid, p. 478
41. Humphreys, Mary Gay, *Catherine Schuyler: A Woman of the Revolution*, p. 232
42. Hamilton, James A., *Reminiscences of James A Hamilton*, p. 3
43. Ibid, p. 4
44. Chernow, Ron, *Alexander Hamilton*, p. 502
45. Ibid, p. 508
46. Ibid, p. 509
47. John Adams to Benjamin Rush, September 1807, *Founders Online*, founders. archives.gov/documents/Adams/99-02-02-5212
48. Chernow, Ron, *Alexander Hamilton*, p. 534
49. "Reynolds Pamphlet", *Founders Online*, founders.archives.gov/documents/ Hamilton/01-21-02-0138-0002
50. Mazzeo, Tilar J., *Eliza Hamilton: The Extraordinary Life and Times of the Wife of Alexander Hamilton*
51. Alexander Hamilton to Elizabeth Hamilton, 21 August 1791, *Founders Online*, founders.archives.gov/documents/Hamilton/01-09-02-0069
52. Chernow, Ron, *Alexander Hamilton*, p. 535
53. George Washington to Alexander Hamilton, 21 August 1797, *Founders Online*, founders.archives.gov/documents/Hamilton/01-21-02-0137
54. Lossing, Benson J, *Life and Times of Philip Schuyler VII*, pp. 460–1

55. Chernow, Ron, *Alexander Hamilton*, p. 529
56. Ibid, p. 544
57. Humphreys, Mary Gay, *Catherine Schuyler: A Woman of the Revolution*, p. 229
58. Boylan, Anne M., *The Origins of Women's Activism: New York and Boston, 1797–1840*, p. 48
59. Alexander Hamilton to Richard Peters, 29 December 1802, *Founders Online*, founders.archives.gov/documents/Hamilton/01-26-02-0001-0055
60. Alexander Hamilton to Elizabeth Hamilton, 25 February 1801, *Founders Online*, founders.archives.gov/documents/Hamilton/01-25-02-0187
61. Alexander Hamilton to Elizabeth Hamilton, 9 March 1801, *Founders Online*, founders.archives.gov/documents/Hamilton/01-25-02-0192
62. Alexander Hamilton to Elizabeth Hamilton, 16 March 1801, *Founders Online*, founders.archives.gov/documents/Hamilton/01-25-02-0195
63. Chernow, Ron, *Alexander Hamilton*, p. 651
64. Ibid, p. 655
65. Lossing, Benson J, *Life and Times of Philip Schuyler VII*, p. 472
66. Sedgwick, John, *War of Two: Alexander Hamilton, Aaron Burr, and the Duel that Stunned the Nation*
67. "Statement on Impending Duel with Aaron Burr, 28 June–10 July 1804," *Founders Online*, founders.archives.gov/documents/Hamilton/01-26-02-0001-0241
68. Chernow, Ron, *Alexander Hamilton*, p. 706
69. Ibid, p. 708
70. Ibid, p. 709
71. Lossing, Benson J, *Life and Times of Philip Schuyler VII*, p. 474
72. Chernow, Ron, *Alexander Hamilton*, p. 724
73. Ibid, p. 3
74. Ibid, p. 725
75. Boylan, Anne M., *The Origins of Women's Activism: New York and Boston, 1797–1840*, p. 104
76. Ibid, p. 48
77. Ibid, p. 148
78. Hamilton, James A., *Reminiscences of James A Hamilton*, p. 65
79. Ibid, p. 66
80. Chernow, Ron, *Alexander Hamilton*, p. 725
81. Ibid, p. 726
82. "Eliza Hamilton's Legacy: An Uptown Library," myinwood.net/eliza-hamiltons-legacy-an-uptown-library
83. Hamilton, James A., *Reminiscences of James A Hamilton*, p. 55
84. Ibid, p. 65
85. Ibid, p. 64
86. The Hamilton-Holly House, Landmarks Preservation Commission October 19, 2004, Designation List 357 LP-2157, media.villagepreservation.org/wp-content/uploads/2020/03/15122925/Hamilton-Holly-House-NYC-LPC-Designation-Report.pdf
87. "The Residence on H Street N.W.: Mrs. General Hamilton" tudorplace.org/wp-content/uploads/2020/08/HStreet-NW-11.28.2018-jw_edited.pdf

88. Fremont, Jessie Benton, *Souvenirs of my Time*
89. Mazzeo, Tilar J., "Eliza Hamilton's Excellent Five-Month Steamboat Ride from New York to Wisconsin," whatitmeanstobeamerican.org/identities/eliza-hamiltons-excellent-five-month-steamboat-ride-from-new-york-to-wisconsin/
90. Gara, Lary, "William S. Hamilton on the Wisconsin Frontier," Wisconsin Historical Society, content.wisconsinhistory.org/digital/collection/wmh/id/26008
91. "The Residence on H Street N.W.: Mrs. General Hamilton" tudorplace.org/wp-content/uploads/2020/08/HStreet-NW-11.28.2018-jw_edited.pdf
92. Chernow, Ron, *Alexander Hamilton*, p. 2
93. Fremont, Jessie Benton, *Souvenirs of my Time*
94. Hamilton, James A., *Reminiscences of James A Hamilton*, p. 65

Chapter 10 – Dolley Payne Todd Madison
1. Côté, Richard N., *Strength and Honor: The Life of Dolley Madison*, p. 34
2. Ibid, p. 40
3. Henry, Patrick, "Give Me Liberty or Give Me Death," 1775, Yale Law School Avalon Project, avalon.law.yale.edu/18th_century/patrick.asp
4. Côté, Richard N., *Strength and Honor: The Life of Dolley Madison*, p. 48
5. Allgor, Catherine, *The Queen of America: Mary Cutts Life of Dolley Madison*, p. 46
6. Côté, Richard N., *Strength and Honor: The Life of Dolley Madison*, p. 20
7. Allgor, Catherine, *A Perfect Union: Dolley Madison and the Creation of the American Nation*, p. 19
8. Ibid, pp. 21–2
9. Côté, Richard N., *Strength and Honor: The Life of Dolley Madison*, p. 100
10. Ibid, p. 106
11. Allgor, Catherine, *The Queen of America: Mary Cutts Life of Dolley Madison*, p. 95, 206
12. Allgor, Catherine, *The Queen of America: Mary Cutts Life of Dolley Madison*, p. 95
13. Abrams, Jeanne E., *First Ladies of the Republic*, p. 207
14. Allgor, Catherine, *A Perfect Union: Dolley Madison and the Creation of the American Nation*, p. 38
15. *James Madison's Montpelier*, Mansion Tour, 2021
16. Chadwick, Bruce, *James & Dolley Madison: America's First Power Couple*, p. 51
17. Allgor, Catherine, *A Perfect Union: Dolley Madison and the Creation of the American Nation*, p. 43
18. Côté, Richard N., *Strength and Honor: The Life of Dolley Madison*, p. 201
19. Allgor, Catherine, *A Perfect Union: Dolley Madison and the Creation of the American Nation*, p. 76
20. Côté, Richard N., *Strength and Honor: The Life of Dolley Madison*, p. 207
21. Ibid, p. 209
22. Chadwick, Bruce, *James & Dolley Madison: America's First Power Couple*, p. 73
23. Côté, Richard N., *Strength and Honor: The Life of Dolley Madison*, p. 219
24. Ibid
25. Ibid, p. 234

26. Dolley Payne Todd Madison to Anna Payne Cutts, 29 July 1805, *Dolley Madison Digital Edition*, Holly C. Shulman. rotunda.upress.virginia.edu/dmde/DPM0094
27. DPTM to James Madison, 23 October 1805, *Dolley Madison Digital Edition*, Holly C. Shulman. rotunda.upress.virginia.edu/dmde/DPM0110
28. James Madison to DPTM, 28 October 1805, *Dolley Madison Digital Edition*, Holly C. Shulman. rotunda.upress.virginia.edu/dmde/DPM0112
29. DPTM to Elizabeth Collins Lee, 26 February 1808, *Dolley Madison Digital Edition*, Holly C. Shulman. rotunda.upress.virginia.edu/dmde/DPM0165
30. Allgor, Catherine, *A Perfect Union: Dolley Madison and the Creation of the American Nation*, p. 137
31. Elizabeth Collins Lee to DPTM, 2 March 1809, in *The Dolley Madison Digital Edition*, Holly C. Shulman. rotunda.upress.virginia.edu/dmde/DPM0189
32. Côté, Richard N., *Strength and Honor: The Life of Dolley Madison*, p. 255
33. Allgor, Catherine, *A Perfect Union: Dolley Madison and the Creation of the American Nation*, p. 157
34. Ibid, p. 174
35. Ibid, p. 171
36. Côté, Richard N., *Strength and Honor: The Life of Dolley Madison*, p. 192
37. Allgor, Catherine, *A Perfect Union: Dolley Madison and the Creation of the American Nation*, p. 207
38. Ibid, p. 188
39. Côté, Richard N., *Strength and Honor: The Life of Dolley Madison*, p. 327
40. Howard, Hugh, *Mr and Mrs Madison's War: America's First Couple and the Second War of Independence*, p. 6
41. "Annual Message to Congress, 4 November 1812," *Founders Online*, founders.archives.gov/documents/Madison/03-05-02-0334
42. Howard, Hugh, *Mr and Mrs Madison's War: America's First Couple and the Second War of Independence*, p. 63
43. DPTM to Hannah Nicholson Gallatin, 29 July 1813, *Dolley Madison Digital Edition*, Holly C. Shulman. rotunda.upress.virginia.edu/dmde/DPM0404
44. *Founders Online*, founders.archives.gov/documents/Madison/03-06-02-0409
45. DPTM to Lucy Payne Washington Todd, 23 August 1814, *Dolley Madison Digital Edition*, Holly C. Shulman rotunda.upress.virginia.edu/dmde/DPM0469
46. Abrams, Jeanne E., *First Ladies of the Republic*, p. 241
47. Côté, Richard N., *Strength and Honor: The Life of Dolley Madison*, p. 301
48. Jennings, Paul, *A Colored Man's Reminiscences of James Madison*
49. Côté, Richard N., *Strength and Honor: The Life of Dolley Madison*, p. 306
50. Allgor, Catherine, *A Perfect Union: Dolley Madison and the Creation of the American Nation*, p. 318
51. Thomas Jefferson to James Madison, 24 September 1814, *Founders Online*, founders.archives.gov/documents/Madison/03-08-02-0217
52. Côté, Richard N., *Strength and Honor: The Life of Dolley Madison*, p. 317
53. Abrams, Jeanne E., *First Ladies of the Republic*, p. 234
54. Elizabeth Collins Lee to DPTM, 4 March 1817, *Dolley Madison Digital Edition*, Holly C. Shulman. rotunda.upress.virginia.edu/dmde/DPM0562

55. John Adams to James Madison, 6 December 1816, *Founders Online*, founders. archives.gov/documents/Madison/99-01-02-5604

56. Côté, Richard N., *Strength and Honor: The Life of Dolley Madison*, p. 329

57. Allgor, Catherine, *A Perfect Union: Dolley Madison and the Creation of the American Nation*, p. 348

58. *James Madison's Montpelier*, Mansion Tour, 2021

59. Allgor, Catherine, *A Perfect Union: Dolley Madison and the Creation of the American Nation*, p. 366

60. Chadwick, Bruce, *James & Dolley Madison: America's First Power Couple*, p. 174

61. *James Madison's Montpelier*, Mansion Tour, 2021

62. Jennings, Paul, *A Colored Man's Reminiscences of James Madison*

63. DPTM to Richard Cutts, 5 July 1836, *Dolley Madison Digital Edition*, Holly C. Shulman. rotunda.upress.virginia.edu/dmde/DPM0879

64. Allgor, Catherine, *The Queen of America: Mary Cutts Life of Dolley Madison*, p. 56

65. Allgor, Catherine, *A Perfect Union: Dolley Madison and the Creation of the American Nation*, p. 380

66. Côté, Richard N., *Strength and Honor: The Life of Dolley Madison*, pp. 351–2

67. Jennings, Paul, *A Colored Man's Reminiscences of James Madison*

68. Allgor, Catherine, *A Perfect Union: Dolley Madison and the Creation of the American Nation*, p. 386

69. Allgor, Catherine, *The Queen of America: Mary Cutts Life of Dolley Madison*, p. 61

70. Ibid, p. 66

71. Jennings, Paul, *A Colored Man's Reminiscences of James Madison*

72. "Becoming America's First Lady," *James Madison's Montpelier*, montpelier.org/learn/dolley-madison-becoming-americas-first-lady

Chapter 11: Revolutionary Women

1. Warren, Mercy Otis, *Poems, Dramatic and Miscellaneous*

2. Abigail Adams to John Adams, 10 December 1775, *Founders Online*, founders. archives.gov/documents/Adams/04-01-02-0221

Bibliography

Abrams, Jeanne E., *First Ladies of the Republic*, (New York University Press, New York, 2018)

Abrams, Jeanne E., *A View from Abroad: The Story of John and Abigail Adams in Europe*, (New York University Press, New York, 2021)

Allgor, Catherine, *A Perfect Union: Dolley Madison and the Creation of the American Nation*, (Henry Holt and Company, New York, 2006)

Allgor, Catherine, *The Queen of America: Mary Cutt's Life of Dolley Madison*, (University of Virginia Press, Charlottesville, 2012)

Arnold, M., and Joyce D. Goodfriend. "Notes and Documents: The Widowhood of Margaret Shippen Arnold: Letters from England, 1801–1803." *The Pennsylvania Magazine of History and Biography*, vol. 115, no. 2, 1991, pp. 221–255. JSTOR, www.jstor.org/stable/20092605.

Atkinson, Rick, *The British are Coming: The War for America, Lexington to Princeton, 1775–1777*, (Henry Holt and Company, New York, 2019)

Berkin, Carol, *Revolutionary Mothers: Women in the Struggle for America's Independence*, (Vintage Books, New York, 2005)

Boylan, Anne M., *The Origins of Women's Activism: New York and Boston, 1797–1840*, (University of North Carolina Press, Chapel Hill, NC, 2002)

Brady, Patricia, *Martha Washington: An American Life*, (Penguin Group, New York, 2005)

Chernow, Ron, *Alexander Hamilton*, (Penguin, New York, 2004)

Chernow, Ron, *Washington: A Life*, (Penguin, New York, 2010)

Côté, Richard N., *Strength and Honor: The Life of Dolley Madison*, (Corinthian Books, Mount Pleasant, South Carolina, 2005)

Daigler, Kenneth A., *Spies, Patriots, and Traitors: American Intelligence in the Revolutionary War*, (Georgetown University Press, Washington DC, 2014)

Davies, Kate, *Catherine Macaulay and Mercy Otis Warren: The Revolutionary Atlantic and the Politics of Gender*, (Oxford University Press, Oxford, 2005)

Diamant, Lincoln, *Revolutionary Women in the War for American Independence: A One-Volume Revised Edition of Elizabeth Ellet's 1848 Landmark Series*, (Praeger, Westport, CT, 1998)

Dolley Madison Digital Edition, rotunda.upress.virginia.edu/dmde.

Fields, Joseph E., *Worthy Partner: The Papers of Martha Washington*, (Greenwood Press, Westport, CT, 1994)

Ford, Corey, *A Peculiar Service: A Narrative of Espionage in and around New York during the American Revolution*, (Little, Brown, & Co, Boston, 1965)

Fremont, Jessie Benton, *Souvenirs of My Time*, (D Lothrop and Company, Boston, 1887)

Founders Online, founders.archives.gov

George Washington's Mount Vernon, mountvernon.org

Gelles, Edith B, *Portia: The World of Abigail Adams*, (Indiana University Press, Indianapolis, 1992)

Hamilton, Alexander, "Reynolds Pamphlet", 1797, *Founders Online*, founders. archives.gov/documents/Hamilton/01-21-02-0138-0002.

Hamilton, James A., *Reminiscences of James A. Hamilton*, (Charles Scribner & Co, New York, 1869)

Howard, Hugh, *Mr and Mrs Madison's War: America's First Couple and the Second War of Independence*, (Bloomsbury Press, New York, 2012)

Humphreys, Mary Gay, *Catherine Schuyler: A Woman of the Revolution*, (Charles Scribner's Sons, New York, 1897)

Hunt, Paula D., "Sybil Ludington, the Female Paul Revere: The Making of a Revolutionary War Heroine," *The New England Quarterly*, volume LXXXVIII, no2 (June 2015), p. 187–222

Jacob, Mark and Case, Stephen H., *Treacherous Beauty: Peggy Shippen, the Woman behind Benedict Arnold's Plot to Betray America*, (Lyons Press, Guildford, CT, 2012)

James Madison's Montpelier, montpelier.org

Jennings, Paul, *A Colored Man's Reminiscences of James Madison*, (Harper Torch Classics, Toronto, 2014)

Journal of the American Revolution, allthingsliberty.com

Johnson, Willis Fletcher, *Colonel Henry Ludington*, (Lavinia and Charles Ludington, New York, 1907)

Kerber, Linda K., *Women of the Republic: Intellect and Ideology in Revolutionary America*, (University of North Carolina Press, Chapel Hill, 1980)

Lossing, Benson J., *Life and Times of Philip Schuyler V.II*, (Sheldon & Co, New York, 1873)

Massachusetts Historical Society, masshist.org

Nagel, Paul C, *The Adams Women: Abigail and Louisa Adams, Their Sisters and Daughters*, (Oxford University Press, New York, 1987)

Nagy, John A., *George Washington's Secret Spy War: The Making of America's First Spymaster*, (St Martin's Press, New York, Norton, Mary Beth, *Liberty's Daughters: The Revolutionary Experience of American Women, 1750–1800*, (Cornell University Press, Ithaca, 1996)

Oberg, Barbara B, *Women in the American Revolution: Gender, Politics, and the Domestic World*, (University of Virginia Press, Charlottesville, 2019)

Pennypacker, Morton, *General Washington's Spies on Long Island and in New York*, (Long Island Historical Society, Brooklyn, 1939)

Ronald, D.A.B., *The Life of John Andre: The Redcoat who Turned Benedict Arnold*, (Casemate, Philadelphia, 2019)

Rose, Alexander, *Washington's Spies: The Story of America's First Spy Ring*, (Bantam Dell, New York, 2006)

Stuart, Nancy Rubin, *The Muse of the Revolution: The Secret Pen of Mercy Otis Warren and the Founding of a Nation*, (Beacon Press, Boston, 2008)

Warren, Mercy Otis and Cohen, Lester H., *History of the Rise, Progress and Termination of the American Revolution: interspersed with Biographical, Political and Moral Observations*, (Liberty Classics, Indianapolis, 1988)

Withey, Lynne, *Dearest Friend: A Life of Abigail Adams*, (Touchstone, New York, 1981)

Young, Alfred F., *Masquerade: The Life and Times of Deborah Sampson, Continental Soldier*, (Alfred A Knopf, New York, 2004)

Index